2615

Edward IV's French Expedition

of 1475

Sir William Brugge, First Garter King of Arms

EDWARD IV's FRENCH EXPEDITION of 1475

The Leaders and their Badges

being

MS. 2. M. 16. College of Arms

edited

with permission of the chapter

by

Francis Pierrepont Barnard

M.A., D.Litt., F.S.A.

First Published *1925*
This Edition Published by
Gloucester Reprints *1975*

This reprint has been authorized by the Clarendon Press Oxford

Gloucester Reprints
32A Rosebery Road
Dursley
Gloucestershire
England

The text has been reproduced from copies kindly lent by
the County Librarian, Devon Library Services, and Essex
County Library.

The text in this reprint has been reduced by 10·5%

The facsimile manuscript has been reduced by 40%

ISBN 0 904586 01 4

Printed in Great Britain by
Redwood Burn Limited, Trowbridge & Esher
Bound by Cedric Chivers Ltd, Bath

PREFACE

The inglorious, but remunerative, expedition to France in 1475, when Edward IV took across the Channel what Comines described as the largest, best disciplined, and most perfectly equipped, army with which any English king had ever invaded his country, is too familiar to need description. The MS. now published for the first time, however, not only throws light upon the field-state and scale of payments, in which respects it supplements Rymer's Foedera, *but also possesses an heraldic interest owing to the information it furnishes as to the badges of the captains. It is remarkable that several of the leaders named in this roll, although persons of the highest distinction as soldiers, or as diplomatists, or as both, notably Sir John Astley, Sir Thomas Borough, Sir Thomas Montgomery, and Sir Richard Tunstall, have been entirely overlooked by the editors of our Biographical Dictionaries. All these were men of no inconsiderable figure in their day, and much of whose work must have been of lasting effect. Some attempt has been made here to atone for this neglect. For the lives of those in the list who have been dealt with in the* Dictionary of National Biography *the reader is*

referred to that work. The MS. *thus has a fourfold importance :
military, financial, armorial, and personal.*

The lists given in Molinet [1] *and Haynin* [2] *contain a number
of names of knights which do not appear in our Roll : perhaps it
may be assumed that these soldiers were not in command of units.*

[1] *Chroniques de Jean Molinet,* first published and edited by Buchon, 1827,
ii, pp. 139–41. Molinet d. 1507.

[2] *Les Mémoires de Jean de Haynin : 1465–77 ;* Mons, 1842, i, pp. 282–5. The
editor of Molinet justly remarks in a note ' Presque tous ces noms sont défigurés de
manière à les rendre presque méconnaissables ', and Haynin's list is little, if any,
better. One is not without a suspicion that some of these strange forms are due to
mis-reading of the original *MSS.* on the part of the editors.

LIST OF WORKS CITED

(Only printed books are included in this list: MSS. used are referred to in the Notes. Transcripts of most of them are in the possession of the Editor.)

Ælianus, *De Instruendis Aciebus*, Cologne, 1580.
Anastatic Drawing Society.
Ancestor, The.
André, *Vita Henrici VII*, Rolls Series.
Anstis, *Register of the Order of the Garter*, 1724.
Archaeologia.
—— *Æliana.*
Archaeological Institute, Proceedings at the Royal.
—— *Journal.*
Arnold's Chronicle, Ed. by Douce, 1811.
Ashmole, *Institution &c. of the Order of the Garter*, 1672.

Bacon, *Historia Regni Henrici Septimi*, Leyden, 1647.
——, *Historie of the Raigne of Henry VII*, 1622.
Beaumont, *Ancient Memorial Brasses*, 1913.
Bedford, *The Blazon of Episcopacy*, 1897.
Beltz, *Memorials of the Order of the Garter*, 1841.
Bessy, Song of Lady, Ed. by Halliwell, 1847.
Birch, *Seals*, 1907.
Blomefield, *History of Norfolk*, 1805–10.
Blore, *Monumental Remains*, 1826.
Blount's Tenures, Ed. by Hazlitt, 1874.
Boutell, *English Heraldry*, 1899.
——, *Heraldry, Historical and Popular*, 1864.
——, *Monumental Brasses and Slabs*, 1847.
Brayley and Britton, *Topographical History of Surrey*, 1850.
Burke, *General Armory*, 1884.

Burke, *Genealogical and Heraldic History of the Commoners*, 1836–8.
Busch, *England under the Tudors*, English Edition, 1895.

C. (A. E.), *The Family of Corbet*, [1914].
Camden Miscellany.
Camden, *Remains*, 1674.
Carlisle, *Endowed Grammar Schools*, 1818.
Cely Papers, Camden Series.
Chronicle of Calais, C.S.
—— *The Grey Friars, London*, Ed. by Howlett in ' Monumenta Franciscana ', R.S.
—— ——, C.S.
Chronicles of London, Ed. by Kingsford, 1905.
—— *The White Rose*, Ed. by Giles, 1845.
Clark, *Mediaeval Military Architecture*, 1884.
Collectanea Topographica et Genealogica.
Collins, *Baronetage of England*, 1720.
Comines, *Mémoires*, Ed. by Dupont, 1840–7.
Cooper, *Annals of Cambridge*, 1842–1908.
Cotgrave, *Dictionarie Fr. and Eng.*, 1632.
Courthope, *Historic Peerage of England*, 1857.
Cowell, *Law Dictionary, or Interpreter*, 1708.
Croke, *Genealogical History of the Croke Family*, 1823.
Croyland Chronicle Continuation, Tr. by Riley, 1854.
Cussans, *Handbook of Heraldry*, 1869.

Dallaway, *Enquiries into Heraldry*, 1793.
——, *History of Sussex*, 1832.
Davies, *Records of the City of York*, 1843.
Demay, *Le Costume de Guerre d'après les Sceaux*, 1875.
Dépêches Milanaises, Ed. by Brown, in ' Calendar of State Papers '.
Devon, *Issue Rolls of the Exchequer*, 1837.
Dickinson, *History of Newark*, 1816.
Dillon and Hope, *The Birth, Life, and Death of the Earl of Warwick*, 1914.
Dingley, *History from Marble*, C.S.
Dorling, *Leopards of England*, &c., 1912.
Doyle, *Official Baronage*, 1886.
Drake, *Eboracum*, 1736.

Ducange.

Dugdale, *Baronage*, 1675-6.

——, *Warwickshire*, 1730.

Edmondson, *Complete Body of Heraldry*, 1780.

Edward VI, *Journal of King*, Clarendon Historical Society, 1884.

Ellis (H.), *History of the Parish of Shoreditch*, 1798.

—— *Original Letters Illust. Eng. Hist.*, 1824-46.

Ellis (W. S.), *Antiquities of Heraldry*, 1869.

English Chronicle, C.S.

Essex Archaeological Society Transactions.

Excerpta Historica, 1831.

Fabyan, *Chronicles of England and France*, Ed. by Ellis, 1811.

Fairholt, *Costume in England*, Ed. by Dillon, 1885.

Farrer, *Church Heraldry of Norfolk*, 1885-7.

Ferne, *Glorie of Generositie*, 1586.

——, *Lacyes Nobilitie*, 1586.

Fleetwood, *Arrival of King Edward IV*, C.S. ; and in ' Chron. of White Rose '.

Fonblanque, *Annals of the House of Percy*, 1887.

Forsyth, *Antiquary's Portfolio*, 1825.

Fortescue, *The Governance of England* (1471-6), Ed. by Plummer, 1885.

Foster, *Pedigree of Croker of Lineham,* in ' Genealogical Account of the Fox Family ', 1872.

——, *Yorkshire Pedigrees*, 1874.

Froissart, Chronicles, Tr. by Johnes, 1848.

——, *Illuminated Illustrations of*, Humphreys, 1884.

Gairdner, *Richard III*, 1898.

G. E. C[okayne], *Complete Peerage*, 1st ed. 1887-98 ; new ed. 1910, &c.

Genealogist, The.

Gibbon, *Introductio ad Latinam Blasoniam*, 1682.

Gibbs and Halliday, *The Courtenay Mantelpiece at Exeter*, 1884.

Godefroy, *Lexique de l'ancien français*, 1881-1902.

Godwin, *The English Archaeologist's Handbook*, 1867.

Gough, *Sepulchral Monuments*, 1786-96.

Grants of Edward V, C.S.

Gregory's Chronicle, C.S.

Grose, *Military Antiquities*, 1801.
Guillim, *Display of Heraldry*, 1724.

Habington (W.), *Historie of Edward IV*, 1640.
——, (Thos.), *Survey of Worcestershire*, Worc. Hist. Soc., 1895–9.
Haines, *Manual of Monumental Brasses*, 1861.
Hall, *Chronicle*, Ed. by Ellis, 1809.
Halliwell, *Dict. of Archaic and Provincial Words*, 1855.
——, *Letters of the Kings of England*, 1846.
Halsted, *Richard III*, 1844.
Harington, *Nugae Antiquae*, Ed. by Park, 1804.
Harleian Miscellany, Ed. by Oldys and Park, 1808–13.
Haynin, Les Mémoires de Jean de (1465–77), 1842.
Hearne's Curious Discourses, 1771.
Henry (Robt.), *Hist. of Gt. Britain*, 1788–9.
Heraldic Exhibition (Society of Antiquaries), 1896.
Herald and Genealogist, The.
Hewitt, *Ancient Armour*, 1855–60.
Historiae Croylandensis Continuatio, Ed. by Fulman, 1684.
Historical MSS. Commission Reports.
Holinshed, *Chronicles*, Ed. by Ellis, 1807–8.
Hope, *Heraldry for Craftsmen*, 1913.
——, *Stall-plates of the Knights of the Garter : 1348–1485*, 1913.
Household Books of John, Duke of Norfolk, and Thomas, Earl of Surrey, Roxburghe
    Club, 1844.
Hunter, *Hallamshire*, 1819.
——, *South Yorkshire*, 1828–31.
Husenbeth, *Emblems of Saints*, 1860.
Hutchinson, *History of Sidmouth* (Unpublished).
Hutton, *Battle of Bosworth*, 1813.

Inquisitiones Post Mortem.

Johannes de Bado Aureo, Ed. by Bysshe, 1654.

Kelham, *Dict. of the Norman Language*, 1779.
Kerry, *The Hundred of Bray*, 1861.
Kingsford, *English Historical Literature in the Fifteenth Century*, 1913.

Lacombe, *Dict. du Vieux Langage françois*, 1766 ; *Supplément*, 1767.

Laing, *Ancient Scottish Seals*, 1850, 1866.

Lancashire and Cheshire, Historical Society of.

Langford Charters (Unpublished).

Larwood and Hotten, *History of Signboards*, 1898.

Lee, *History of the Church of Thame*, 1883.

Leigh, *Accedence of Armorie*, 1597.

Leland, *Collectanea*, 1774.

——, *Itinerary*, Ed. by L. T. Smith, 1906–10.

Letters of Margaret of Anjou, C.S.

Letters and Papers, . . . Henry VI, R.S.

—— *and Papers, Richard III and Henry VII*, R.S.

Lincolnshire Pedigrees, Harleian Society.

List of Sheriffs, Public Record Office, 1898.

Lords' Committees, Reports from the, 1820–9.

Lower, *Curiosities of Heraldry*, 1845.

——, *Patronymica Britannica*, 1860.

Lydgate, *Troy Book*, Ed. by Bergen, E.E.T.S., 1906.

Manning and Bray, *History of Surrey*, 1804–14.

Marchegay, *Historia Gaufridi Ducis* (by Jean of Marmoutier, 12th cent.), Soc. de l'hist. de France, Paris, 1856.

Markham, *Richard III*, 1906.

Materials for the Reign of Henry VII, R.S.

Mayhew and Skeat, *Concise Dict. of Middle English*, 1888.

Medallic Illustrations of British History, B.M., 1885.

Metcalfe, *Book of Knights*, 1885.

Mirror for Magistrates, Ed. by Haslewood, 1815.

Miscellanea Genealogica et Heraldica.

Molinet, Chroniques de Jean, Ed. by Buchon, 1827.

Money, *History of Newbury*, 1887.

Monstrelet, *Chronicles*, Tr. by Johnes, 1840.

Montfaucon, *Antiquities of France*, 1750.

Monumenta Vetusta.

Morant, *History of Essex*, 1816.

More, *Richard III*, Ed. by Lumby, 1883.

Moule, *Bibliotheca Heraldica*, 1822.

Nichols, *History of the County of Leicester*, 1795–1815.
——, *Wills of the Kings and Queens of England*, 1780.
Nicholson, *Leges Marchiarum*, 1747.
Nicolas, *Battle of Agincourt*, 1827 and 1832.
——, *Scrope and Grosvenor Controversy*, 1833.
——, *Siege of Carlaverock*, 1828.
——, *Testamenta Vetusta*, 1826.
——, *Wardrobe Accounts of Edward IV*, 1830.
Noble, *History of the College of Arms*, 1805.
Norman, *London Signs*, 1893.
Notes and Queries.

Olivier de la Marche, Ed. by Beaune and D'Arbaumont, 1883–4.
Oman, *Art of War*, 1924.
Oxford English Dictionary.

Papworth, *Ordinary of British Armorials*, 1874.
Paston Letters, Ed. by Gairdner, 1872–1907.
Patent Rolls, Calendar of (1452–85), 1897–1910.
Paul, *Heraldry in Relation to Scottish History and Art*, 1900.
Percy's (Bp.) Folio MS., Ed. by Hales and Furnivall, 1868.
Percy (Bp.), *Reliques of Ancient English Poetry*, 1839.
Pierce the Ploughman, Ed. by Skeat, 1867.
Pixley, *History of the Baronetage*, 1900.
Planché, *The Pursuivant of Arms*, 1859.
Plumpton Correspondence, C.S.
Pole, *Collections towards a Description of Devon*, 1791.
Political Poems, R.S.
—— *Songs*, C.S.
Pollard (A. F.), *The Reign of Henry VII*, 1913.
Polydore Virgil, *Historiae Anglicae*, Leyden, 1651.
—— Vergil, *Henry VI—Richard III*, English Version, C.S.
Poulson, *History of Holderness*, 1840.
Prestwich, *Respublica*, 1787.
Prince, *Worthies of Devon*, 1810.
Privy Council, Proceedings of the, Ed. by Nicolas, 1834–7.

Proceedings of the Society of Antiquaries.
Promptorium Parvulorum, C.S.
Purey-Cust, *Heraldry of York Minster*, 1896.

Raine, *History of North Durham*, 1852.
Ramsay, *Lancaster and York*, 1892.
Ransford, *The Origin of the Ransfords*, 1919.
Reliquary, The.
Retrospective Review, The.
Return of Members of Parliament, 1878.
Risdon, *Chorographical Description of Devon*, 1811.
Rogers, *Sepulchral Effigies of Devon*, 1877.
Rolls of Arms.
Rotuli Parliamentorum.
Round, *The King's Serjeants*, 1911.
Rows Rolls, Ed. by Courthope, 1859.
Ruding, *Annals of the Coinage*, 1840.
Rutland Papers, C.S.
Rymer's *Foedera.*

Sallust.
Salmon, *History of Hertfordshire*, 1728.
Sandeman, *Calais under English Rule*, 1908.
Sandford, *Genealogical History of England*, Ed. by Stebbing, 1707.
Scofield, *Life and Reign of Edward IV*, 1923.
Shakespeare.
Shaw, *Knights of England*, 1906.
Six Town Chronicles, Ed. by Flenley, 1911.
Skeat, *Etym. Eng. Dict.*, 1882.
Skelton, *Works*, Ed. by Dyce, 1843.
Smyth (John), *Lives of the Berkeleys (1066–1618)*, Ed. by Maclean, 1883–5.
Somersetshire Archaeological Society's Proceedings.
Spelman, *Glossarium*, 1687.
Spener, *Insignium Theoria*, Frankfurt, 1690.
Staffordshire, Collections for a History of (William Salt Archaeological Society)
Stark, *History of Gainsborough*, 1843.

State Papers, R.S.
Statutes of the Realm, 1816.
Stonor Letters, C.S.
Stothard, *Monumental Effigies*, 1817–32.
Stow, *Survey of London*, Ed. by Kingsford, 1908.
Stratmann, *Mid. Eng. Dict.*, Ed. by Bradley, 1891.
Streatfield, *Excerpta Cantiana*, 1836.
Strutt, *Regal and Ecclesiastical Antiquities*, 1793.
Supplementary Letters and Papers, Hen. VI, R.S.
Surrey Archaeological Collections.
Surtees, *History of Durham*, 1816–40.
Sussex Archaeological Society's Collections, and Record Society Publications.
Symonds, *Diary of the Marches of the Royal Army, 1644*, C.S.

Tanner, *Notitia Monastica*, 1695.
Taylor (Arthur), *The Glory of Regality*, 1820.
—— (Isaac), *Words and Places*, Ed. by Palmer [1909].
Thoresby, *Ducatus Leodiensis*, Ed. by Whitaker, 1816.
Three Fifteenth Century Chronicles, C.S.
Topographer, The, 1792.
—— *and Genealogist, The.*
Turner and Parker, *Domestic Architecture of the Middle Ages*, 1851–9.

Upton, *De Studio Militari*, Ed. by Bysshe, 1654.

Viollet-le-Duc, *Dict. du Mobilier français.*
Visitations :—Bedfordshire, Harleian Society.
        Berkshire, Harleian Society.
        Buckinghamshire, Harleian Society.
        Cambridgeshire, Harleian Society.
        Cheshire, Harleian Society.
        Cornwall, Harleian Society.
        Derbyshire, *The Genealogist*, New Series, viii.
        Devonshire, Harleian Society.
        ——, Ed. by Vivian, 1895.

Visitations :—Essex, Harleian Society.

Norfolk, Harleian Society.

Nottinghamshire, Harleian Society.

Oxfordshire, Harleian Society.

Shropshire, Harleian Society.

Suffolk, Ed. by J. J. Howard, 1866.

Sussex, Harleian Society.

Warwickshire, Harleian Society.

Worcestershire, Harleian Society.

Yorkshire (Dugdale's), *The Genealogist,* New Series, xx.

—— (Glover's), Ed. by Foster, 1875.

—— (Tonge's), Surtees Society.

Vulgate.

Walden (De) Library, *Banners, Standards, and Badges,* 1904.

Waller, *Monumental Brasses,* 1864.

Walpole, *Royal and Noble Authors,* 1759.

Warkworth's Chronicle, C.S.

Waurin, *Recueil des Chroniques,* R.S.

Weekley, *Romance of Names,* 1914.

——, *Surnames,* 1917.

Weever, *Funeral Monuments,* 1767.

Westminster, Antiquities of St. Peter's, 1722. [Jodocus Crull.]

Whitaker, *History of Richmondshire,* 1823.

——, —— *Whalley,* 1872–6.

Willement, *Heraldic Notices of Canterbury Cathedral,* 1827.

——, *Regal Heraldry,* 1821.

Wills from Doctors' Commons, C.S.

Worcester, William of, *Annales,* R.S.

—— ——, *Collections,* R.S.

—— ——, *Itineraria,* Ed. by Nasmyth, 1778.

Wright, *Roll of Caerlaverock,* 1864.

Wriothesley's Chronicle, C.S.

Yorkshire Archaeological and Topographical Journal.

Young, *Grey and Hastings Controversy,* 1841.

Jon Elryngton tresorer of the kyngꝭ housholde ꝫ
hath payed

And John Dorell and John ffitzherbert hand payed of M̃M̃M̃M̃ d̃c̃c̃c̃xl li. ꝭꝛ ꝫ

kyngꝭ of Armes ⸬ ⸬ ⸬ Geralde
purseuantꝭ ⸬ ⸬ ⸬ my

Et And on the pꝑe lord Audeley Cr Byshon lords baliard
Enres hath besoyned wyth them into ffrotengꝫ of Gorcz ⸬

kyng Edward
the iiij.

The Duc off Clarence ⸬ iō chenaherꝭ c la
A . M̃ . blake bulle

The Duc of gloucestez ⸬ iō chenaherꝭ c la
A . M̃ . whytt bore

The Duc of norffolke ⸬ ⸬ chlꝛꝭ eǧ la
A . ccc . whytt lyon

The Duc off Suffolke ⸬ ⸬ chlꝛꝭ eǧ la
A . ccc . lyon of golde the kꝛo fforched

The Duc off Bokyngham ⸬ ⸬ chlꝛꝭ eǧ la
A . ccc . the stafford knot . ꝭ dom

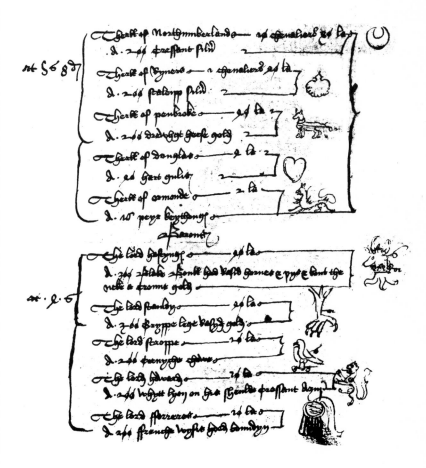

The lord Bray Padou ———— 10 ta
A . iij treff passant throuenth thrame gold wyth in
the compaff off the treff a grei feld

The lord Bray Erldom ———— 10 ta
A . red plake bagyd staff

The lord ffhtwarens ———— 10 ta
A ho Borders knott

The lord Cobhm ———— 6 ta
A ho the plake farzyn hede

The lorde Lyfle ———— 1 ta
A . ho hon feld thdu ynit a holefart thround gold
enarmede arnr

The lord Clynton ———— A mullet
The lord Bourde ———— 2 ta
Bar an Andre gold
Baneretts

Sir John Afteley ———— a ta
A . 12

Sir Willm Aparre ———— 10 ta
A red maydyn hed

Sir Thomas Montgomeryo — 10 ta
A 100

Sir Thomas Boroug̃h ———— 10 ta
A   at the armys of an ermie & the garnedot

Sir Raufe Haftynge ———— 8 ta
A 100 thaffont feld wyth 3 Cyftryg̃ fhdnzt

Sir John ... stewys — — ...
& so matyn filid

Sir Willm Stanlow — ...
& so gar gede filid

Sir Robert tarbost of tymeo — ...
& so the vogat monke

Sir John radcliff fitz wot — ...
& so garbrale filid

Sir thomas edward — ...
& so palet filid

Sir humffrey talbot — ...
& so venyngtonde filid on stand a mollet

Sir thomas trays — ...
& so stalyng leder filid

Sir John armidell — ...
& so an dobory

Sir rychard dunstalus — ...
& so the vogut dole

Sir James Harryngton — ij̄ li̇
d iC lyonys hede fild or

Sir Robert Chamberleyn — xxij̄ li̇
d iiijd feyre gede d̄ azur

Sir Wᵐ Roos — ij̄ li̇
d iC slade saboyn hede vasyl

Sir John Hazliwyn — xx s li̇
d li̇ slade sarezyn hede cope

Sir John Sherrerd — ij li̇
d vj. fild passant & maskill gede gold

Sir John Maleverer — iij li̇
d xl vosytt grenfoid de berant

Sir Lawrence Raynford — xij li̇
d vj s l̇ fild

Sir Nicolas Langford — iij li̇
d iij n wolvnggg fild

Sir John Danaye — iij li̇
d xl lyngforne gede vasyg fild

Sir James Radcliff — ij li̇
d xij

Sir Wᵐ Denssell — vj li̇
d viij slade as gede vasyg & bind the nek frame gold

Sir Rychard Brandon — ij li̇
d lyon gede vasyg & gold

Sir Rychard Corbett — iij li̇

Sir John Scrobber — vj li̇

Sir Simond Mountford ● flonredly & gonly

Sr Dodeley dene of the kynge chapell at ʒ d. iij jo² ⅠHC
a grat Chyld

¶ ¶ iti Chapell

Sr perse Courteney d saint Antony chose d xviij

Sr John gunnthrope d Salutop got gold ond the
Salutop d thow Hode passe sevi

Sr Hartop d ffatop d golve god ffilate d xviij   }
Sr of the ordnance pyke by John stykynd   2 ———— at ꝑ d jo² jij jo²
Sr of the kynge Courtt Richard Harnot ———— at ꝗ s ij d v iij jo²
¶ speyes   2 ———————————— at 12 d ij jo²
d lance   2 ———————————— at 18 d ij jo²

Mayontony Roroy Marche   2 ———— at 18 d ij jo²
ffezattz ffcanntz at Armes   2 ———— at 2 d ij jo²
pursivantz   2 ———————————— at 18 d ij jo²
Collin Wayde and Edmond Gregory   2 ———— at 2 at 12 d ij jo²
Comptroller of the ordonance John rose at ꝑ d ij jo²
The Clerke of the ordonance Thomas Hongh at iiij d dʒ

Item Joloyers   2 ———— 8.   Item Carpenters   2 — 19
Item Masons   2 ———— 2 d   Item Smethes   9 d
Item Salvers   Item plomes
Item Tynners   Item Horsharnosmakers
Item Souyers   Item Cartes

Item All banez berrers and standarez berers to Have
doble wage aftyr as they are off descent or degree

ij the constable to delyu the waghe worde to the kyng
wythyt adven he shall delyuer hyt to the marshall
the marshall to advertyse the arme

iij A flyer to be made be for the kyng bret
aduyson or frent where the vache for thatt
myght first shall resort vnto dyscrete men
of arme aduyson dygcharge et̄c

When the kyng or any other armee first &
dysoldyth theyr lancers hyt vsade be doon by
sadde and dyscret innocent tanncestlours some
of theym waryeng of age beseshyng the
larophest cause why to theentent thatt there
shuld bee founde noo vnfaythfulnes in the sayd
armee but thatt he doeth hit apon a Just
titulle and quarell vnche doon to comamde
the chyef gerannt to vnrolle hit and the armee
to make hym knyght thatt berryth the sayd
lancere yf he bee not before and comamde
hym to hold fast and to ryde forthe in the
name off god /zc/

A declaracion Afwell of Capitengnes theire Speires and Archers
Reteigned wyth our Sou[er]eigne lord Kyng Edward the iiij[th] in his s[er]uife of
Guerre into his Duchie of Normandye and his Realme of ffraunce as of
theire wages for the Second q[ua]rter paid by John Sorell and John
ffitzherberd tellers of the Kynges mony in his Receyt at Canterbury
the moneth of Jun the xv yere of the Reigne of our faid fou[er]eigne
lord Kyng Edward the iiij[th] that is to fey

v Duk[es] — { Speres — cccxxxiiij — } viij[M] Dvij[C] xxviij*li*
{ Archers — mmdcccij — } viijs iiijd [1]

vj Erles — { Speres — ciiij[xx] and vj — } — mmmdciiij xixli iijs [2]
{ Archers — miiij — }

xiij Barons — { Speres — ciiij[xx] xviij — } — v[M] ccccxxxli viijs vjd [3]
{ Archers — mdviij[C] xlvij — }

xij Baronettes [4] — { Speres — iiij[xx] xiiij — } — mmdcciiij vjli xixs vjd [5]
{ Archers — dcccxxxiij — }

viij Knyghtes — { Speres — iiij[xx] xiij — } — mmdlxiijli xviijs vjd [6]
{ Archeres — viij[C] xl — }

iij xiij[xx] — { Squiers & } Speres — cciiij[xx] xiij — } — vij[M] cccviijli ixd [7]
{ Gentilmen } Archers — viijcxl — }

onners } Artificers } v[C] lxiij — mccciiij[xx] xviijli xvs iiijd [9]
ethers [8] } & other }
owyers }
other }

Some total { Speres — mciiij[xx] xviij }
{ Archers — ix[M] dciiij[xx] xv } xj[M] cccc4lvij } xxxij[M] xvli xiijs xd [11]
{ Artificers — dlxiiij [10] }
{ & other }

---

[1] £9,228 8s. 4d. [2] £3,699 3s. 0d. [3] £5,430 8s. 6d. [4] i. e. Bannerets : see on
is word Pixley, *Hist. of the Baronetage*, pp. 1-8. [5] £2,886 19s. 6d. [6] £2,563 18s. 6d.
£7,308 0s. 9d. [8] i. e. Fletchers. [9] £1,378 15s. 4d. [10] This was 563 in the
receding entry ; and the archers' total is 8,666, not 9,695. [11] £32,015 13s. 10d.

B

trezorer John Elryngton Treforer of the Kynges Guerres
    hath payed   } MDCV*li* xvj*s* vııj*d*

And John Sorell and John ffitzherbert haue payed—xxx ccccıx*li* xvıj*s* ıj*d*

ıııj Kynges of Armes { heraldes————ıııj
                 purf[*er*]uantz————v

And ou[*er*] this John lord Audeley & Galliard lorde
Duras hath Reteyned wyth theym into Breteigne of Archers MM } MMMMDL *l*

Kyng Edward

the ıııj[th]

                      The Duc off clarence————10 cheualiers. c La[*nces*].
                      A[*rchers*] 1000. blake bulle.
                      The Duc of gloucefter————10 cheualiers. c La.
                      A 1000. Whitt bore
at 13*s* 4*d*   The Duc of norffolke————2 chlrs. 40 La.
(per day for himself)   A. 300. Whytt lyon.
                      The Duc of Suffolke————2 chlrs. 40 La
                      A. 300. lyon of gold the kew (queue) forched
                      The Duc off Bokyngh[*a*]m—4 chlrs. 40 La
                      A. 400. the ftafford knot. Re Dom[2]

---

[1] £30,409 17*s*. 2*d*.

[2] *Reversus domum*, 'He returned home'.

t 10s The marquis of Dorffett

t 6s 8d [1] Therll of Northumberland———— 10 cheualiers   40 La
A. 200   Creffant filu[er]
Therll of Ryuers————————2 cheualiers   40 La
A. 200   fcaleipp filu[er]
Therll of penbroke——————40 La
A. 200   Drewhgt (draught) horfe gold
Therll of Douglas——————4 La
A. 40   hart gulis
Therll of ormonde——————2 La
A. 16   peyr keythonges [2]

Barons

The lord haftynges——————40 La
A. 300   Blake Boull hed Rafid hornes & pys (breast) & bout the neke a Croune gold
The lord ftanley——————40 La
A. 300   Gryppe (griffin's) lege Rafyd gold
The lord fcroppe——————20 La
A. 200   Cornyche chowe (Cornish chough)
The lord howard——————20 La.
A. 200   Whytt lyon on his fheulde[r] Creffant Azur
The lord fferreres——————20 La
A 200   ffrenche wyfis hood boundyn

at 4s

---

[1] The writer has set down 5s. in error for 6s.   Half a mark was the daily war-wage of an earl.
[2] For ‘ gryphongs ’, griffins.

The lord Grey Codon————————10 La
A. 155 treffe paffant Thorough Croune gold wyth in
the Compafe of the treffe a grei (badger) filu[er]
The lord Gray Rythyn————————10 La
A. 140 Blak Ragyd ftaffe
The lord ffitzwaren————————10 La
A 50 Boufers Knott
The lord Cobh[a]m————————5 La
A 50 the Blake faryn (saracen's) hede
The lorde Lyfle————————7 La
A. 50 lyon filu[er] fhowyng holeface Cround gold
enarmede azur
The lord Clynton————————A mulet gold
The lord Boyde————————2 La
A 20 an Anker gold

Banerettes

Sir John afteley ————————2 La
A. 12
Sir Will[ia]m aparre ————————16 La
A 140 maydyn hed
Sir Thomas montgomery————————10 La
A 100
Sir Thomas Borough————————16 La
A [blank] al the armur of An erme (arm) & the gauntelot
Sir Rauffe haftynges————————8 La
A 100 fhafront filu[er] wyth 3 Eyftryges (ostrich's) ffedyrs

r John ffenys————————4 La
  40 ma[r]tyn ſilu[er]
r Will[ia]m ſtanley———— 2 La
  20 hart hede ſilu[er]
r Robert Tailboſſe of Kyme——12 La
  80 the whyt Boull
r John Radeclyff ffitzwat[er]——6 La
  70 garbrale ¹ ſilu[er]
r Thomas howard————————6 La
  40 ſalet ſilu[er]
r humffrey Talbot———— 10 La
  100 Renynghonde (running hound) ſilu[er] on ſhau[l]d[er] a mollet
r Thomas gray————————8 La
  80 ſkalyng lader ſilu[er]
r John Arundell———————— 2 La
  20 an Akkorn
r Rychard Dunſtalle————10 La
  100 the whytt Coke

---

¹ coudière.

Knyghtes

Sir James haryngton————————10 [and] 2 La
A 100 lyonp[ar]tes [1] hed filu[er] [2]
Sir Robert Chamberleyn————————10 [and] 2 La
A 100 ffryrs (friar's) gerdill Azur
Sir Will[ia]m Norys————————10 [and] 2 La
A 100 Blake Rawyn (raven's) hede Rafyd
Sir John harlwyn————————3 La
A 50 Blake farezyn hede Cope (couped)
Sir John fferrers————————2 La
A 15 filu[er] paffant [3] a mafkell gold
Sir John maleuerer————————3 La
A 30 whytt greyhonde [c]urrant
Sir lawrence Raynford————————12 La
A 60 l[ys ?] filu[er]
Syr Nycolas langford————————8 La
A 60 ij whyngges filu[er]
Sir John Sauage————————3 La
A 30 Vnycorne hede Rafyd filu[er]
Sir James Radcleffe————————1 La (i. e. himself)
A 12 [4]
Sir Will[ia]m Truffell————————6 La
A 60 Blake as hede Rafid & bout the nek Croune gold
Sir Rychard Brandon————————1 La (i. e. himself)
A [blank] lyon hede Rafyd gold
Sir Rychard Corbett————————3 La
Sir John Crokke————————6 La
Sir fimond mounford flourdelys goulys

---

[1] Probably =Lionpard's, i. e. Leopard's, head.
[2] 'or' added here as a correction. 10 2 is a short way of expressing the addition $\frac{10}{2}$.
[3] Some omission before 'silver'. [4] No badge given.

r Dodeley Dene of the Kynges chapell at 4s p[or] ¹ Jo[u]r
grat Sylu[er]

[emoran]d[um] la Chapell ²

r perife (Piers) Courteney A scant (error for ' seant ', = saint) ⎫
    Antony Crofe Azur   ⎪
r John gounthrope A fawter gold ou[er] the   ⎬ at 4s p[or] Jo[u]
wter A lyon hede rafed filu[er]   ⎪
r Smyrte gartier A Brode Arowe hed Blake Armyned ⎭

r of the Ordenance pykes v[i]z John fturgyn——————at 5s 8d ³ p[or] Jo[u]r
r of the Kynges Tenttes Rychard garnet————— at 3s 4d p[or] Jo[u]r
[emoran]d[um] fcurers (scourers, scouts) ⁴————at 12d p[or] Jo[u]r
lance————————————————————at 18d p[or] Jo[u]r
arenfceux Noroy marche——————————at 28d p[or] Jo[u]r
eralld f[er]geauntz at Armes——————————at 24d p[or] Jo[u]r
rf[er]u[a]ntz (pursuivants)———————————at 18d p[or] Jo[u]r
ill[ia]m Warde and Edmond Gregory—————at 12d p[or] Jo[u]r
mptroller of the Ordonance Will[ia]m roofe—— at 4s p[or] Jo[u]r
e Clerke of the Ordonance Thomas Bonys———— - at 4d ⁵

[e]m Bowyers———8.	It[e]m Carpenters————19
e]m mafons——24	It[e]m Smethes——32
e]m fawers——	It[e]m plomers——
e]m Turners——	It[e]m horfharnefmakers——
e]m Coupers——	It[e]m Carters——

e]m All baner berrers and ftandarez berers to haue
ble wages aftyr as they Are of aveour ⁶ or degree

---

¹ Or ' par '.   ² The rest of the personnel of the King's chape
³ An unusual amount, but so the *MS.* reads.
⁴ ' The Kynge sent scorers to aspie '. (Fleetwood, *Arrival of King Edward IV*, p. 7.)
⁵ Apparently altered in the MS. to 24d.
⁶ ' Behaviour ' or ' conduct '. This short form without the English prefix appe
aviour ' several times in Shakespeare : *e. g. Merry Wives*, i. iii, 86,

m[emoran]d[um] the connftable to delyu[er] the Wa[c]he worde to the Kyng
whych dowen (done) he fhall delyu[er] hyt to the marfchall
the marfchall to advertyfe the Arme (army)

m[emoran]d[um] A ffyer to be made be for the Kynges Gret
pavelyon or Tent where the Wache for thatt
nyght furft fhall Refort vnto Afwell men
of Arme (men-at-arms) As Archers &c

When the Kyng or Any other prince ffurft
difployth theyr baners hyt wolde be doon by
fadde and difcret Auncyent Counceillours fome
of theym hooryd (hoary) of age Schewyng the
lawffull cawfe why to thentent thatt there
fhuld bee fownde noo wyldfulnes in the faid
prince but thatt he doeth hit apon a Juft
cawfe and quarell wiche doon to comaunde
the chief herauld to vnrolle hit and the prince
to make hym Knyght thatt berreth the fayd
baniere yf he bee not before and comaunde
hym to hold faft and to Ryde forthe in the
name of god &c

No. 1. 'John Sorell', a 'teller of the kynges mony in his Receyt at Canterbury.' I have been unable to identify the family of this official with any certainty. The name occurs in the Eastern Counties. On July 1, 1462, a commission was issued to him under which he was to take ships, masters, mariners, and victuals within the counties of Norfolk and Suffolk for the King's fleet against his enemies.[1] In May, 1471, he received the grant of tronage and pesage [2] in the port of Ipswich,[3] and again in Aug. 1474, but this time at Southampton and adjacent ports,[4] whence Edward at one time intended to sail in this expedition with either Guienne or Normandy as his objective. Later in the same year he acted as receiver of the tenths in Norfolk, Suffolk, Cambridgeshire, and Hunts,[5] and we come across him finally as troner and peser in the port of Southampton in Oct. 1478.[6]

No. 2. 'John Fitzherberd', a 'teller of the kynges mony in his Recyt at Canterbury.' John Fitzherbert, of Etwall and Coterall, Derbyshire, Esq., Remembrancer of the Exchequer,[7] was perhaps the second son of Nicholas Fitzherbert, of Norbury in that county, Esq.,[8] by Alice, a daughter of Henry Booth, of

[1] *Pat. Rolls, 1461–7*, p. 201.

[2] Tronage was the toll paid for the weighing of wool by the standard trona, or beam (public balance) ; pesage the toll paid for the similar weighing of merchandize generally.

[3] *Ibid., 1467–77*, pp. 259–69.   [4] *Ibid.*, p. 468.   [5] *Ibid.*, p. 496, Nov. 28.

[6] *Ibid., 1476–85*, p. 117. It was not considered necessary to burden this book with every minor office or grant relating to the persons here commemorated.

[7] *Ibid., 1476–85*, p. 202 ; *Collect. Topog. et Geneal.*, i, pp. 268–9. 'Rememorator in Scaccario' : *Visit. Oxon.*, Harl. Soc., p. 147.

[8] Kt. of the shire for Derbyshire in 1446 and 1452–3 (*Return of Memb. Parl.*, pp. 335, 347), and Sheriff of Notts and Derbyshire in 1452–3 (*Proc. of Privy Council*,

Harlaston, Staffordshire.[1] John Fitzherbert was still holding office as Teller on Feb. 14, 1479,[2] and at Easter, 1480.[3] On Sept. 21, 1485, he was re-granted for life the post of King's Remembrancer in the Exchequer, with such emoluments as he had lately enjoyed when holding the same office,[4] and on Oct. 20 of that year there is record of a grant to him of a certain waste in Derbyshire for twenty years at an annual rent,[5] also of a lease for seven years of lead mines in that county to him and Sir John Savage, jun.[6] 'Johannes Fitzherbert de Norbury' was appointed one of the Derbyshire commissioners in 1496 for raising the subsidy to provide means of 'defence ayenfte the cruel Malyce of the Scottis',[7] who had received Warbeck as 'King Richard IV'. He married Joan, a daughter of Robert Babington, of Lower Kiddington[8] and Asterley, Oxon., Esq., Hereditary Keeper of the Royal Palace of Westminster, and Head Warden of the Fleet Prison, by Helen, daughter of Richard Illingworth, 'Baro Scaccarii', K.B., and died on Nov. 18, 1502.[9]

vi, p. 272; 'Pedigrees from the Plea Rolls', *Genealogist*, N.S., xviii, p. 186; xx, p. 96). He was named in the indictment of 1454 (see under No. 50 below), and had died in 1473 (*Archaeol. Journal*, 1914, p. 383).

[1] *Coll. Top. et Gen.*, *ibid.*, and ii, p. 95; viii, pp. 328–9; 'Pedigrees from the De Banco Rolls', *Gen.*, N.S., xxiii, p. 92. In *Gen.*, N.S., vii, p. 131, however, he is said to have been grandson of Nicholas and Alice, and s. & h. of their son Rafe, whose wife's name is not given.   [2] Anstis, *Regist. of the Garter*, ii, p. 354.

[3] Devon, *Issue Rolls of Exchequer*, p. 499.

[4] *Materials Reign Hen. VII*, i, p. 26.

[5] *Ibid.*, p. 95; and see *Pat. Rolls, 1461–7*, p. 422.

[6] No. 51 below. *Materials Reign Hen. VII*, i, p. 310.

[7] *Rotuli Parl.*, vi, p. 517.   [8] *Aliter* Coddington and Cuddington.

[9] *Visit. Oxon.*, H.S., pp. 146–7; *Visit. Essex*, H.S., p. 63; *Visit. Notts.*, H.S., p. 7. She is variously called Joane, Johanna, Mary, Margaret, and Dorothea.

No. 3. 'John Elryngton Treforer of the Kynges Guerres.'
John Elrington was of Udimore, near Rye, and a royal licence to
crenellate his manor-house there was granted him in 19 Edward
IV.[1] It is doubtful whether he was not a knight at the date
of this·expedition, for if the entry can be trusted in detail, in
12 Edward IV[2] 'Johannes Elrington, miles, Thesaurarius
Hospitii Regis', had obtained a licence to crenellate his manor-
house of Dixtherne, Sussex.[3] This, now known as Great Dixter,
near Northiam, about five miles North of Udimore, is a timber
house which still survives. It was an Etchingham property,
and came to him with his second wife.[4] He appears in the
Tellers' Roll for the first quarter's expenses of this campaign
in a military capacity also, himself serving as a man-at-arms and
bringing thirty archers.[5] In the same roll the wages of one
Matthew Scarden for that quarter, 45*s.* 6*d.*, are paid through
Elrington as Treasurer of the King's Wars.[6] At the contract of
marriage between Richard, Duke of York, second son of
Edward IV, and Anne, daughter of John Mowbray, Duke of
Norfolk,[7] on Jan. 15, 1477, Elrington, then Treasurer of the

[1] (March 4, 1479—March 3, 1480.) Turner and Parker, *Dom. Arch. of Middle
Ages*, iii, p. 422 ; Godwin, *Eng. Archaeol. Handbook*, p. 249.

[2] Mar. 4, 1472—Mar. 3, 1473.

[3] Turner and Parker, iii, p. 422 ; Godwin, p. 238.

[4] See below, and *Sussex Archaeological Society's Collections*, lii, p. 23.

[5] Rymer's *Foedera*, xi, p. 845. The edition by Holmes is used here as a rule.
' Johanni Elrington Armigero Thefaurario Guerrae Domini Regis pro uno Homine
ad Arma (*i. e.* himself) & pro xxx Sagittariis lxxv*l.* xviij*d.*' This payment was for
91 days. ' Armigero ' may be an error for ' militi ' : such slips are not unknown
in the *Foedera* ; yet he is described as an esquire in *Pat. Rolls*, July 3, 1476, p. 596,
which should settle the matter.

[6] *Foed.*, xii, p. 15. Thus he was acting in a double capacity.   [7] No. 8 below.

Household, received his Knighthood of the Bath.[1] The knights made on that occasion were elected on the 17th and dubbed on the 18th.[2] On Jan. 8, 1478, he was returned as knight of the shire for Middlesex,[3] and in 1479 served as sheriff of Surrey and Sussex.[4] King Edward kept Christmas, 1481, at Windsor, and, among the notables there who made New Year's gifts to the heralds, ' Sir John Elrington, Treasurer of the King's House ', gave 20s.[5] In the following year he is again acting as Treasurer of the King's Wars : ' Easter, Anno 22 Ed. IV, To Sir John Elryngton, Knight, the King's Treasurer at War, by the hands of Richard, Duke of Gloucester,[6] viz. for the wages of 1,700 fighting men, retained by the said Duke to accompany him in the war against the Scotch ; viz. from the 11th August until the end of fourteen days the next following,—595l. . . . To Sir John Elryngton, Knight, the King's Treasurer at War, in part payment of the wages of 20,000 [7] men-at-arms, going upon a certain expedition with the Duke of Gloucester against the Scots ; paid to his own hands—4,504l. 11s. 8½d. . . . To the same Treasurer, as a reward given to divers soldiers, as well in the retinue of the Duke of Gloucester as in the retinue of the Earl of Northumberland [8] and others, for their expenses in going from the town of Berwick to their own homes ', three sums

[1] This would suggest that probably he was already a Knight Bachelor.
[2] Shaw, *Knights of England*, i, p. 138 ; Metcalfe, *Book of Knights*, p. 5.
[3] *Return Memb. Parl.*, p. 364.
[4] Appointed Nov. 5 : *List of Sheriffs, Public Record Office*, p. 137.
[5] *Hearne's Curious Discourses*, i, p. 151. [6] No. 7 below.
[7] On this number see Ramsay, *Lancaster and York*, ii, p. 442 ; but it is perhaps only a clerical error for 2,000. [8] No. 12 below.

amounting to nearly £795.[1] During this campaign Elrington
was created a Banneret in Scotland by the Duke of Gloucester.[2]
Like Montgomery and Borough, he was exempted from the
Sumptuary Act of 1482.[3] In connexion with the preparations
for the coronation of Edward V the following entry is extant :
' Warrant for payment of 14*l.* 11*s.* 5*d.* to John Belle, in full
contentacion of 32*l.* 2*s.* 7*d.* for certain stuff of wild fowl of him
bought by Sir John Elrington, ayenst that time that the coronation
of the bastard son of King Edward should have been kept and
holden.'[4] This entry was, of course, made after Bishop Stillington's revelation of the illegitimacy of the young prince. Elrington
was present at the coronation of Richard III on July 6, 1483,[5]
and died that year.[6] From a grant made on Sept. 20, 1485, we
know that he had held the office of Keeper, or Clerk, of the
Hanaper of the Chancery.[7] He married, as his first wife,
Maud . . . ,[8] and, as his second wife, Margaret, daughter and heir
(or coheir) of Sir Thomas Etchingham, of Etchingham, Sussex,
Kt., and relict of Sir William Blount, eldest son of Walter, Baron
Mountjoy.[9] His will, dated at Newcastle-on-Tyne, July 11,

[1] Devon's *Issues*, pp. 501-2. Detailed orders to Elrington in these matters
are recorded in *Foedera*, xii, p. 158, dated June 30, 1482.

[2] July 24, 1482. Shaw, ii, p. 17 ; Metcalfe, p. 6. The former adds ' probably
on the conclusion of the Treaty between the Duke of Gloucester and the Duke of
Albany and the Scottish nobles near Edinburgh '.

[3] *Rot. Parl.*, vi, p. 221 ; and see under Nos. 31, 32, below.

[4] *Harl. MS. 433, Art. 1651.*

[5] Holinshed, iii, p. 398.　　　　[6] *Sussex Arch. Soc. Collect.*, lii, p. 23.

[7] *Mat. Reign H. VII*, i, p. 16. Since 1473 in fact : *Pat. Rolls, 1476-85*, p. 495 ;
1467-77, pp. 396, 398.

[8] Streatfield, *Excerpta Cantiana*, 1836, Pedigree facing p. 5.

[9] *Visit. Worc.*, H.S., p. 20, where she is called Martha, d. & h. of Thos., Lord

1482, was proved[1] by Dame Margaret.[2] An abstract of it was printed by Sir Harris Nicolas.[3] In it Elrington describes himself as 'Treasurer of the Household', orders that his body be buried in the Church of Shoreditch, to which he had given a chantry,[4] and leaves his wife Margaret 100 marks and the 'stuff' at Dixson [Dixter] or at Hoxton. On July 26, 1486, Margaret Elrington, widow, was granted the custody of the manor-house of Thame, *alias* Igham, Sussex, for ten years at an annual rent of 40*s*.,[5] and at Michaelmas that year Richard and Nicholas Colepepper and their wives sued her for the manor of Dixsterne. The result is not stated.[6] On Aug. 2, 1487, she took as her third husband Thomas Combe, of Sussex, and at Easter, 1488, was again a widow.[7] She, too, was buried in St. Leonard's, Shoreditch,[8] where an altar-tomb, with recumbent effigies of herself and Elrington, existed till it was destroyed

Etchingham. Sir William Blount died *v.p.* before 1474, but she had issue by him. ' John Blount, Lord of Mountjoie, sued John Elryngton, Armiger, and Margaret his wife, for the manor of Belton [Rutland], which Richard Duddeley and John Lovedale had granted to Walter Blount, Kt., and the heirs male of his body, *temp.* Ric. 2. . . . Verdict for the plaintiff.' No date given. ('Pedigrees from Plea Rolls': *Gen.*, N.S., xx, p. 28.)

[1] *P. C. C.*, Feb. 3, 1483; *Visit. Sussex*, H.S., p. 125.

[2] *Pat. Rolls*, *1476–85*, p. 495; *Visit. Salop.*, H.S., p. 56; *Gen.*, N.S., xxi, p. 246; *Excerpt. Cant.*, *loc. cit.*; Alex. Croke, *Genealogical Hist. of Croke Family*, ii, pp. 202, 366; *Visit. Essex*, *1558*, H.S., p. 49, where he is called Sir John Elrington ' of Shordish ', but other details there are wrong.

[3] *Testamenta Vetusta*, p. 347.   [4] Ellis, *Hist. Shoreditch*, pp. 6, 7.

[5] *Mat. Reign H. VII*, i, p. 524.

[6] 'Pedigrees from the De Banco Rolls', *Gen.*, N.S., xxii, pp. 86–7.

[7] 'Ped. De Banco', *Gen.*, N.S., xxiii, pp. 150, 155.

[8] *Visit. Essex*, *1558*, H.S., i, p. 49; *Gen.*, N.S., xxi, p. 246; *Hist. Croke Fam.*, *loc. cit.*; *Stonor Letters*, i, p. 123; Stow, ii, p. 75.

at the taking down of the old church in 1736. Weever,[1] writing
in 1631, speaks of 'this defaced monument'. The mischief
was probably done by the Edwardian Protestants. In the vestry
of the new church are three drawings, made in 1735, two of the
tomb and one of windows, which show the arms of Elrington
and Etchingham.

No. 4. 'John lord Audeley.' John Tuchet, 6th Baron
Audley, succeeded his father in 1459 (see *Dict. Nat. Biog.,
s. n.* Touchet). In the present expedition he and Lord Duras [2]
were to serve under the Duke of Brittany at 4*s.* per day each,[3]
with 2,000 archers at 6*d.* per day, for the first quarter of 91 days,
and £4,586 was advanced to them for that purpose.[4] For the
second quarter, as we have seen in our *MS.,*[5] they were paid
£4,550.

No. 5. 'Galliard lorde Duras.' Galeard Durefort, Seigneur
de Duras in Guienne, had been since 1453 a refugee here and
a pensioner of the English King (see *D. N. B., s. n.* Duras).
The terms on which he served have been given under No. 4 above.

No. 6. 'The Duc off clarence.' The retinue of George
Plantagenet, Duke of Clarence, brother of Edward IV (see
D. N. B.), in this expedition consisted for the first quarter of 120
men-at-arms, himself reckoned in,[6] and 1,000 archers. His pay
as a Duke was the usual mark a day ; 20 of his men-at-arms
received 2*s.* a day as being Knights, the remaining 99 the

[1] *Fun. Mon.*, p. 211 ; Ellis, *op. cit.*, pp. 51, 52, gives a description, and his
Pl. VI drawings, of this monument.   [2] No. 5 in this Roll.

[3] The regular pay of a Baron on military service.

[4] *Foedera*, xi, p. 791 ; xii, p. 12.

[5] Fol. 1 *verso*.

[6] The leader is always included in the number stated.

customary 1s. of an esquire or other man-at-arms. In addition each man-at-arms was given 6d. a day 'ultra de regardo'. This *reward*, or *bonus*, commonly appears in the Tellers' Rolls. The archers had 6d. a day. The sum total advanced to him for the first quarter, of 91 days, was £3,193 6s. 10d.[1] In the second quarter, as our *MS*. shows,[2] his following was 10 Knights only, 100 men-at-arms, and 1,000 archers. Under the Proclamation of Feb. 1, 1475, all these leaders and their retinues, 'in their best and most defensible array were to muster at Portes Down in the county of Southampton' on May 26 following.[3]

BADGE. 'blake bulle.' The Black Bull was one of the badges of the House of York. Clarence was the district about the town, castle, and honour of Clare,[4] and in a window at Windsor was *A Bull sable corned and hoofed or*, and over it a scroll inscribed 'Ex honore de Clare'.[5] This attribution is borne out by other evidence. 'The bargens[6] of the honor of Clare, in Cambridgeshire, is a blak bull wt hornys, clees,[7] and membres[8] of golde.'[9] Again, 'The blacke bull, golden collar, for Clare'.[10] See, too, *Digby MS. 82, init.*:[11] 'The Bages that he beryth by the Honor

---

[1] *Foed.*, xi, p. 845. These rates of pay were the same as in the Agincourt campaign: see Nicolas, *Battle of Agincourt*, 2nd ed., 1832. A Knight-Banneret received the wages of a Baron, 4s. a day, as will be seen. [2] Fol. 1 *verso*.

[3] *Foed.*, xi, pp. 848–9. For the reason see under Sorell, No. 1 above. Eventually the embarkation was made from the Kentish ports.

[4] Edmondson, *Complete Body of Heraldry*, i, p. 97.

[5] So Sandford, *Genealogical Hist. Eng.*, pp. 403–4. [6] Badges.

[7] Claws, *i. e.* hoofs. [8] *Pudenda*.

[9] *Harl. MS. 4632, circa* 1522–34, *Coll. Top. & Gen.*, iii, p. 55.

[10] *Harl. MS. 5854, f. 23.*

[11] Bodl.; printed in *Archaeologia*, xvii, p. 226.

of Clare ys a blacke Bolle, rowghe,[1] his Hornes, and his cleys, And membrys of Gold.' The Bull of Clare is still to be seen carved on the N. side of the Perpendicular pulpit in the 'Yorkist' Church of Fotheringhay, and is found among Inn-signs.[2] It appears also as a supporter on the seal of this Duke.[3] He kept, too, a 'Noir Toureau Pursuivant'.[4] The following extract from Upton,[5] on badges, may not be out of place here : 'Ifta figna non funt fua Arma, fet folummodo figna per que ipforum feudatarii & vaffalli ab aliis cognofcuntur.' Or, as John Blount, of All Souls, Oxford, in his unpublished translation of Upton,[6] has it : 'Thefe bages be not ther owne aremes, but onely certen markes & fygnes wherby there feedmen & vaffalls may be knowne frome other.'[7] Way was probably right in saying[8] that the badge was the origin of uniform.

No. 7. 'The Duc of gloucefter.' Richard Plantagenet,

[1] *i. e.* ruffling, savage, shown in its fullest grandeur. Compare the uses of 'ruff' and 'rufl' in, *e. g.*, Leigh's *Accedence of Armorie*, fol. 104 *b* ; Ferne's *Glorie of Generofite*, p. 94, and *Lacyes Nobilitie*, p. 24 ; also Halliwell's *Dict. Arch. & Prov. Words*, *s. v.* 'Ruffle'.

[2] See Larwood and Hotten, *Hist. of Signboards*, p. 133, which is taken from Bagford's *MS.* list of signs that originated in badges in *Harl. MS. 5910, ii. 167.* Bagford was a friend of Hearne : see the latter's *Remains.*

[3] Sandford, p. 436 ; Hope's *Garter Plates*, lxiv, and his *Heraldry for Craftsmen*, p. 207.

[4] Edmondson, i, p. 129 (on the authority of *Cotton MS. Domitian A. ix, n. 20*) ; Thynne, Lancaster Herald in 1605, cited in *Hearne's Cur. Disc.*, i, p. 160.

[5] *De Studio Militari* (*c.* 1436), Ed. by Bysshe, p. 35.

[6] *MS. c.* 1490–1500, *penes me.* It is clear from internal evidence that Blount's version was not made from any one of the six codices upon which Bysshe's edition was based.

[7] 'Might I not know thee by thy household badge ?' (Shak., *Hen. VI, B. v.* i. 201).   [8] *Promptorium Parvulorum*, C.S., i, pp. 20–1, note.

386   C

Duke of Gloucester, afterwards Richard III, does not appear in the Tellers' Roll for the first quarter of this expedition, but in our *MS.*[1] he brings for the second quarter 10 Knights, 100 other men-at-arms, and 1,000 archers, he himself receiving a Duke's pay, 13*s.* 4*d.* a day. This distinguished soldier,[2] as might be expected, was the only one among the leaders, from the King inclusive downwards, who preferred blows to bribes, and wished to fight.

BADGE. ' whitt bore.' As the phrase went, ' The Duc of Gloster gave a Whitt Bore '.[3] According to Sandford [4] Richard's badge of the White Boar was derived ' ex Honore de Windsore '. Is this notion based on one of the exploits of the traditional Guy of Warwick? ' But first, neare Winsor, I did slaye / A bore of passing might and strength ; / Whose like in England never was / For hugenesse both in bredth and length.' [5] Or may ' Bore ' have been merely an anagram of *Ebor*, referring to the House of York, like the well-known alerion of Loraine? In June, 1483, as a response to a letter from the Duke of Gloucester, the City of York agreed to send 300 horse to London to support the Protector against the Queen's party, and these were to wear both the cognizance (badge) of the Duke and that of the City ; [6] and 8,000 boar badges were made and ' wrought upon fuftian ' at 20*s.* per thousand for Richard's coronation ; [7] while ' four ftandards of farcenett with boars ', and ' thirteen thoufand

---

[1] Fol. 1 *verso.*

[2] ' Horribili vigilantia ac celeritate plenus ', as the hostile Polydore Virgil styles him (*Hist. Angl.*, Leyden, p. 701).

[3] *Harl. MS. 304, f. 12.*   [4] p. 430.

[5] Percy's *Reliques of Anc. Eng. Poetry*, iii, p. 149.

[6] Davies, *Records of the City of York*, pp. 152–4.

[7] ' Wardrobe Accounts of 1483 ' : *Archaeologia*, i, p. 394.

quinyſans of fuſtian with boars' were ordered on Aug. 31 following for the same event.[1] In the *Rows Roll*[2] Richard is shown twice as King standing on a Boar, as is his son Edward, Prince of Wales. The reference to the 'hog' in the Colyng-bourne distich[3] is too familiar to need quotation, and is, of course, in accord with the usage of the times, as shown in the political poems of the period, and indicated in the lines, 'For where I meant the King by name of hog, / I only alluded to his badge the bore'.[4] Richard is spoken of by his badge in *Les Douze Triomphes de Henri VII*,[5] where he is compared with the Boar of Arcadia slain by Hercules, *i. e.* Henry VII : 'De ce senglyer c'est droit que je l'aplique au roy Richard.' Similarly, in line 13 of *The Rose of England* : 'A beast men call a bore', and again in line 32, 'The bore soe white', and elsewhere in the same poem.[6] Oddly enough, it does not occur in *The Song of Lady Bessy*. Richard's boar-badge is carved on the south side of the pulpit in Fotheringhay Church, also on the soffit of the bay-window of the withdrawing room at Barnard Castle, which was a property of his.[7] A cut of this is given in Halsted's *Richard III*.[8] Cooper, in his *Annals of Cambridge*,[9] states[10] that Richard III gave to Queen's College 'a silver seal matrix whereon is engraved his cognizance the boar'. This is not now in the possession of the College, nor is there any record of it

---

[1] Drake, *Eboracum*, p. 117. 'Quinyſans' are cognizances.

[2] Ed. by Courthope, Nos. 17, 63, 64.

[3] For whose case see Gairdner, *Richard III*, pp. 186–92.

[4] *Mirror for Magistrates*, Pt. II, i, p. 377.

[5] Bernard André, *Hist. Regis Henrici Septimi*, R.S., p. 138.

[6] *Bp. Percy's Folio MS.*, iii, p. 190.   [7] Clark, *Mediaeval Mil. Arch.*, i, p. 210.

[8] i, p. 346.   [9] i, p. 225, note.   [10] On the authority of *Harl. MS. 433, ff. 68, 87.*

there.[1] *A boar argent, armed, bristled, and membered or* was used as a sinister supporter by Richard,[2] and both his supporters are sometimes white boars.[3] Sandford [4] says that in his time [5] there was over the gate of the Library at Cambridge a rose carved in stone, with a boar as sinister supporter. This has long disappeared. He also states [6] that on the West side of the steeple at Wolverhampton were Richard's arms in stone supported by two boars. These, too, are gone, perhaps destroyed at the recent ' restoration ' of the Church. As Duke of Gloucester, Richard had, besides a Gloucester Herald, a ' Blanke-Sanglier ' Pursuivant,[7] and, as King, a ' Blanc Sanglier ' Herald ; [8] also at Bosworth a Pursuivant with the same title.[9]

No. 8. ' The Duc of norffolke.' John Mowbray, 5th Duke of Norfolk [10] and Earl Marshal (see *D. N. B.*), received for the first quarter £1,013 17s. 10d. as payment for 40 men-at-arms, including himself, and 300 archers.[11] His following for the second quarter, as we see, was the same with the addition of two Knights.[12]

[1] *Ex inform.* the President of Queen's, Jan. 20, 1923. Among the relics found on Bosworth Field was a gold ring with a white boar enamelled on it. There is an illustration of this in Hutton's *Battle of Bosworth*, p. 263, and fig. 9. Its attribution, however, is doubtful. See, too, the almost contemporary illustration of Richard's badge in ' Prince Arthur's Armory ', given in *Cat. Her. Exhib. Burl. Ho.*, Pl. XXXIII ; also Richard's letter of Dec. 6, 1483, to the authorities at Gloucester ordering that his badge alone should be worn in that city. (Ellis, *Letters*, Series 3, i, p. 113.)

[2] *Harl. MS. 4632*, in *Coll. Top. & Gen.*, iii, p. 57.

[3] *Royal MS. 18. A. 12*, in Willement's *Regal Heraldry*, Pl. XIII, fig. 1 ; also *Vincent MS. 152, f. 53.*   [4] p. 430.   [5] That is between 1660 and 1677.

[6] p. 430.   [7] *Hearne's Cur. Disc.*, i, p. 160.

[8] *Letters & Papers, Rich. III & Hen. VII*, R.S., i, pp. 25, 35.

[9] Edmondson, i, p. 127 ; Noble, *College of Arms*, pp. 57, 58, 73.

[10] Margaret Plantagenet, Duchess of Norfolk, being reckoned as the first of that title.   [11] *Foed.*, xi, p. 846.   [12] *MS.* fol. 1 *verso.*

BADGE. ' Whytt lyon.' This badge, *A white lion rampant*, was taken from the Duke's arms, being either that from the Mow-bray coat, *Gules, a lion rampant argent*, or that from the Segrave coat, *Sable, a lion rampant argent, crowned gold*, brought in by the Mowbray–Segrave marriage three generations earlier. In *Harl. MS. 4632* [1] the badge of the Duke of Norfolk is given as *A lion rampant argent*, which the editor of the catalogue in *Coll. Top. & Gen.*[2] considered to be the white lion of Segrave.[3] In the list of badges in the *Wroxton MS.*[4] we read ' The duke of Northfolke is yᵉ Whyte lyon rampand, and for yᵉ lordeschipe of Sedgrave the Whyte lyon passand wᵗ a crone of golde upō his head '. In all the early Rolls of Arms, however, the Segrave lion is rampant. The father of the Duke of our Roll is referred to by his badge : ' To se þe . . . Lione brought to a bay ' ; [5] and again at Towton : ' the White Lyon, ful worthely he wrought.' [6] So, too, his grandfather, the Mowbray Duke of Norfolk who died in 1432, in the line ' The White Lioun is leyde to slepe '.[7]

No. 9. ' The Duc of Suffolke.' This was John de la Pole, 2nd Duke of Suffolk (see *D. N. B.*), whose muster in the first quarter for the invasion of France was 40 men-at-arms, himself included, and 300 archers, for which he received £1,013 17*s*. [10*d*.].[8]

---

[1] *circa* 1522–34.   [2] iii, p. 65.

[3] For these two bearings see, *e. g.*, Willement, *Heraldic Notices of Cant. Cath.*, pp. 131–2 ; also *Archaeologia*, lxvi, pp. 541–2 ; and for a Mowbray coat of this period the ' Fifteenth Century Bk. of Arms ', from *Harl. MS. 2169*, in *The Ancestor*, iii, p. 202, No. 86.

[4] *Herald & Genealogist*, vii, p. 337 : 1st list of badges, early 16th cent.

[5] ' Political Poem ', *c.* 1460 : *Archaeologia*, xxix, p. 341.   [6] *Ibid.*, p. 345.

[7] *Political Poems*, R.S., ii, p. 222 ; *Excerpta Historica*, p. 161 ; and *Retrospective Review*, ii, p. 515.

[8] *Foed.*, xi, p. 846 ; the same number and sum as the Duke of Norfolk.

For the second quarter his numbers were identical, save for the addition of two knights, as in the case of the Duke of Norfolk.[1]

BADGE. 'lyon of gold the kew forched.' This badge is the main charge from the arms of Burghersh. *Argent, a chief gules, over all a lion rampant tail-forked or*, which is quartered with those of De la Pole on Suffolk's Garter-plate.[2] The Burghersh coat was brought in by Chaucer, the Duke's mother, Alice, being daughter and heir of Thomas Chaucer, of Ewelme, Oxon., Esq., by Matilda, daughter and coheir of Sir Thomas Burghersh, of Ewelme.[3] 'The yelowe lyon w^t ye ii tayles for his mother,' says the *Wroxton MS.*[4]

No. 10. 'The Duc off Bokyngh[a]m.' Henry Stafford, 2nd Duke of Buckingham (see *D. N. B.*), does not appear in the Tellers' Roll for the first quarter of this 'viage', but in our *MS.*[5] he contributes 4 knights, 40 other men-at-arms, and 400 archers. The Roll tells us that he went home. He is not in either Molinet's or Haynin's list.

BADGE. 'the stafford knot.' Knots, or twists, such as this[6] are supposed by some to have been intended to represent the initial letters of their respective houses, or possibly monograms.[7] For examples of the Stafford Knot see, *e. g.*, the seal of this Duke given in *Archaeologia*, xxxviii, Pl. XIV, fig. 5; also Hope's *Heraldry for Craftsmen*, p. 185, from a brass of 1413 at Exeter

---

[1] *MS.*, fol. 1 *verso*.   [2] Hope, *G.P.*, lxxix.

[3] G. E. C., 1st ed., vii, p. 306.

[4] 1st list of badges : *Her. & Gen.*, vii, p. 337.   [5] Fol. 1 *verso*.

[6] Except, of course, the Harrington 'knot', so called, which is no knot, but merely the fret from the arms of that family.

[7] Compare abroad the badge of 'L'Ordre du Noeud', for which see Montfaucon, *Antiquities of France*, i, p. 57 *et seq.*, and Plates CXIII, CXV–CXVIII.

to Canon William Langeton ; the counter-seal of Humphrey, Earl of Stafford, on a deed of May 17, 1438, figured in *Archaeologia, ibid.*, No. 4ᵃ ; and the standard, *c.* 1475, of our man given in Boutell's *English Heraldry*, 1899, p. 260. It is still to be seen on the gateway of Maxstoke Castle, Warwickshire, a Stafford property.

No. 11. ' The marquis of Dorſſett ' (see *D. N. B.*). Thomas Grey, Baron Ferrers of Groby, b. 1451, was the eldest son of the Queen by her first husband, John, Baron Ferrers of Groby, usually known as Sir John Grey. On August 14, 1471, he had been created Earl of Huntingdon, a title which he soon after resigned to the King, and upon April 18, 1475, on the eve of this expedition, had been promoted to be Marquis of Dorset.[1] He is not in the Tellers' Roll for the first quarter, and no following is given in our *MS.* We see, however, from the latter that the pay of a Marquis on service was 10*s.* per day.[2]

BADGE. None is given in the *MS.* His son and heir, Thomas, who succeeded in 1501, bore as a badge on his standard a unicorn ermine surrounded by sun-rays,[3] and a unicorn ermine supported the staff of his banner.[4] In the list in *Harl. MS. 4632, ff. 209–25,* compiled between 1522 and 1534,[5] *On a sun or a unicorn ermine* is given as a crest (or badge ?) of Grey, Marquis of Dorset.[6]

No. 12. ' Therll of Northumberland.' Henry, 4th (Percy) Earl of Northumberland (see *D. N. B.*), received for the first

---

[1] G. E. C., new ed., iv, p. 418; Courthope, p. 164; Ashmole, *Ord. of Garter,* p. 107 ; Doyle, i, p. 617, who has May 30th.   [2] Fol. 2 *recto.*

[3] *MS. i. 2, Coll. of Arms,* in *Excerpt. Hist.,* p. 52, and in ' De Walden Library ', *Banners, Standards, & Badges,* p. 98.

[4] De Walden, p. 38.   [5] Printed in *Coll. Top. & Gen.,* iii, pp. 49 *et seq.*

[6] See No. 47 below.

quarter of this enterprise £1,249 14s. 8d., his following being
60 men-at-arms, and 350 archers. His pay as an Earl was 6s. 8d.
a day ; 9 of the other men-at-arms had 2s. as knights, the
remaining 50 1s., and all of the above 6d. a day each extra as
' reward '. The archers were paid the usual 6d. apiece.[1] In
the second quarter his retinue had shrunk to 40 men-at-arms
and 200 archers.[2]

BADGE. ' Creſſant ſilu[er].'[3] ' The erle of Northumberland
geveth the mone.'[4] The father of this nobleman was buried,
as is supposed, with many other Percies, in the N. aisle of St.
Denis, York, under the large blue stone near the window in
which his crescent appears ; and his son and heir, Henry Algernon
Percy, bore on his standard, as one of his badges, the silver
crescent. This standard is accompanied by eleven smaller ones,
on seven of which the crescent is shown.[5] Hutton [6] quotes from
' Tenne Strange Prophecies ', 1644, a story relating to the
Earl's betrayal of Richard III, in which he is designated after
his badge, as ' the moon '. In 1403 the adherents of the House
of Percy are spoken of as wearing ' leurs cressans as braas '.[7]
There are numerous early literary references to this badge.
Henry, 1st (Percy) Earl of Northumberland [8] is described as

---

[1] *Foed.*, xi, p. 847.   [2] *MS.*, fol. 2 *recto*.   [3] It was sometimes gold.
[4] *Wroxton MS.*, 1st list ; *Her. & Gen.*, vii, p. 338.
[5] *MS. 1. 2. Coll of Arms*; in *Excerpt. Hist.*, p. 334. See, too, De Walden,
p. 258 ; and *Harl. MS. 4632*, in *Coll. Top. & Gen.*, iii, pp. 62, 66, under ' The
Herlle of Northethomberland ' and ' Cont de Northumberland '.
[6] *Bosworth*, p. 223.
[7] ' Au bras '. Fonblanque's *Annals of the House of Percy*, i, pp. 230, 534.
[8] Succ. 1377, d. 1408.

'The Crescent'.[1] Similarly 'The Lucetts[2] and the Cressawnts
both, The Skotts fought them agayne'.[3] To take a later
example, from 'The Rising in the North' of 1569, 'Erle Percy
there his ancyent[4] spred, / The Half-Moone shining all soe
faire.'[5] On a seal, of 1396, of Henry, 1st (Percy) Earl, as sheriff
of his county, is a castle within a crescent, and Longstaffe[6]
thought that the crescent originally had reference to the shire,
not to the Percy family, because a castle with three crescents on
it appears upon the seal of John Heron, of Chipchase, as sheriff
of Northumberland in 1444. One of the badges of the Ducal
House of York was the lion of March within a crescent, and
York was, of course, the old capital of Northumbria.[7] In the
ceiling of the Percy chantry-chapel[8] at Tynemouth Priory is
the Percy crescent and shacklebolt on a shield.[9] The anagram
on 'Henricus Percius' cited in Camden's *Remains*[10] may be
given here : 'Percius "hic pure sincerus", Percia Luna /
Candida tota micat, pallet at illa polo.' A silver crescent of the
Duke of Northumberland is shown in Hope's *Heraldry for
Craftsmen*, pp. 311–12, and there is a cut of a similar badge in
Coll. Top. & Gen.[11] On the chancel stalls of Wakefield Church

[1] Longstaffe in *Archaeologia Æliana*, 1860, p. 173, quoting Gower, *Harl. MS.*
6291.   [2] Luces, or pike, of the Lucy family.

[3] Percy, *Reliques*, i, p. 31, 'Battle of Otterbourne' (1388), ll. 69, 70. A 15th-
century poem.   [4] *Ancien*, probably a corruption of OF. *enseigne* (Skeat).

[5] Percy, *Reliques*, i, p. 293, ll. 105–6; and the lines, *temp.* Hen. VII, there
quoted, which give an imaginary origin for this badge; also ll. 139–42 of the same
poem.   [6] *Arch. Æliana, loc. cit.*, pp. 179–80.

[7] Leland, *Collectanea*, ii, p. 619; Willement, *Reg. Her.*, p. 47.

[8] Mid. 15th cent.   [9] *Arch. Journal*, 1910, p. 25.   [10] Ed. of 1674, p. 189.

[11] iii, p. 76. See also the illustration in *Her. Exhib. Burl. Ho.*, p. 27, and the
bequest in 1430, there cited, of a silver crescent.

are Percy crescents of *c.* 1470,[1] and others exist in Great Sandal Church, Yorkshire.[2]   See, too, the panel and miserere at All Saints, Wakefield.[3]   This badge also was used as a tavern-sign, and occurs in Bagford's list as ' Crescent or Halfe Moune, þe Earle of Northumberland '.[4]   The case will be remembered of James Percy, the Dublin trunk-maker, who, in 1670, claimed the titles and inheritance of the Percies, alleging, among his proofs of descent, that he was born, as he said other Percies had been, with a mole like a half-moon on his body.[5]

No. 13. ' Therll of Ryuers.'   This was Anthony Wydville, Baron Scales *iure uxoris*, Elizabeth, daughter and heir of Thomas, Baron Scales, and, from 1469, 2nd Earl of Rivers (see *D. N. B.*). His name does not appear in the muster for the first quarter, but for the second quarter he took to France two Knights, 40 men-at-arms, with himself, and 200 archers.[6]

BADGE.   ' ſcaleipp ſilu[*er*].'   This badge was taken from the canting arms of Scales : *Gules, six escallops 3, 2, and 1 argent.* In Middle-English ' scale ' is found in the sense of ' shell ',[7] and in medieval heraldry the shell is almost always the escallop of the pilgrim.   ' The lorde Skales is the scalop schelles.' [8]   An escallop argent is given as the badge of ' Skalles ' in *Harl. MS. 4632.*[9] During this invasion of France ' an English herald called Scales was made prisoner ', and letters found on him were read by the

---

[1] An illustration of one of them is given in *Her. & Gen.*, vii, p. 353.

[2] *Ibid.*, vi, p. 671.

[3] *Yorks. Archaeol. & Top. Journal*, i, p. 149.

[4] Larwood and Hotten, *op. cit.*, p. 133.   [5] Fonblanque, ii, p. 485.

[6] *MS.*, fol. 2 *recto.*   [7] Stratmann, p. 522 ; see, too, Skeat, *s.v.*

[8] *Wroxton MS.*, 1st list ; *Her. & Gen.*, vii, p. 338.

[9] *Coll. Top. & Gen.*, iii, p. 74.

French King.[1]   According to Edmondson,[2] this Earl Rivers
had a Scales Pursuivant in 1477, but he states no authority.
In the passage from Monstrelet 'herald' may have been a vague
term for an officer of arms of any rank.[3]

No. 14. 'Therll of penbroke.' William, 2nd (Herbert)
Earl of Pembroke, afterwards Earl of Huntingdon (see *D. N. B.*),
was only fourteen at the time of this expedition. He is not mentioned in connexion with the first quarter, but in the second
quarter brought 40 men-at-arms and 200 archers.[4]

BADGE. 'Drewhgt horſe gold.' In heraldry a draught-
horse is distinguished by having a collar and traces, or shafts,
and is so drawn in our *MS.* The horse, however, does not occur
as a charge in early English armory, hence we seem debarred
from finding the origin of this badge in the arms brought in by
any family alliance. In Rymer[5] we read of 'Draught Horſeȝ
for the Cariage of our Ordenance', and if we could find that
Pembroke held any special office or command in relation to the
artillery, the explanation might lie there.

No. 15. 'Therll of Douglas.' James, 9th and last Earl of
Douglas, and 3rd Earl of Avondale, head of the Black Douglases,
was a refugee from Scotland (see *D. N. B.*). The Tellers' Roll

---

[1] Monstrelet, ii, p. 415.   [2] i, p. 129.

[3] Doyle, iii, p. 144, is in error about the arms of this Earl Rivers, and gives no
evidence. Rivers, of course, would have no right to quarter Scales. His true
bearings are shown on his tabard in the well-known illumination of 1477 in the
Lambeth Library (*MS.* 265), which has often been reproduced; as, *e. g.*, in
Walpole's *Royal & Noble Authors*, 1759, i, Frontispiece, and in Strutt's *Regal
& Ecclesiastical Antiquities*, Pl. XLVII.

[4] *MS.*, fol. 2 *recto*. The presence of this lad furnishes us with an example of
the practice of children of great houses attending the wars for the purpose of
military education.   [5] *Foed.*, xii, p. 158; June 30, 1482.

for the first quarter shows that he brought 4 men-at-arms, himself counted in, and 40 archers, for which he was paid £141 16s. 2d. His personal wage was that of an English Earl, half a mark daily.[1] In the second quarter his contingent was the same.[2]

BADGE. ' hart gulis.' This was taken from the well-known charge in the Douglas coat. See, for example, the Garter-plate of this nobleman,[3] and the description of Lifton Church, Devon, in *Symonds's Diary*.[4]

No. 16. ' Therll of ormonde.' John Butler, 6th Earl of Ormond (see *D. N. B.*), brought to the muster for the first quarter 2 men-at-arms, that is 1 besides himself, and 16 archers, for which he received a payment of £73 11s. 2d. ;[5] in the second quarter his numbers were the same.[6]

BADGE. ' peyr keythonges.' This must be an error for ' gryphongs ', *i. e.* griffins, as the drawing shows. The colour is not stated, perhaps because in early armory the griffin is usually gold. Carrick MacGriffin [7] was an ancient manor of the Butlers. The arms of this lordship, quartered by the Earls of Ormond, *Argent, a lion rampant sable, on a chief gules a swan with wings expanded of the first between two annulets or*, were, according to legend, those of the Griffiths, or Griffins, descendants of Griffith, Prince of Wales in the eleventh century, who migrated to Ireland and were the original lords of Carrick MacGriffin.[8] The worthlessness of the story need not prevent its being an explanation

---

[1] *Foed.*, xi, p. 844.   [2] *MS.*, fol. 2 *recto*.   [3] Hope, *G. P.*, lxxii.

[4] *Diary of the Marches of the Royal Army, July 31, 1644*, C.S.

[5] *Foed.*, xi, p. 846.   [6] *MS.*, fol. 2 *recto*.

[7] Now Carrick (' crag ') on Suir. So called from a large rock in the bed of the river.   [8] *Her. & Gen.*, i, p. 286.

of the origin of this badge. Later the griffin appears as a supporter used by the various branches of the Butlers of Ireland. In some cases it is, as here, what the heraldry books call the wingless, or male, griffin, which has two horns, and golden rays proceeding from its body. On the seal (1446) of James Butler, the 5th Earl, the sinister supporter is a horned griffin.[1] The supporter of the Ormond banner in *MS. 2 M. 16. Coll. of Arms*, of this period, has the rays, but no horns.[2]

No. 17. 'the lord hastynges.' William Hastings, 1st Baron Hastings (see *D. N. B.*), took to France for the first quarter 40 men-at-arms, 'seipso computato ut barone', and 300 archers, for which he received £966 18s. 6d., including his own pay of 4s. a day as a Baron,[3] and in the second quarter his following was the same.[4]

BADGE. 'Blake Boull hed Rasid hornes & pys [5] & bout the neke a Croune gold.' The same badge had been used by his grandfather Sir Ralph Hastings as early as 1397.[6] This badge is similar to the crest on the Garter-plate of Lord Hastings,[7] where, however, the breast is not gold, but the mane is, and the erasing is concealed by the crown, as in the two seals reproduced by Hope.[8] On the other hand this Hastings crest as it appears

---

[1] Doyle, iii, p. 674, and see p. 158, Rochford. [2] De Walden, p. 51.

[3] *Foed.*, xi, p. 846. [4] *MS.*, fol. 2 *recto*.

[5] OF. for *poitrine*, 'breast'. *Pis contre pis*, 'breast to breast'. (Godefroy, *Lexique de l'ancien français*; Lacombe, *Dict. du Vieux Langage françois*; Kelham, *Norm. Dict.*) Variant forms occur in Middle English, the nearest to this being 'pisan', found for a breast-plate, or gorget, in *Sir Gawayne and the Green Knight (c.* 1360), l. 204 (Stratmann, *s.v.*). [6] Hope, *H. for C.*, p. 174.

[7] Hope, *G. P.*, lxvii. [8] *Ibid.*, and in *H. for C.*, pp. 140, 204.

on the roundel of 1587, being set on a torse, shows the erasing.[1]
The 3rd Baron, grandson of our Lord Hastings, bore, as one of
the badges on his standard, in the French expedition of 1513,
' A bulls hed sabull rassed wyth a crown about his neck gold.'[2]
The same badge is seen on the standard of ' The Lord Hastynggis '
in *MS. I. 2. Coll. of Arms* ;[3] and in *Harl. MS. 4632*[4] it is
A bull's head erased sable ducally gorged and armed or.

No. 18. ' The lord Stanley.' This was Thomas, 2nd Baron
Stanley (see *D. N. B.*). There went with him to France in the
first quarter 40 men-at-arms, himself counted in, and 300 archers,
in payment for which he had £966 17s. 6d.,[5] and in the second
quarter his muster was the same.[6]

BADGE. ' Gryppe [7] lege Rafyd gold.' In this connexion,
however, it is always regarded as an Eagle's Leg. The ' Eygell's
fett '[8] is taken from the familiar Stanley crest : ' A Eygelle gold
wyth swedylled chyld in the fette.'[9] The eagle's claw badge
is found on the seal of this Lord Stanley as Earl of Derby and
Seneschal of Macclesfield in 1485.[10] So, in *MS. I. 2. Coll. of
Arms* ' Eagle's Legs erased at the thigh and erect or ' are dis-

---

[1] *Archaeologia*, lxx, p. 63, No. 12, and Pl. II, 12.

[2] *Cotton MS. Cleopatra C. v.*

[3] In *Excerpt. Hist.*, p. 321.   [4] In *Coll. Top. & Gen.*, iii, p. 67.

[5] *Foed.*, xi, p. 845.   [6] *MS.*, fol. 2 *recto*.

[7] Vulture. *Prompt. Parv.* ; Stratmann ; Halliwell, &c., *s.v.*

[8] *Cotton MS. Cleopatra C. v*, describing the badges borne on the standard of
the grandson and immediate successor of the Lord Stanley of this Roll in the
Expedition to France of 1513.

[9] *Ibid.*, and see the Garter-plates of this peer and his father in Hope's *G. P.*,
lxii and lxxxvi.

[10] Hope, *H. for C.*, p. 183, and *G. P.*, lxxxvi.

played as badges on the banner of the 2nd Earl of Derby.[1] Again, in *Harl. MS. 4632*, in the case of the great-grandson of our man, 'Conte Derby' gives as badge *An eagle's leg erased at the thigh or*.[2] It is carved on the Warden's stall in Manchester Cathedral.[3] In *The Song of Lady Bessy* [4] this badge is repeatedly referred to as Lord Stanley's : 'The Eagle's foot should be pulled down' ; [5] 'He drew an Eagle foot on the door truely' ; [6] 'Twenty thousand Eagle feet' ; [7] 'Ten thousand eigle feete to fighte' ; [8] 'And xx.tie thowsand eigle feete.' [9] See, too, the variant *Ladye Bessiye* in *Bishop Percy's Folio MS*.[10] He is alluded to in a similar way in *The Rose of England*,[11] as 'an Egle gleaming gay'. In the same poem he is 'my ffather the old Egle',[12] pointing, of course, to his having married the Dowager Countess of Richmond.[13] The 'gripes ffoot' badge of 'þe Ld. Stanley' occurs also as a tavern-sign.[14]

No. 19. 'The lord Scroppe.' The retinue of John, 5th Baron Scrope of Bolton (see *D. N. B.*), in the first quarter consisted of 20 men-at-arms and 200 archers, for which he received £602 17s. 6d. ; [15] in the second quarter his muster was the same.[16]

---

[1] *Excerpt. Hist.*, p. 332.

[2] Tarbock, a branch of the Lathom House, used the same, but as a charge on the shield : *Arch. Journal*, vi (1851), Pl. XXII, p. 202 ; *Coll. Top. & Gen.*, vii, pp. 7, 18. [3] *Arch. Journal, ibid.*, Pl. XXV, p. 207.

[4] Ed. by Halliwell, 1847. [5] Version, i, p. 5. [6] *Ibid.*, p. 23.

[7] *Ibid.*, p. 25, where, and in the two next quotations, the badge is identified with his followers. [8] Version, ii, p. 46.

[9] *Ibid.*, p. 62. [10] Hales and Furnivall, iii, pp. 319–63.

[11] *Ibid.*, p. 190, l. 21. [12] *i. e.* Henry Tudor's step-father.

[13] *Ibid.*, p. 191, l. 35. It is engraved upon the silver clasp of her *MS.* Prayer Book shown on p. 51 of *Her. Exhib. Bur. Ho.* [14] Bagford's List, *loc. cit.*

[15] *Foed.*, xi, p. 844. [16] *MS.*, fol. 2 *recto.*

BADGE. ' Cornyche chowe.' In the contemporary *Verses on the Battle of Towton* this Lord Scrope is referred to as ' þe Cornysshe Chowghe ' ;[1] and in the *Wroxton MS.* we find ' The lorde Scropilton ye cornysse crowe '.[2] Cornish choughs also appear as badges displayed on his standard by (probably) his grandson Henry, 7th Baron.[3] Two Cornish choughs were later used as supporters by Scrope of Bolton.[4] Our Lord Scrope's first wife, who was living at the date of this expedition, was Joan, daughter of William, 4th Baron Fitzhugh,[5] and *A Cornish Chough proper* was a Fitzhugh crest.[6] It seems likely, therefore, that this was the source of the badge.[7]

No. 20. ' The lord howard.' John, 1st Baron Howard (see *D. N. B.*), does not appear in the Tellers' Roll for the first quarter, but in the second quarter he brings 20 men-at-arms and 200 archers.[8]

BADGE. ' Whytt lyon on his fheulde[r] Creffant Azur.' On this White Lion see under the Duke of Norfolk above [9] and Sir Thomas Howard below.[10] In *MS. I. 2. Coll. of Arms* [11] the Lord Howard used, as the badge on his standard, a Lion rampant argent, &c., with a crescent on his shoulder for difference. That compilation is retrospective as well as contemporary, and the Lord Howard referred to is this leader. There is extant a letter from

---

[1] *Archaeologia*, xxix, p. 345.   [2] *Her. & Gen.*, vii, p. 338.
[3] *MS. i. 2. Coll. of Arms*, in *Excerpt. Hist.*, p. 62, and reproduced in De Walden, p. 104.   [4] *e. g.* Willement, *Her. Cant. Cath.*, p. 109, note.
[5] Nicolas, *Scrope & Grosvenor Controversy*, ii, p. 61 ; G.E.C., new ed., v, Ped. between pp. 668–9.   [6] Burke.   [7] I have not found it earlier.
[8] *MS.*, fol. 2 *recto*.   [9] No. 8.   [10] No. 38.
[11] *Excerpt. Hist.*, p. 62, and De Walden, p. 105.

him to John Paston, written a few days after the landing of Henry Tudor in August, 1485, in which he requests the former to meet him at Bury St. Edmunds and bring ' seche company of tall men as ye may goodly make at my cost and charge, be seyd [*besides*] that ye have promysyd the King ; and I pray yow ordeyne them jakets of my levery '.[1] The White Lion rampant of ' Norfolk and all þe Hawardes ' is found as a Tavern-sign.[2]

No. 21. ' The lord fferreres.' Sir Walter Devereux, of Weobley, Herefordshire, 7th Baron Ferrers of Chartley, son and heir of Sir Walter Devereux, of Weobley, by Elizabeth, daughter and heir of John Merbury, Esq., was born about 1432.[3] Since 1350 no summons to Parliament had been issued to Ferrers of Chartley. The 6th Baron died without issue in 1450, and Devereux, who had married his daughter and heir, Ann Ferrers, was summoned as Lord Ferrers on Feb. 20, 1462.[4] We meet with him first in 1455 as Sheriff of Gloucestershire.[5] In 1459, during the temporary collapse of the Yorkist party, he, then a simple esquire,[6] made submission, with others, to Henry VI ; when ' many men, bothe knyghtys and squyers, come whythe syr [7] Water Deverose, in hir schyrtys and halters in hyr hondys, fallynge by-fore the kynge, and alle hadde grace and marcy bothe of lyffe and lym '.[8] He had been attainted in the Coventry Parliament of that year,[9] and, though spared, was deprived, with

---

[1] *Paston Letters*, iii, p. 321.
[2] Bagford's List, *ut supra*.   [3] G. E. C., new ed., v, p. 597.
[4] *Ibid.*, p. 598 ; Courthope, p. 186.
[5] *List of Sheriffs*, p. 50 ; appointed Nov. 4.   [6] *Rot. Parl.*, v, p. 349.
[7] *Sic*. A mistake.   [8] *Gregory's Chronicle*, C.S., pp. 206–7.
[9] *Rot. Parl.*, *ibid.* ; *English Chron.*, C.S., p. 83.

D

certain reservations, of all his possessions. On Feb. 12, 1460, he is still only ' armiger '.[1] Upon the 17th of August following, by which time the Yorkists had retrieved their position, he was appointed by that party to keep order for them in Wales,[2] and on Oct. 4 of the same year we find him returned as Knight of the shire for Herefordshire.[3] He is included by William of Worcester [4] in the list of those present with Edward at Mortimer's Cross on Feb. 2, 1461, and described there as ' Dominus Walterus Deveris, dominus Ferreres de Charteley ', but doubtless this description applies to him as he was when the Chronicler wrote. He was with the Yorkist magnates who forgathered at Baynard's Castle on the succeeding 3rd of March and agreed that Edward, Duke of York, must be King of England,[5] on the 29th he was created Knight Bachelor by Edward at Towton,[6] and he took part in the Scotch expedition of 1462.[7] Exemption was granted him from the Act of Resumption of 1467–8.[8] He was a witness when Henry Percy,[9] whose Lancastrian father had been slain at Towton, was released from the Tower and took the oath of fealty to the Yorkist King on Oct. 27, 1469 ; [10] was one of the persons ordered to raise men and do their best to arrest Clarence and Warwick in March and April of 1470 ; [11] was among those who, on July 3, 1471, after Edward's restoration, took the oath recognizing the latter's son as heir to the throne ; [12] and on

[1] *Foed.*, xi, p. 443.   [2] *Proc. Priv. Coun.*, vi, pp. 304–5, and lxxxvi.
[3] *Return Memb. Parl.*, p. 355.   [4] *Itineraria*, ed. Nasmith, 1778, p. 328.
[5] *Wilhelmi Wyrcester Annales*, R.S., p. 777.
[6] *A. Wood MS. F. 11* ; Shaw, ii, 13.
[7] *Three 15th Century Chronicles*, C.S., p. 157.   [8] *Rot. Parl.*, v, p. 580.
[9] No. 12 above.   [10] *Foed.*, xi, pp. 648–9.
[11] *Ibid.*, xi, p. 656.   [12] *Ibid.*, xi, p. 714.

Aug. 27 following was empowered to receive the submission of, and issue pardons on behalf of the King to, Lancastrian rebels in S. Wales and the Welsh Marches.[1] On April 24, 1472, he received the Garter.[2] In the Act of 1472–3 conferring the Dukedom of Cornwall on Edward's elder son any interests of Lord Ferrers were protected,[3] as also they were in the Act of Resumption of 1473.[4] For the invasion of France in 1475 he brought in the first quarter a contingent of 20 men-at-arms at 4s. and ' 19 other men ' at 1s. a day each, for which he was paid £602 17s. 6d.,[5] in the second quarter the same number of lances and 200 archers,[6] and was a signatory to the truce of August 13th with the French King.[7] He attended the coronation of Richard III,[8] but soon after his loyalty to him seems to have wavered, since he gave shelter for a time to Buckingham [9] and Piers Courtney [10] in his house at Weobley ; [11] and again, in 1485, if we may trust a line in *Lady Bessy*,[12] he seems to have had personal communication with Henry Tudor. However, in the end, according to most accounts, he fought and fell in Richard's army at Bosworth.[13] The *Croyland Continuation* [14] says that he

---

[1] *Ibid.*, xi, pp. 719–20.

[2] Beltz, *Order of the Garter*, No. 206 ; Hope, *G. P.*, lxxvii.

[3] *Rot. Parl.*, vi, p. 16. Cf. Nos. 31, 32, 44 below. [4] *Ibid.*, p. 77.

[5] *Foed.*, xi, p. 845. [6] *MS.*, fol. 2 *recto*. [7] *Foed.*, xii, p. 15.

[8] *Excerpt. Hist.*, p. 384 ; Holinshed, iii, p. 398. [9] No. 10 above.

[10] No. 59 below. [11] *Croyland Cont.*, p. 568. [12] i, p. 30 ; ii, p. 67.

[13] Polydore, p. 714, English Version, C.S., p. 244 ; More, *Richard III*, p. 125 ; Davies, *York Records*, p. 217 ; ' Poem of Bosworth ffeilde ', *Bp. Percy's Folio MS.*, iii, pp. 244, 257 ; *Chronicles of London*, p. 278 : ' slayn . . . the lorde forrers ' ; and Halliwell's *Letters*, i, p. 169 : ' slain upon the same field . . . Sir Walter Deveres '.

[14] p. 574.

fled without fighting. Perhaps the truth is that he was killed in the pursuit, during which the chief slaughter took place. His attainder is recited in the Act of the first year of Henry VII.[1]

BADGE. ' ffrench wyfis hood boundyn.' In *Harl. MS. 4632*, compiled between 1522 and 1534, it is called simply *A hood argent*. His grandson and namesake, the 9th Baron and 1st Viscount Hereford, who died in 1558, displayed on his standard the same badge,[2] and upon the latter's stall-plate as Knight of the Garter, are two badges : on the dexter side the hood, on the sinister the canting horse-shoe of Ferrers. Why the badge is here called ' a French wife's hood ' is a mystery. This hood, or *chaperon*, was worn by both sexes long before and long after the time we are dealing with, and is well illustrated in an illumination in the Harleian Froissart,[3] reproduced by H. N. Humphreys in *Illuminated Illustrations of Froissart*.[4] The grandmother of this nobleman was a Roche,[5] and one meaning of *Rochet* in O.F. is a ' hood '.[6] Was, then, this badge a play on her surname ?

No. 22. 'The lord Grey Codon.' Henry, 7th Baron Grey of Codnor, in Derbyshire, succeeded in 1444,[7] at the age of nine. Originally a Lancastrian, he was with Margaret's army at her victory in the Second Battle of St. Albans on Feb. 17,

[1] *Rot. Parl.*, vi, p. 276 ; and see *Plumpton*, p. 48.

[2] *MS. I. 2. Coll. of Arms* ; in *Excerpt. Hist.*, p. 332.

[3] *Harl. MS. 4379–80.*

[4] 1844, Pl. III. See, too, Dillon's *Fairholt*, i, pp. 174, 177 ; ii, p. 119 ; Viollet-le-Duc, *Dict. du Mobilier français*, iii, p. 141 ; Montfaucon, *Antiq. Fr.*, ii, p. 4, and Pl. CLV.

[5] G. E. C., new ed., v, Ped. of F. of C. between pp. 596-7.

[6] Ducange, *Gloss. française* ; also Godefroy.

[7] G. E. C., 1st ed., iv, p. 98.

1461,[1] but changed sides after the next fight, Edward's triumph at Towton,[2] took part in the Scotch expedition of 1462,[3] and was with the head-quarters at Warkworth Castle that year.[4]   His name is not in the Tellers' Roll for the first quarter of the 1475 enterprise, but for the second quarter he brought 10 men-at-arms and 155 archers.[5]   In 1478 he was holding office as Deputy Lieutenant of Ireland.[6]   He attended the coronation of Richard III,[7] and, if the ' Poem of Bosworth ffeilde ' is to be relied upon, stood by him in that campaign.[8]   This does not seem to have done him much harm with the new King, for we find him appointed on Feb. 27, 1486, a commissioner of the Royal mines for twenty years.[9]   He took part in Henry's siege of Boulogne in Oct. 1492,[10] and died on Apr. 8, 1496.[11]   It is outside our limits here, but perhaps of interest to note that he was a student of Alchemy, and one of the persons to whom a licence was granted for the transmutation of metals.[12]   He

---

[1] *Wil. Wyrc. Ann.*, p. 776.   He had been falsely reported killed during the Queen's march southwards from York to St. Albans (*Three 15th Cent. Chron.*, p. 161).

[2] *Lords' Reports*, iv, pp. 932, 954.   [3] *Three 15th Cent. Chron.*, p. 157.

[4] *Excerpt. Hist.*, p. 365.   [5] *MS.*, fol. 2 *verso*.

[6] *Devon's Issues*, Easter, 18 E. IV.

[7] *Ashmole MS. 863*, p. 437 ; *Excerpt. Hist.*, p. 384.

[8] *Bp. Percy's Fol. MS.*, iii, p. 244, l. 237.   [9] *Mat. Reign H. VII*, i, p. 316.

[10] *Chronicle of Calais*, C.S., p. 2.   This was the expedition that ended in the Peace of Étaples, when Henry VII followed the financial precedent set by Edward IV in 1475 at Pecquigny, and allowed himself to be bought off by the French King Charles VIII.   [11] *G. E. C., loc. cit.*

[12] ' Grant, during pleasure, to Henry Grey of Cotenore, knight, . . . of power and authority to labour, by the conning of philosophy, transmutation of metals . . . at his own cost, so that he shall answer to the King if any profit grow.' (*Pat. Rolls, 1461–7.* p. 285, Oct. 21, 1463.)

married, in 1454, as second wife, Katherine, daughter of
Henry[1] Strangways, of South House, Yorks., by Katherine,
daughter of Ralph Nevill, Earl of Westmorland, and relict of John
Mowbray, Duke of Norfolk,[2] and left no issue.[3] By his will,
dated Sept. 10, 1492,[4] he directs that he be buried 'in the
Chancel of Our Lady in the Fryers of Aylesford',[5] and mentions 'Margaret that was my wife' and 'Katherine that was
my wife, which was the Duchess of Norfolk's daughter', but
later in the will apparently refers to the latter as alive, which she
must have been, for she married again one Ailmer.[6]

BADGE. 'treffe paffant Thorough Croune gold wyth in the
Compafe of the treffe a grei filu[er].' Here we seem to have
a combination of badges.[7] 'Gray', a well-known synonym for
badger,[8] is, of course, a cant on the name. See the seal of his
grandfather.[9] This tress, or plait of hair, is shown on the standard
of John Zouche, of Codnor, who used the same badge.[10]

No. 23. 'The lord Gray Rythyn.' Anthony Grey, eldest
son of Edmund, 4th Baron Grey of Ruthin, who had been created
Earl of Kent in 1465, as a return for his desertion of the cause of
Henry VI, was styled, as in our MS., Lord Grey de Ruthin.[11]

[1] Thomas ?   [2] No. 8 above.

[3] *Dugdale's Visit. Yks.*, in *Gen.*, N.S., xx, p. 182 ; G. E. G., *loc. cit.*

[4] *Test. Vetust.*, p. 411.

[5] A Carmelite House founded in 1240 by his ancestor Richard Grey of Codnor,
2nd Baron by Tenure.   [6] *Test. Vetust.*, *loc. cit.*, note.

[7] Like the Falcon and Fetterlock.

[8] Stratmann, *s.v.* 'grai' ; Mayhew and Skeat, also Halliwell, *s.v.* 'gray'.

[9] Hope, *H. for C.*, p. 183.

[10] *MS. I. 2. Coll. of Arms*, reproduced in de Walden, p. 163. For the wearing
of a tress from a lady's head, or her manche, see *Polit. Songs*, C.S., p. 3.

[11] G. E. C., 1st ed., iv, p. 106 ; Leland, *Itin.*, i, p. 103.

'The lord Grey Ruffyn' was with King Edward 'in his jorny in to Scottlong' in Dec., 1462.[1] According to the Tellers' Roll for the first quarter of 1475, he brought 16 men-at-arms and 140 archers, receiving £439 1s. 6d. ; [2] in the second quarter 10 men-at-arms and the same number of archers as before ; [3] and was one of the signatories to the treaty between the English and French sovereigns on August 29 of that year.[4] He married Joan, daughter to Richard Widville, and sister of Elizabeth, Queen of Edward IV, and died, v. p. and s. p. in 1480.[5] There is a brass to him in St. Albans Abbey.[6]

BADGE. 'Blak Ragyd Staffe.' This badge of Grey de Ruthin, which seems to be merely suggested by the surname, 'grey-stock', had been used also by his father, as is shown by a line in the *Verses on the Battle of Towton* : 'þer was the Blak Ragged Staf, þt is boþe trewe and goode ' ; [7] by his grandfather, Sir John Grey, of Ruthin, K.G., who died, v. p., in 1439, for it appears upon the lining of the mantling on his Garter-plate ; [8] and by his nephew, Richard, 6th Baron Grey of Ruthin, and 3rd (Grey) Earl of Kent : *A ragged staff in bend sable.*[9] It is still to be seen among the badges in the fifteenth-century oak roof of the N. aisle in Ruthin Church, and in Bagford's list of inn-signs is the Black Ragged Staff for the Earl of Kent.[10]

---

[1] *Three 15th Cent. Chron.*, p. 157.   [2] *Foed.*, xi, p. 845.
[3] *MS.*, fol. 2 *verso*.   [4] *Foed.*, xii, p. 15.   [5] G. E. C., *loc. cit.*
[6] Haines, i, p. 86 ; Boutell, *Mon. Br.*, p. 73 ; *Topographer*, 1792, iv, p. 119 ; Gough, *Sepul. Mon.*, iii, p. 269 ; Beaumont, *Anc. Memorial Brasses*, p. 31.
[7] *Archaeologia*, xxix, p. 345. It is probably a *gré*, or scaling-stock, with the treads outside. See the step-stick in Guillim, p. 113, and No. 40 below.
[8] Hope, *G. P.*, liv.   [9] *Harl. MS. 4632*, in *Coll. Top. & Gen.*, iii, p. 66.
[10] Larwood and Hotten, *loc. cit.* According to C. E. Young, York Herald, *Grey*

No. 24. ' The lord ffitzwaren.' Fulke Bourchier, 10th Baron Fitzwarine, was born on Oct. 25, 1445, and succeeded on Dec. 12, 1469.[1] He died at the age of 33, and the shortness of his life may explain the fact that there is little mention of him of interest or importance in the records and chronicles of the period. He was one of the persons ordered in March and April, 1470, to arrest Clarence and Warwick.[2] For the first quarter of 1475 £193 7s. 6d. was paid to him for bringing 10 men-at-arms and 50 archers ;[3] in the second quarter his contingent numbered the same.[4] He married Elizabeth, sister and coheir [5] of John, 2nd Baron Dinham,[6] died on Sept. 18, 1479, and was buried in Bampton Church, N. Devon.[7] Only a portion of his tomb remains.[8] In case of accidents during this expedition, he made his will on Apr. 1, 1475,[9] in which he says ' If I die beyond the seas I will that my body be buried near to the place of my death ; but if in England, then in the Chapel of Our Lady adjoining to the Church-yard at Bawnton near to the grave of the Lady Thomasine my mother ', and directs that a ' fair stone of marble

and Hastings Controversy, the Ragged Staff Sable was a badge of Hastings. It was Anthony's great-grandfather, Reginald, 3rd Baron Grey of Ruthin, who was the successful petitioner in that famous coat-armour case, heard in the Court of Chivalry.

[1] G. E. C., new ed., v, p. 745.

[2] *Foed.*, xi, pp. 655–6.   [3] *Ibid.*, p. 845.   [4] *MS.*, fol. 2 *verso*.

[5] *Pat. Rolls, 1476–85*, p. 190 ; Courthope, p. 160 ; *Visit. Devon, 1620*, H.S., p. 34, and *Gen.*, N.S., xxxvi, p. 18, mistakenly say daughter and heir, the next following authorities correctly having sister.

[6] *Coll. Top. & Gen.*, iv, p. 361 ; *Lincs. Peds.*, H.S., iii, p. 852.

[7] *I. p. m.* 19 E. IV, vol. iv, p. 397, No. 76 ; *Gen.*, N.S., xxii, p. 180, ' Pedigrees from the De Banco Rolls ' ; G. E. C., *loc. cit.*

[8] *Ex inform.* the Rev. E. V. Cox, Vicar of Bampton.

[9] *Test. Vetust.*, p. 341.

with an inscription thereon ' be laid on the tombs of his father, his mother, and himself respectively, and appoints Elizabeth his wife his executrix. His will was proved on Nov. 10, 1480.

BADGE. ' Boufers Knott.' This badge, like the bougets in the Bourchier coat, is a cant upon the surname, and is supposed to represent two B's in cipher. Bowser Knots are to be seen on the above-mentioned tomb at Bampton ; [1] also on the brass in the ' Bowser Chapel ' at Little Easton, Essex, to this Lord Fitzwarine's uncle, Henry Bourchier, Earl of Essex,[2] on the West door there, and on the Bowser Bell [3] still hanging in the tower and still in use.[4] His grandson, the last Bourchier Earl of Essex, used as his badge *A Bourchier Knot argent.*[5] The stall-plate of another of his uncles, John Bourchier, 1st Baron Berners, K.G.,[6] has the lining of the mantling powdered with Bowser Knots and water-bougets set alternately ; [7] while on the standard of ' Bousser Lord Barnys ', *i. e.* John, 2nd Baron Berners, a cousin of our leader,[8] the badge takes the form of ragged staves twisted into Bourchier Knots, this variant form of the Knot being taken from another badge on the same standard composed of an eagle (or falcon) perched upon a ragged staff.[9] This eagle is found as a Bourchier badge in the East window of

---

[1] Hamilton Rogers, *Sepulchral Effigies of Devon*, p. 85.

[2] Died 1483. Weever, p. 386; Willement, *Her. Cant. Cath.*, p. 23, note d ; Waller, *Mon. Brasses*, Pt. XIV ; Haines, ii, p. 56.

[3] Weever, p. 387.

[4] *Ex inform.* the Rev. R. L. Gwynne, Rector of Little Easton.

[5] *Harl. MS. 4632.*   [6] Died 1474.   [7] Hope, *G. P.*, lxiii.

[8] The Translator of Froissart, Huon of Bordeaux, Marcus Aurelius, &c.

[9] *MS. I. 2. Coll. of Arms,* in *Excerpt. Hist.*, p. 334 ; reproduced in De Walden, p. 260.

the Dean's Chapel at Canterbury Cathedral.[1] In *Harl. MS. 4632*[2]
the same form of the Knot is described as *A Bourchier Knot
ragulée argent*. In the Chapel of St. Edmund at Westminster
Abbey is the matrix of a brass[3] to Sir Humphrey Bourchier, son
of the 1st Baron Berners, and so another cousin of our Lord
Fitzwarine, who was killed on the Yorkist side at the battle of
Barnet. On it the strap of an elbow-cop is shown in the form of
a Bourchier Knot. This is repeated six times, cut in the Purbeck
marble.[4] A third uncle of Lord Fitzwarine, Thomas Bourchier,
Cardinal-Archbishop of Canterbury, used the same badge,
which, as well as the eagle referred to, remains in the East
window of the Dean's and of St. Michael's Chapels in his
Cathedral,[5] where it is twined round the pall on his tomb ;[6]
it also commemorates him in the vaulting of the Divinity School
at Oxford. In *Harl. MS. 4632*,[7] again, ' Thomas Bowcer '
displays as badges *Three Bourchier Knots or and a Falcon argent* ;
and, once more, in the same *MS.* there occurs, under ' Bousser ',
A Bourchier Knot or. The Knot appears on the Seal of Wantage
School,[8] in memory of the association of the Fitzwarines with the
town and locality. This seal is still used by the Governors.[9]

[1] Willement, *op. cit.*, p. 37.   [2] *Coll. Top. & Gen.*, iii, p. 67.
[3] The effigy has been lost at some time since 1722.
[4] One is illustrated in Hope, *H. for C.*, p. 186 ; and see Gough, ii, Pl. LXXXVI*,
p. 220 ; Boutell, *Heraldry, Hist. & Pop.*, p. 285. This monument is described as
complete in *The Antiquities of St. Peter's, or the Abbey Church of Westminster*,
i, pp. 59–60.   [5] Willement, *op. cit.*, pp. 37, 42.
[6] Gough, *loc. cit.* A cut of this is given in Cussan's *Handbook of Heraldry*, p. 122.
[7] *Coll. Top. & Gen.*, iii, p. 62.
[8] Illustrated in Carlisle, *Endowed Grammar Schools*, i, p. 43.
[9] *Ex inform.* Mr. Walter Money, F.S.A. The Knot also appears in the E. window at Ripple Church, Worcestershire. (Habington, *Survey of Worc.*, ii, pp. 267–8.)

No. 25. 'The lord Cobh[a]m.' John, 2nd (Brooke) Baron Cobham of Kent, succeeded in 1464, and was a minor on Dec. 10, 1467.[1] He was made Knight Bachelor by Edward IV 'in the field of Grafton besydes Tewkesbury' after the battle, May 4, 1471 : [2] the field called by Leland *Gastum*.[3] In the following year a dispute arose between him and Thomas Stonor, of Stonor, Oxfordshire, concerning the manor of Cliffe, in Kent, and in a letter of about that time [4] William Swan complains to his master, the above Thomas Stonor, that 'my lady of Cobham on Saturday last sent hir men, and havyn fette [5] awey my susterys corn and catell and stuff, all þat she left in þe plase, and havyn broke up every dore and locke, and set hem wyde opyn for every thyng to go in, and also have fett aweye a cowe of herys, þat was with novyne '.[6] Ten years later, at the end of 1482, the quarrel was still unsettled.[7] In the first quarter of 1475 his contingent numbered 5 men-at-arms and 50 archers, for which his remuneration was £159 5s.[8] In the second quarter his following was the same.[9] He was present at the coronation of Richard III,[10] whom he supported against Buckingham,[11] and also at that of Elizabeth of York on St. Catherine's Day, 1487.[12] During October and November, 1492, he was one of the 'optimi bellopotentes'[13]

---

[1] G. E. C., new ed., iii, p. 346.
[2] *A. Wood MS. F. 11* ; *Paston*, iii, p. 9 ; Shaw, ii, p. 14 ; Metcalfe, p. 3.
[3] *Itin.*, iv, p. 162.   [4] *Stonor Letters*, i, p. 137.   [5] Fetched.
[6] Mine own. See *O. E. D.*, *s.v.* 'nowne'.   [7] *Stonor Letters*, ii, p. 155.
[8] *Foed.*, xi, p. 846.   [9] *MS.*, fol. 2 *verso*.   [10] *Excerpt. Hist.*, p. 384.
[11] *Pat. Rolls, 1476–85*, p. 433.
[12] Leland, *Collect.*, iv, p. 230 ; Holinshed, iii, p. 398.
[13] Polydore, p. 741, who describes him here, and elsewhere, as ' Ioannes Polus Cobani regulus '. The ' Polus ' is explicable by the fact that his great-great-

who took part in the abortive siege of Boulogne, when Henry VII allowed himself to be bought off very much after the fashion of Edward IV in 1475; and he assisted in the defeat of the Cornish rebels who advanced into Kent in 1497.[1] His death took place on March 9, 1512,[2] and, according to some authorities,[3] he was buried, with his second wife Margaret Nevill, who had died on Sept. 30, 1506,[4] in Cobham Church. His effigy is gone from the brass there,[5] and seems to have been missing as far back as Dingley's time,[6] for he mentions only Margaret's.[7] Whether it was still there in Weever's day[8] is not clear from his description,[9] but it is said to have survived till 1597.[10] This brass was engraved after his wife's decease and probably in his lifetime, for it bears her death-date, but not his.[11] It seems likely, however, that his body was actually buried in the Grey Friar's Church, London: 'In tumba elevata ad finem . . . altaris juxta hostium[12] sub cruce jacet dominus Johannes Cobham baro de comitatu Cancie.'[13]

grandfather was Sir John de la Pole, who married Joan Cobham, daughter of John de Cobham, 3rd Baron Cobham of Kent, and *suo jure* Baroness Cobham (G. E. C., new ed., iii, pp. 345–6; Courthope, p. 118). The use of *regulus*, however, for *baro* or *dominus*, is unusual; indeed Polydore, in an earlier passage (p. 719), writes ' regulos . . . vulgus dominos vocat '. But *regulus* in record Latin usually either means ' King's son ' or stands for *Comes*, *i. e.* ' Count ' or ' Earl ', just as *subregulus* = ' Viscount '.

[1] Polydore, p. 761; Bacon, *Hen. VII*, p. 166; *Harl. Misc.*, vi, p. 578.
[2] G. E. C., new ed., iii, p. 347.   [3] *Gen.*, N.S., xxxiii, p. 61.
[4] *Gen., ibid.*, and N.S., xxxvi, p. 16.   [5] Haines, ii, p. 96.
[6] *c.* 1680–5.   [7] *Hist. from Marble*, C.S., ii, p. cccxxvi.
[8] *c.* 1631.   [9] p. 122.
[10] *Proc. Somerset Archaeol. Soc.*, 1899, Pt. II, but no authority is given there.
[11] *Ibid.*, and Dingley, *loc. cit.*   [12] *Ostium.*
[13] *Coll. Top. & Gen.*, v, p. 387; Stow, i, p. 321.

BADGE. 'the Blake faryn [1] hede.' The badge of Cobham is given in *MS. I. 2. Coll. of Arms* [2] as 'A man's head in profile, wreathed round the temples argent and sable'; and in *Harl. MS. 4632* [3] as 'A man's head in profile sable, couped gules, wreathed round the temples or'. In *Cotton MS. Cleopatra C. v.* the badge on the standard of this Lord Cobham's son and heir, Thomas, in 1513, is given as *A dolfyn's head sable, with a wreath about the same silver and sable*. There is obviously an error of metathesis here, 'dolfyn's' for 'foldyn's', *i. e.* 'soldan's'. Our Lord Cobham's mother was Elizabeth Touchet, daughter of James, 5th Baron Audley,[4] and the Touchet crest was 'A Sarazins hed sable, &c.' [5] Bagford's *MS. List* of Inn-signs derived from family badges has 'Sarason Head, ye Ld. Audley and ye Ld. Cobham'.[6] This, however, can only have been a coincidence, not the origin of Lord Cobham's badge, for the Black Saracen's Head had served long before as the crest of the Cobhams. It is seen on the Garter-plate of Reginald, 1st Baron Cobham of Sterborough, Kent, who died in 1361, younger son of John, 2nd Baron Cobham, of Kent,[7] and on the brass at Lingfield, Surrey, to the former's son and heir of the same name, who died in 1403.[8] The crest of 'Lord Brooke' is described in *Harl. MS. 4632* [9] as 'On a wreath or and sable a man's head affrontée sable ducally crowned or'. And, again, in Wall's

---

[1] Saracen's.   [2] *Excerpt. Hist.*, p. 335.   [3] *Coll. Top. & Gen.*, iii, p. 67.
[4] G. E. C., new ed., iii, p. 346; *Gen.*, N.S., xxviii, pt. i, p. 62.
[5] 'Wall's Bk. of Crests' (*c.* 1530), *Ancestor*, xii, p. 72, *s.v.* Audeley, Baron.
[6] Larwood and Hotten, p. 134.   [7] Hope, *G. P.*, xxxii.
[8] Haines, ii, p. 202; Boutell, *Mon. Brasses & Slabs*, p. 60; Waller, Pt. VI;
Brayley and Britton, *Top. Hist. Surrey*, iv, p. 167. The matrix alone of the crest is left.
[9] *Coll. Top. & Gen.*, iii, p. 73.

Book of Crests,[1] 'Broke Baron beryth to his crest a sarazins hede caboched long here and berd sable crouned gold langued geules leying on the mantel geules doubled argent'. The relic in Cobham Church is well known : the armet, with a wooden soldan's head (funeral) crest attached,[2] of George, 4th (Brooke) Baron Cobham of Kent,[3] grandson of our man.

No. 26. 'The lorde Lyſle.' Edward Grey, 2nd son of Edward, 6th Baron Ferrers of Groby, and therefore uncle of the Marquis of Dorset,[4] was born before 1439. On the eve of this expedition, being husband of Elizabeth *suo jure* Baroness Lisle, he was created by patent of March 14, 1475, Baron L'Isle of Kingston L'isle, Berks.[5] His contribution to the expeditionary force for the first quarter was 7 men-at-arms and 50 archers, and his payment £172 18*s.* ;[6] for the second quarter his muster was the same.[7] Although he was the younger brother of the Queen's first husband, Sir John Grey, he abandoned her party after the death of Edward IV, and supported the Protector Gloucester before his assumption of the crown,[8] to which presumably he owed his advancement to the rank of Viscount on June 28, 1483.[9] He officiated at Richard's coronation,[10] and assisted him in the repression of Buckingham's rising,[11] but it is clear

[1] *Ancestor*, xii, p. 71.

[2] Illustrated in Hope, *H. for C.*, p. 133 ; and described in *Archaeol. Journal*, 1881, pp. 509–10, and figs. 33–4 (helm only) ; also *Heraldic Exhib. Cat. Soc. Antiq.*, p. 3.   [3] D. 1558.   [4] No. 11 above.

[5] G. E. C., 1st ed., v, p. 116; Courthope, pp. 291–2; Smyth, *Lives of Berkeleys*, ii, pp. 29, 115.   [6] *Foed.*, xi, p. 846.   [7] *MS.*, fol. 2 *verso*.

[8] 'Stallworth's Letters ', in *Stonor Letters*, ii, p. 161. *Excerpt. Hist.*, pp. 13–17.

[9] G. E. C., *loc. cit.*, Courthope, p. 292.

[10] *Holinshed*, iii, p. 398 ; *Excerpt. Hist.*, p. 384.

[11] *Pat. Rolls*, 1476–85, p. 479.

from *Lady Bessy* that at the end of the latter's reign he was in treasonable correspondence with Henry Tudor.[1] 'The Vicomte Lifley' was at the coronation of Elizabeth of York,[2] and was manifestly trusted by Henry, for on Sept. 22, 1485, he received the grant for life of the Stewardship of the Duchy of Lancaster in Warwickshire and the Seneschalship of the Castle of Kenilworth,[3] while on July 5 in the following year he was appointed a justice of oyer and terminer of all treasons, &c.[4] He was a leader of the King's army in 1487,[5] and so probably present at Stoke, and was among those called upon on Dec. 13, 1488, to help in raising archers in Warwickshire for the expedition of 1489 to Brittany.[6] His death took place on July 17, 1492.[7] He married (1) Elizabeth, sister and heir of Thomas, 2nd Viscount L'Isle ;[8] (2) Jane, relict of Sir Robert Drope, Lord Mayor of London in 1474–5.[9] There is an abstract of his will in *Testamenta Vetusta*,[10] in which he directs that he be buried in 'the new tomb in the new Chapel of Our Lady, by me begun, in the College of Astley,[11] where the body of Elizabeth lieth. To Jane my now wife, &c.' There are recumbent effigies

---

[1] i, pp. 27, 30 ; ii, pp. 64, 67. In these four lines his name is spelt in as many different ways to suit the rhyme.

[2] Leland, *Collect.*, iv, p. 230. [3] *Mat. Reign H. VII*, i, p. 553.

[4] *Ibid.*, i, p. 482. [5] Leland, *Collect.*, iv, p. 210.

[6] *Foed.*, xii, p. 357, Nos. 4, 9 above, and Nos. 31, 32, 36, 37, 41, 45, 51, 56, 57 below, were also engaged upon the same work. [7] G. E. C., *loc. cit.*

[8] She died Sept. 8, 1487. (Courthope, p. 292; Doyle, ii, p. 399.)

[9] Fabyan, p. 664; G. E. C., *loc. cit.* For Drope's canting arms, which perhaps show how his name was pronounced, see Gibbon, *Lat. Bl.*, p. 35.

[10] pp. 410, 466. Proved Aug. 26, 1492.

[11] A collegiate church in Warwickshire.

in alabaster of him and his wives in the present Church at Astley, to which they were removed about 1580.[1]

BADGE. 'lyon ſilu[er] ſhowyng holeface cround gold enarmede azur,' a badge taken from his arms : 'Goulys a lyon paſſaunt[-guardant] of sylvyr crownyd wᵗ golde.'[2] This was a Lisle, not a Grey, coat, and occurs frequently as such in the early Rolls of Arms.[3]

No. 27. 'The lord Clynton.' John (Clinton, or Fiennes), 6th Baron Clinton, was aged 30 and more at his succession in 1464, when his father died,[4] but was never summoned to Parliament.[5] He is not in the Tellers' Roll for the first quarter of 1475, and no retinue is given him in our *MS.* His father had been a prominent soldier on the Lancastrian side till 1459, thenceforward on the other, and by Henry VI's Coventry Parliament of that year was attainted as a Yorkist, but his honours and estates were restored to him on the accession of Edward IV.[6] Of the son I have found no record of military service other than that which is furnished by the present Roll. In a brief reference to him, however, in *The Ancestor*[7] there is a suggestion that about 1483 some of his activities were being engaged upon

[1] *Ex inform.* the Rev. J. F. H. Carr-Gregg, Vicar of Astley. A photograph shows him to be wearing a mail standard and the collar of SS. For some family quarrels of the Greys of this house see *Lives of the Berkeleys*, ii, pp. 116–17, 127.

[2] 'Fifteenth Cent. Bk. of Arms,' *Ancestor*, iv, p. 230.

[3] *e. g. Acre, Camden, First Dunstable, Parliamentary, Second Calais*, and *Willement Rolls*, also in the Canterbury Cloisters, ranging from 1192 (?) to 1411.

[4] *I. p. m.*, 4 E. IV, vol. iv, p. 324, No. 22.

[5] G. E. C., new ed., iii, p. 316 ; Courthope, p. 116.

[6] *Foed.*, xi, p. 447 ; *Rot. Parl.*, v, p. 348.

[7] viii, p. 185. This statement is perhaps based upon *Pat. Rolls, 1476–85*, pp. 425–6. On piracy at this time by persons of 'respectability' consult Fortescue, pp. 19, 232–3.

piracy in the Channel. He died on Feb. 29, 1488, and was buried in the Church of the Grey Friars in London : ' sub cruce de lapidibus mamoreis jacet dominus Johañes Clynton baro.'[1] Lord Clinton married (1) Elizabeth, daughter of Richard Fiennes, Baron Dacre, by Joan, *suo jure* Baroness Dacre ; (2) Anne, said to be daughter of Sir Humphrey Stafford.[2]

BADGE. 'A mulet gold.' This badge, the rowel of a spur, is taken from the Clinton coat : ' Silver, a chief azure with two pierced mullets gold.'[3] In the arms of his grandfather the mullets are pierced gules.[4] The same badge is given for Clinton in *Harl. MS. 4632.*[5] This nobleman's father, however, used as his badge at Towton ' a Kay '.[6]

No. 28. 'The lord Boyde.' Robert, Lord Boyd, son and heir of Sir Thomas Boyd, of Kilmarnock, was, like the Earl of Douglas,[7] an exile from Scotland and a pensioner of Edward IV (see *D. N. B.*, and *G. E. C.*, new ed., ii, p. 260). For the first quarter he brought two men-at-arms, himself being one of them, and 20 archers, his payment for which was £70 19s. 6d. He received the usual remuneration of a Baron, that is 4s. a day.[8] His contingent in the second quarter was the same.[9] In the *Dict. Nat. Biog.* he is said to have died soon after Nov. 22, 1469. Our Roll disproves that, and his death must have taken place

---

[1] *Coll. Top. & Gen.*, v, p. 280; Stow, i, p. 320.   [2] *G. E. C.*, *loc. cit.*

[3] ' Fifteenth Cent. Bk. of Arms ', *Ancestor*, iv, p. 229.

[4] Willement, *Her. Cant. Cath.*, p. 53, No. 13, and p. 80, No. 99 ; *Archaeologia*, lxvi, p. 478 ; Blore, *Hen. IV*, p. 21.   [5] *Coll. Top. & Gen.*, iii, p. 67.

[6] ' Verses on the Battle of Towton ', *Archaeologia*, xxix, p. 346. An early pronunciation of ' key ': see Skeat. Or is it ' *ca* ', a chough ?

[7] No. 15 above.   [8] *Foed.*, xi, p. 848.   [9] *MS.*, fol. 2 *verso.*

E

at some time between 1475 and Oct. 1482,[1] when the title and estates were restored to his grandson.[2]

BADGE. ' an Anker gold.' After searching in vain for any reason why Lord Boyd should have chosen an anchor for his badge, I applied to Sir James Balfour Paul, who was good enough to take up the hunt, but without result. There is no such charge in the arms of his mother, a coheir of Gifford, but it may have been brought in with her coat. Failing this, I would suggest that possibly it symbolized the exile's hope of return to his country : ' spem, quam sicut anchoram habemus ',[3] which one of the educated clergy with whom he came into contact, such as Dudley, Courtney, or Gunthorpe,[4] might conceivably have suggested to him as appropriate to his circumstances. Emblems were already in the air, and soon to become very prominent in art, literature, religion, and education.

No. 29. ' Sir John afteley.' Sir John Astley,[5] Knight and Banneret, the famous champion, was the son and heir of Sir Thomas Astley, of Nailstone,[6] Leicestershire, and of Patshull and Aston, Staffs., by Elizabeth, daughter and heir of Sir Richard Harcourt. The surname was taken from the lordship of Astley in Warwickshire.[7] On Aug. 29, 1438, he, then an Esquire, challenged, and fought in single combat at Paris, Pierre de Masse, of Pontoise, Esquire. The matter was settled by Astley's

---

[1] G. E. C., new ed., ii, p. 260.

[2] *Ex inform.* Sir James Balfour Paul, Kt., Lord Lyon King-of-Arms.

[3] *Vulgate*, Heb. vi. 10.   [4] Nos. 58, 59, 60 below.

[5] Or Ashley.   [6] Or Nelston.

[7] *Visit. Salop.*, H.S., p. 18 ; Dugdale, *Warwicks.*, 1730, i, p. 106. He was second son according to *Visit. Essex*, H.S., i, p. 138.

running his lance through the other's head.[1]   He had a similar encounter, while still an Esquire, on Jan. 30, 1442, in Smithfield, with ' Sir Philip Boyle ', of Aragon,[2] in the presence of Henry VI, when again he ' had the felde ',[3] though on this occasion he did not kill his adversary.[4]   According to one account Boyle, who is there styled a Catalan, was the challenger,[5] as the wording in which he describes his mission seems to indicate.[6]   In acknowledgement of his prowess in this duel, Astley ' of the kynges honde was made Knyght in the felde for his wele doynge.   And the lord of Aragon after that offered up his harneys at Wyndsore.' [7] Astley was at the same time granted an annuity of 100 marks from the customs of Southampton.[8]   A contemporary illustration of a third duel in which he was engaged, with an unidentified opponent, has been published by Lord Dillon in *Archaeologia*.[9]

[1] See Lord Dillon's paper in *Archaeologia*, lvii, Pt. I, pp. 35–6, and Pl. V.

[2] He is called ' the lord beuf (or Beaufe) Arogoner ' in *Chronicles of London*, p. 150.   On the other hand, there is an entry in Devon's *Issues*, p. 442, ' To Sir Philip Boyle, Kt., & a baron of Arragon, who lately, upon royal licence granted him, performed certain feats of arms in the presence of the said Lord the King in Smithfield, with John Asteley, a faithful and beloved subject of the said Lord the King.   In money paid him in discharge of 100*l*. which the said Lord the King commanded to be paid to the said Philip to be had of his gift.'

[3] *Three 15th Cent. Chron.*, p. 63.

[4] *Archaeologia, ibid.*, pp. 36–8, and Pl. VI.   The illustrations there given are from a contemporary *MS.* once in the possession of Astley himself.

[5] *Greg. Chron.*, p. 220.

[6] *Archaeologia, ibid.*, p. 37.

[7] *Three 15th Cent. Chron.*, p. 64.   Also *Six Town Chronicles*, p. 116; *Chron. Lond.*, p. 150.

[8] *Rot. Parl.*, v, pp. 188, 546; Dugdale, *Warwicks.*, i, p. 110, and see Plate facing p. 111.   [9] *Ibid.*, Pl. IV, p. 33.

He assisted ' as councellor ' at similar fights in 1446[1] and 1453,[2] being evidently an accepted authority in such affairs.[3] On March 21, 1462, he became a Knight of the Garter,[4] and grants of £40 a year were twice made to enable him to support the dignity.[5] He accompanied Edward IV in his Scottish expedition of 1462,[6] and in the following year, on the surrender of Alnwick, was appointed Captain of the town : ' the knight that fought so manly in Smethefylde with an alyon that calengyd '.[7] Sir Ralph Grey, of Heaton, who, as the leading local magnate, had hoped for this post, stirred with jealousy, ' by fals treson toke the sayde Sy[r] John Ascheley presoner and delyveryd hym to Quene Margarete '.[8] He was sent to France.[9] While still a prisoner abroad, he was appointed *Vexillarius Regis*,[10] and is said to have been ransomed in Dec. 1466.[11] We meet with him again in the capacity of a ' counsellor ' in a duello,[12] this time a friendly one : that between Lord Scales[13] and Anthony, Count

---

[1] *Proc. Privy Council*, vi, p. 55.

[2] *Ibid.*, pp. 129, 134, 139. See Nos. 31 and 49 below.

[3] See, too, Anstis, ii, p. 206.

[4] Beltz, No. 192 ; Hope, *G. P.*, No. lxix ; Dugdale, *Warwicks.*, *loc. cit.*

[5] *Rot. Parl.*, v, p. 580 ; July 13, 1461 ; *Pat. Rolls, 1461–7*, pp. 10, 190 ; *1476–85*, pp. 157, 377 ; *Archaeologia, ibid.*, p. 32.

[6] *Three 15th Cent. Chron.*; p. 157.

[7] *Greg. Chron.*, p. 220 ; also *Wil. Wyrc. Ann.*, p. 781 ; *Pat. Rolls, 1461–7*, p. 262.

[8] *Greg. Chron.*, *loc. cit.* ; also *Wil. Wyrc. Ann.*, *loc. cit.*

[9] *MS. Coll. of Arms. L. 9*, cited in the Notes to *Warkworth's Chron.*, C.S., p. 38, and in *Chron. of the White Rose*, p. lxxxviii, where, too, Ralph Gray's subsequent degradation from knighthood and execution are recorded. *Pat. Rolls, 1461–7*, pp. 358, 379 ; Ashmole, p. 622 ; Anstis, i, p. 179.   [10] Anstis, *ibid.*

[11] So *Archaeologia, ibid.*, p. 33.   [12] *Excerpt. Hist.*, p. 202.

[13] No. 13 above, Nos. 15 and 49 being Astley's coadjutors.

de la Roche, known as 'the Bastard of Burgundy ',[1] fought in Smithfield on June 11 and 12, 1467.[2] 'The Lord Scales had the worship of the felde.'[3]   A safe-conduct had been issued ' Pro Bastardo Burgundiae super punctis armorum perficiendis '.[4] The annuity of £40 granted to Astley on July 13, 1461, was protected in the Act of Resumption of 1473.[5] In the Tellers' Roll for the first quarter of 1475 he is entered as receiving £45 10s., for one man-at-arms, that is himself, and 12 archers, and from the same entry we learn that he was by that time a Banneret.[6] His pay on service as such would be, we have seen, 4s. a day, the same as that of a Baron. For the second quarter he was joined by an additional lance.[7] A further grant of £60 a year was made to him in 1479.[8] On the occasion of the funeral of Edward IV at Westminster, Apr. 17, 1483, he was one of the four knights who bore the canopy over the corpse,[9] Sir William Parr [10] being one of the others, and he was present at the coronation of Richard III on July 6 following.[11] Presumably he was not with Richard at Bosworth, for on Dec. 7, 1485,

---

[1] Son of Duke Philip the Good, and therefore half-brother of Charles the Bold.

[2] *Olivier de la Marche*, iii, pp. 51-4; *Three 15th Cent. Chron.*, pp. 92, 181; *Paston*, iii, p. 486, and *Supplement*, pp. 117–20; ' Hearne's Fragment ', *Chron. W. R.*, p. 19; *Greg. Chron.*, p. 236; *Excerpt. Hist.*, pp. 171–212; *Monstrelet*, ii, p. 345; *Wil. Wyrc. Ann.*, p. 787; *Chron. Grey Friars*, p. 21; *Archaeologia*, xxix, p. 135.

[3] *Arnold's Chron.*, p. xxxv.   [4] *Foed.*, xi, p. 573.   [5] *Rot. Parl.*, vi, p. 82.

[6] *Foed.*, xi, p. 846: ' miles ac Bannerettus '. Under the Ordinances of John Tiptoft, Earl of Worcester, Constable of England, dated May 29, 1466, the banner of a Banneret was to be three feet square, and a Banneret's command was 100 men. (Harington, *Nugae Antiquae*, i, p. 8.)

[7] *MS.*, fol. 2 *verso*.   [8] *Pat. Rolls*, 1476–85, p. 132, Jan. 27.

[9] *Lett. & Pap.*, i, p. 5; *Archaeologia*, i, p. 377.

[10] No. 30 below.   [11] Holinshed, iii, p. 398; *Excerpt. Hist.*, p. 384.

he received from Henry VII the grant of an annuity for life
of £40 out of the farm or issues of the City of Winchester, and
£60 a year at the receipt of the Exchequer ;[1] and what was
apparently this £100 a year received protection in the Act of
Resumption of 1485.[2] Again, at Easter in the next year, a
further annuity of £60 for life was bestowed on him under the
Great Seal.[3] On July 27, 1486, the grant of Dec. 7, 1485,
'being insufficient in law', he surrendered it and received in
its stead three annuities, of £40, £20, and £20 respectively.[4]
According to Beltz,[5] he died about 1488, Sir John Savage[6]
succeeding to his stall on Nov. 16 in that year. There is evidence,
however, that he had either died or become incapable before
Aug. 19, 1486, for on that date a payment of 100s. on account of
his annuity was made to his wife Margery.[7] In any case he was
certainly dead by Nov. 8, 1486, since £10 was then paid to his
'widow Margery as due to him from his annuity while he lived',[8]
and on Dec. 18 following a further sum of £8 6s. 8d. was paid
to 'Margere, widow of John Asteley, Knight, deceased, due to the
said John in his lifetime'.[9] Further, on May 10, 1487, there is an
entry of a grant for life to Dame Margery Asteley, widow of Sir
John Asteley, Knight, of an annuity of £10.[10] There is in Patshull
Church a 16th-century tomb erroneously assigned to him.[11]

BADGE. His badge, *A cinquefoil ermine*, is drawn only, not

[1] *Mat. Reign H. VII*, i, p. 203.   [2] *Rot. Parl.*, vi, p. 345.
[3] *Mat. Reign H. VII*, i, p. 404.   [4] *Ibid.*, p. 524.
[5] p. clxviii.   [6] No. 51 below.   [7] *Mat. Reign H. VII*, i, p. 573.
[8] *Ibid.*, ii, p. 99.   [9] *Ibid.*, ii, p. 102.   [10] *Ibid.*, ii, p. 153.
[11] *Visit. Salop.*, H.S., p. 18. Was he the Sir John Asteley (or Ashley) buried
the White Friars' Church in London (Stow, ii, pp. 46, 364) ?

described, in our *MS*. This was taken from the arms of Astley :
Azure, a cinquefoil ermine and a label of three points of the same.[1]
In the background of Plate V in *Archaeologia* [2] stands an heraldic
officer with the arms of Sir John Astley on his tunic : not a
tabard, as one would rather expect at this time. Camden [3] says :
' In Leiceftershire and the Countrey confining, divers bare
Cinquefoyles, for that the ancient Earls of Leicefter bare *Gueles
a Cinquefoile Ermyn.*' The seal of Robert de Bellomont, surnamed ' Bossu ', 2nd Earl of Leicester, who died in 1168, bore
a large cinquefoil ermine, as did that of his grandson Robert,
the 4th Earl, surnamed ' Fitz-Parnell ', who died in 1206.[4]
A variant of this badge was used, among others, on his standard
by Richard Astley, of Staffordshire, in Henry VIII's French
expedition of 1513 : 'synkfoylls hermen perced with bessantes
(for a difference) '.[5]

No. 30. ' Sir Will[ia]m aparre.' This was Sir William Parr,
of Kendal, Westmorland, Knight and Banneret, grandfather of
Queen Catherine Parr (see *D. N. B.*).[6] His name is not in the

---

[1] See Hope, *G. P.*, No. lxix, where the powdering of his mantling with cinque-
foils is one of the comparatively few examples of badges on garter-plates. One or
two others have been noticed here. Compare, too, *Archaeologia*, lvii, Pt. I, p. 31,
and Pl. VII.   [2] *Archaeologia, loc. cit.*   [3] *Remains*, p. 231.

[4] Planché, *Pursuivant*, p. 106 ; Doyle, ii, p. 337 ; Nichols, *Hist. Leic.*

[5] *Cotton MS. Cleopatra C. v.*

[6] As to ' A Parr ', the preposition in this instance is certainly ' of ', not ' at ',
though the latter is common enough in the case of names of humbler persons, as
in ' Athill ', ' Atwood ', &c. ' A' Parr ', then, which occurs often at this period,
is merely a misspelt variant for ' O' Parr ' ; and in the *Paston Letters* (iii,
p. 123) we have ' Syr John off Parre ' in full. Similarly, we find as a tavern-sign
' The Pinder a Wakefielde ' (Larwood and Hotten, pp. 75-6 ; Norman, *London*

Tellers' Roll for the first quarter of the enterprise of 1475, but for the second quarter his contribution to the forces was 16 men-at-arms and 140 archers.[1]

BADGE. 'maydyn hed.' His son, 'Syr Thomas Ap per Knyght', father of Queen Catherine Parr, bore as a badge on his standard *A woman's head affronté couped at the shoulders argent, crined or, vested gules, fimbriated or.*[2] The badge of 'Pare' given in *Harl. MS. 4632*[3] is *A maiden's head full-faced proper vested gules, crined or.* Catherine Parr, as Queen, used a modification of this: *A maiden's head crowned and bust issuant from a Tudor rose.*[4]

No. 31. 'Sir Thomas montgomery.' Sir Thomas Montgomery, Knight and Banneret, 2nd son of Sir John Montgomery, K.B., of Falkbourne, near Witham, Essex, was born in 1433.[5]

Signs, p. 196; &c.). If the place Parr had been a mere spot or simple homestead, 'at' would have been natural, but since it was the manor of the Parr family, the phrase, undistorted, would be 'Sir William of Parr'. Parr is a manor and township in the parish of Prescot, S. Lancashire, of which manor the Parrs were lords. On all fours with this are 'Syr Edward A Borough' (*Lett. & Pap. R. III & Hen. VII,* i, p. 401), younger son of No. 32 below, and 'Sere William a Stanley' (Warkworth, p. 14. No. 35 below). I have touched upon this because some appear to think that 'A Parre' is Welsh, and equivalent to 'Ap Harry', *i.e.* 'Parry'.

[1] *MS.*, fol. 2 *verso.*

[2] *MS. I. 2. Coll. of Arms,* in *Excerpt. Hist.,* p. 330; De Walden, p. 237.

[3] *Coll. Top. & Gen.,* iii, p. 74.

[4] Willement, *Reg. Her.,* p. 75, and Pl. XVII, d., from *MS. L. 14. Coll. of Arms, f. 105*; who adds that the maid's head badge was derived from Ros of Kendal. See, too, *Her. and Gen.,* iv, p. 449. For the maiden's head used as a crest by her brother William Parr, Marquis of Northampton, see *Her. Exhib. Burl. Ho.,* p. 15.

[5] *Supplementary Lett. & Pap.,* H. VI, p. 435; Anstis, ii, p. 403. There is a short sketch of his life in Anstis, but so many new sources of informa-

His father, probably the first of his surname to settle in Essex, and perhaps originally from Scotland, as is suggested by the similarity of his arms [1] to those of Montgomery, Earls of Eglinton,[2] became very prominent at the English Court,[3] and died 27 Hen. VI.[4] His mother was Elizabeth, daughter of Thomas Boteler, of Sudeley,[5] and relict of (1) Sir Henry Norbury, and (2) Sir William Heron, commonly known as Lord Say. She died in 1464.[6] In her will, dated Jan. 31 in that year, she appoints her son Sir Thomas an executor, and directs that he keep all her servants half a year ' yf they be not soner provyded of service '.[7] Falkbourne Hall is of brick, and was built by Sir John and his son Thomas : the licence to crenellate was granted in 1439 or 1440.[8] Thomas was aged 30 at the time of his mother's death, and was then son and heir, his elder brother John having been executed upon Tower Hill in Feb. 1462, by Edward IV for his adherence to Henry.[9] This very able

tion have become available since that writer's time that it was necessary to compile an entirely fresh account of a person of such importance.

[1] *Gules, a chevron ermine between three fleurs-de-lys or* (Ashmole, p. 713 ; as on the brasses in Falkbourne Church).

[2] Anstis, *ibid.* ; Morant, *Essex*, ii, p. 116. Compare, too, the seal (1392) of John Montgomery, Lord of Eagleshame, which is differenced with an annulet (Laing, *Anc. Scottish Seals*, Pt. II, p. 123, and Frontispiece, fig. 8).

[3] Anstis, *ibid.*   [4] *I. p. m.*, vol. iv, p. 239, No. 36.

[5] Anstis, *ibid.* ; Morant, ii, p. 116.

[6] *I. p. m.*, 5 Ed. IV, vol. iv, p. 330, No. 21 ; G. E. C., 1st ed., vii, p. 63 ; *Coll. Top. & Gen.*, vi, p. 154 ; *Letters of Margaret of Anjou*, C.S., p. 105 ; Anstis, ii, p. 204.

[7] *Coll. Top. & Gen.*, iii, p. 106.

[8] *Arch. Journal*, 1913, p. 126, and Pl. III. See, too, Dr. Round in *Trans. Essex Archaeol. Soc.*, N.S., xv (1921), p. 36 and Frontispiece.

[9] Anstis, ii, pp. 204–5 ; *Wil. Wyrc. Ann.*, p. 779 ; *Coll. Top. & Gen.*, iii, p. 106.

and supple soldier and diplomat contrived to keep in favour
with all the Kings during whose unquiet and difficult reigns
he lived : Henry VI, Edward IV, Richard III, and Henry VII.
While yet a lad, he held office at the court of Henry VI. Thus,
on July 18, 1446, despite his extreme youth,[1] we find the following
record of payment for the services named : ' To Thomas Montgomery, Esq., one of the Marshals of the King's Hall, who,
at the especial request of the said Lord the King, attended at
different times upon divers persons to his great detriment and
charge; viz. first upon the Duke of Norfolk, at Killingworth
and within the Tower of London ; secondly upon John Astley ;[2]
thirdly upon Eleanor Cobham[3] from Ledys[4] to London ; and
fourthly upon John Davy, an appellant : also because he restored
into Chancery the King's letters patent granting him £20 per
annum to be cancelled. In money paid to him by assignment
made this day—£40.'[5] Anstis[6] adds what would seem almost
incredible, even in a youth of his evident precocity, that his
business with Davy was to teach him points of arms ' such as he
could ' against the time he[7] should combat at Smithfield. He
was associated with Astley[8] in assisting at appeals of battle in
1446 and again in 1453.[9] In 28 Hen. VI[10] he was protected in
the Act for the Resumption of Crown Grants ' fo that our faid
grauntȝ exceede not xxiij *li.* yerly, the which we wol he have

---

[1] There seems to be no doubt of his identity.　　　　[2] No. 29 above.

[3] This was the Duchess of Gloucester, the victim of the famous witchcraft
case : see, *e. g., Eng. Chron.*, pp. 57–60.

[4] Leeds Castle, Kent, in the chapel of which her trial for sorcery had been
held five years before : see Clark, *Med. Mil. Arch.*, ii, p. 182.

[5] Devon, *Issues*, p. 459.　　　[6] ii, p. 205.　　　[7] *i. e.* Davy.

[8] No. 29 above.　　　[9] See below : *Proc. Priv. Coun.*, vi, pp. 55, 134.

[10] Sept. 1, 1449—Aug. 31, 1450.

and rejoife, accordyng to oure Letters Patente3 made unto
hym : Confideryng that he is a yonger Brother and hath no
thyng to lyve upon, favyng oonly of oure yift '.[1]   From 28 to
38 Henry VI [2] he had the custody of the Exchange and of
the Mint at the Tower, as well as the Keepership of the Dies,
while still remaining Marshal of the King's Hall, and described
as an Esquire of the Body.[3]   As to the fiscal posts, this can only
mean that he received the emoluments attached to them, which
possibly was not unusual.   In 1453 we meet with him in association with Astley [4] and Rainford [5] as a counsellor in the Iyalton
v. Norreys Appeal of Battle.[6]   Edward IV dubbed him Knight-
Bachelor at Towton ; [7] on July 8 following he was nominated
for life Steward of Havering-at-the-Bower and of the Castle of
Hadley, in Essex ; [8] on the 22nd of the same month he was
appointed one of the King's Carvers with a stipend of £40
annually for that service ; [9] on the 25th he became ' lynge (link)
armurer ' at the Tower ; [10] and by Nov. 24, at any rate, was
King's Knight.[11]   He took part in the expedition to Scotland of
1462,[12] and the same year saw him Sheriff of Norfolk and Suffolk.[13]

[1] *Rot. Parl.*, v, p. 193.   [2] 1449-60.

[3] *Pat. Rolls*, 1452–61, pp. 88, 246, 469, 481 ; Ruding, *Annals of the Coinage*,
i, pp. 28, 47, 58 ; ii, pp. 144, 196.   These appointments at the Mint were continued
by Ed. IV (*Pat. Rolls*, 1461–7, pp. 23, 124, 213).

[4] No. 29 above.   [5] No. 49 below.

[6] *Proc. Priv. Coun.*, vi, pp. 129, 139.

[7] March 29, 1461.   *A. Wood MS. F. 11* ; Shaw, ii, p. 13 ; Metcalfe, p. 2.

[8] *Pat. Rolls*, 1461–7, pp. 18, 46, 382.

[9] *Ibid.*, pp. 79, 125, 180, 213 ; *Rot. Parl.*, v, pp. 475, 582.

[10] *Pat. Rolls, ibid.*, p. 126.   [11] *Pat. Rolls, ibid.*, p. 79.

[12] *Three 15th Cent. Chron.*, p. 157.

[13] Appointed Nov. 7, 1461 ; *List of Sheriffs*, p. 87 ; *Paston*, ii, p. 253.

In the third year of Edward IV[1] he acted as ambassador to Scotland, then was sent in the same capacity to the Court of Charolais to treat of a marriage between him and the King's sister and afterwards attend her on her journey; and was also empowered to deal with the ambassadors of Louis XI.[2] In 1464 he is again holding office as Sheriff, this time of Anglesea.[3] The year 1466 finds him employed on commissions to negotiate with the Duke of Burgundy and with the French King,[4] and once more Sheriff of Norfolk and Suffolk.[5] In the Tourney at Eltham in April, 1467, he was one of the four opposed to the King and three others; [6] on May 19 he was returned to Parliament as knight of the shire for Essex; [7] and on June 11 and 12 of the same year he acted as one of the counsellors of the Bastard of Burgundy in the duel between him and Scales.[8] From the Act of Resumption of 1467–8 he received exemption.[9] He does not seem to have been a man of many mistakes, but it is recorded that he and Sir Thomas Borough [10] were considered responsible for ill advice given to the King in persuading him that it was not necessary to take the field against Clarence and Warwick in June, 1469.[11] He appears on July 9 of that year in a public capacity again as the bearer of letters from Edward to those two noblemen and George Nevill, Archbishop of York, urging

[1] March 4, 1463—March 3, 1464.
[2] Anstis, ii, p. 206.
[3] Appointed July 30: *List of Sheriffs*, p. 236.
[4] *Foed.*, xi, pp. 563–5.
[5] Appointed Nov. 5: *List of Sheriffs*, p. 87.
[6] *Paston*, ii, p. 303. Rivers (No. 13 above) was on the King's side.
[7] *Return Memb. Parl.*, p. 357.
[8] No. 13 above. *Excerpt. Hist.*, p. 210.
[9] *Rot. Parl.*, v, 582.
[10] No. 32 below.
[11] Waurin, v, p. 581.

them to join their sovereign in suppressing ' Robin of Redesdale's ' rebellion,[1] and in the succeeding October in a private
capacity as one of the supervisors of the will of Sir Robert Darcy,
of Maldon, for which he was to receive as an honorarium a pipe
of red wine.[2] On the 14th of that month he was holding the post
of ' Knight for the Body of the King ', and was given for life
the Constableship of Bristol and of Caen in Normandy.[3] At
the time of the brief restoration of Henry VI in 1470 the Warwick-
Clarence party contrived to capture him, and John Paston writes,
' Sir T. Mongomere and Joudone be takyn ; what shall falle of
hem I can not sey '.[4] His usual address, or good fortune, however,
saved him, for in the ensuing spring we read of him as among the
leaders [5] who joined Edward at Nottingham after the landing at
Ravenspur.[6] Like the others, evidently he agreed with the
sentiment ' I came to serve a King and not a Duke ', put in his
mouth by Shakespeare,[7] referring to Edward's statement that
he had returned only to recover his Dukedom of York, not the
throne. As Habington has it,[8] ' Neither could they juſtifie
their taking armes to ſettle a ſubject in his inheritance.' In
1472 he is a feofee of the estate of Elizabeth, widow of John
de Vere, Earl of Oxford, whose son John [9] was then holding

[1] *Paston*, ii, pp. 360–1. For the doubtful identity of this person see Gairdner,
Paston, Suppl., p. cclxxiv ; Ramsay, ii, pp. 338–9.   [2] *Weever*, pp. 368–9.

[3] *Pat. Rolls, 1467–77*, p. 173 : Oct. 20.

[4] *Paston*, ii, p. 412 : Oct. 12, 1470.

[5] Nos. 30, 32, 43, and 45 of this Roll were others.

[6] Hall, p. 292 ; Holinshed, iii, p. 306 : ' boldlie affirming to him that they
would serve no man but a king '.

[7] *3 H. VI*, iv, 7, where he is misnamed John.   [8] *Hist. Ed. IV*, p. 76.

[9] Afterwards Earl of Oxford.

St. Michael's Mount against Edward IV.[1]   In the Act of 1472-3
conferring the Dukedom of Cornwall on the elder son of the King,
it was provided that nothing in it should be to the prejudice of
any interests of Montgomery's,[2] so, too, in the Act of Resumption
of 1473.[3]   He was appointed on June 26, 1474, steward of the
lands in Essex of Francis, son and heir of Sir John Lovel, during
his minority, from which we learn that he was by then a Banneret,[4]
and later in the year was sent to negotiate with the Emperor
Frederick and the King of Hungary for an alliance against
Louis XI.[5]   Shortly before this he had bought from the Earl
of Kent the manor of Braxted Magna in Essex for 1,000 marks,[6]
so that his financial position was apparently assured ;   and
Geoffrey Poole, of Wythune, Bucks., Esq., in his will, dated
Oct. 12 in the same year, left lands in Stoke Mandeville, in that
county, to his son Henry, with remainder to Montgomery and
his heirs.[7]   In January, 1475, he was acting as ambassador with
Morton [8] to Charles the Bold, at that time engaged upon his
siege of Neuss,[9] and on May 3 he received the Stewardship
of the King's Forest of Essex for life.[10]   He contributed to the
expeditionary force in that year, for the first quarter, 10 men-at-
arms and 100 archers, receiving as payment £307 2s. 6d., and
was still Knight for the Body of the King.[11]   For the second

---

[1] Blomefield, *Norfolk*, i, p. 82.

[2] *Rot. Parl.*, vi, p. 16.   Compare Nos. 21, 32, 44 of this Roll.

[3] *Ibid.*, pp. 81, 90.   [4] Anstis, ii, p. 207.   [5] *Foed.*, xi, pp. 834-6 : Dec. 2.

[6] Anstis, *loc. cit.*   [7] Proved March 21, 1475.   *Test. Vetust.*, p. 338.

[8] Then Master of the Rolls.

[9] *Paston*, iii, pp. 123, 129 : Jan. 17, Feb. 15.

[10] *Pat. Rolls*, 1467-77, p. 528.   [11] *Foed.*, xi, p. 846.

quarter his contingent was the same,[1] and he was a person of sufficient consideration to be a signatory to Edward's proposals of Aug. 13 to the French King ; in fact was among those who advised the King to make terms with Louis.[2] Comines[3] tells us that he was among the English leaders whom the latter thought it worth while to bribe, as being an important and trusted servant of King Edward, ' fort privé de luy '.[4] Under the treaty Margaret of Anjou was to be handed over to Louis on his payment of her ransom, and the custody of ' the Lady Margaret ', whose title of Queen was not recognized by the Yorkists, was meanwhile entrusted to Montgomery.[5] Next year this ' Pere-gregius Eques '[6] received the Garter,[7] succeeding to the stall vacated by Duras.[8] On March 12, 1477, his name occurs in a feoffment made by Thomas Cornwaleys of the latter's lands in Whitechapel ;[9] in the summer he was deputed to negotiate with the Ambassadors of France ;[10] and at the end of the year is once more serving as knight of the shire for his county.[11] In 1477 a licence was issued to him and others for the establishment of a Gild of the Fraternity of Jesus at Pritwell in Essex,[12] and in the winter he was sent as ambassador to deal with Edward's sister, the Duchess of Burgundy, in the matter of the equalization

---

[1] *MS.*, fol. 2 *verso.* [2] *Foed.*, xii, p. 15 ; *Pat. Rolls, 1467–77*, p. 571.

[3] Dupont, i, p. 360. [4] *Ibid.*, p. 389.

[5] *Foed.*, xii, pp. 21–2 : Nov. 13, 1475 ; *Pat. Rolls, 1467–77*, p. 571.

[6] Anstis, ii, p. 203. [7] Beltz, No. 218, and p. lxxii : Nov. 14, 1476.

[8] No. 5 above, who had surrendered the Order on Nov. 4, with Edward's permission, on swearing allegiance to the French King and receiving back his estates in France. [9] ' Early London Deeds ' : *Gen.*, N.S., iv, p. 106.

[10] *Foed.*, xii, p. 45. [11] *Return Memb. Parl.*, p. 363 : Dec. 16.

[12] *Pat. Rolls, 1476–85*, p. 34.

of the coinage of the two countries, and also to treat with the envoys of the Dukes of ' Ostriche ' and Burgundy.[1] We next meet with him at Bruges, where, in 1480, he is acting as ' Consiliarius Regis', when Maximilian and Mary, 'Dukes' of Austria and Burgundy, took oath to observe the Treaty of marriage between Philip, Count of Charolais and Edward IV's daughter Anne.[2] An inquisition taken at Penn, in Buckinghamshire, on Jan. 28 of this year had found that John Hunden, late Bishop of Llandaff,[3] and Sir Thomas Montgomery might assign to the Prioress and Convent of Dartford, Kent, in part of a grant of 100 marks, £5 yearly rent in Isnehamstede Chene ;[4] on the last day of August he receives, as a Knight for the King's Body, from the Royal Wardrobe, a gift of crimson cloth of gold for the covering of his ' brygandyn ' ;[5] and Ann, Duchess of Buckingham, appointed him one of the executors of her will, proved Oct. 31 ensuing.[6] On Feb. 14, 1481, he, with others, founded the Gild, or Fraternity, at Ulting, in Essex.[7] In November, 1481, he again comes in for a pipe of wine, or rather its monetary equivalent, apparently 100 shillings, though in a less reputable manner. Richard Cely and his father, of Alveley, in South Essex, had been indicted for driving a hart across the Thames which was subsequently killed at Dartford, in Kent, nearly opposite to the Cely home,[8] ' the qweche hartte ', writes Richard

---

[1] *Foed.*, xii, p. 96 : Dec. 18, 1478.   [2] *Ibid.*, p. 139 ; Anstis, ii, p. 208.
[3] Resigned 1476.
[4] Isenhamsted Chenies, Bucks. *Arch. Journ.*, xxxvi, p. 260; *I.p.m.*, 19 E. IV, vol. iv, p. 398, No. 80.
[5] Nicolas, *Wardrobe Accounts of Ed. IV*, p. 162. See No. 32 below.
[6] *Test. Vetust.*, p. 357.   [7] *Pat. Rolls, 1476–85*, p. 255.
[8] See, too, Nos. 33, 39 below.

to his brother George at Calais, 'whe nevyr se ner knew of
and thys day I have ben w^t master Mwngewmtré and geven
hym the whalew of a pype whyn to have ws howt of the boke
hevir hyt be schewyd the Kyng and so he has promysed me.
. . . I pray yow at hys comyng [to Calais] whate apon hym
and thanke hym for us for he has beyn howr spessyall good
master in thys mater . . . hyt have coste myche mony byt and
Sur Thomas Mongewmbre had not beyn howr goode master
hys ¹ wholld acoste myche mor '.² He appears among the witnesses to the confession, made at Westminster on Aug. 8, 1482,
of John Edward to having calumniated the Earl of Rivers, the
Marquis of Dorset,³ and Richard Radcliffe.⁴ In King Edward's
last year Montgomery and Sir Thomas Borough,⁵ with a few
other of the sovereign's intimates, were especially exempted from
the Sumptuary Act of 1482, and, under it, had permission to
wear cloth and fur, purple and cloth of gold alone being excepted.⁶
Towards the end of the reign he was appointed Treasurer of
Ireland for life,⁷ and was one of the executors of Edward's will,
in which capacity he received a bequest of £40.⁸ He attended
the coronation of Richard III,⁹ and was one of the dignitaries
to whom were made gifts of cloth of gold and silk for the cere-

---

¹ This.
² *Cely Papers*, pp. 73–80. Montgomery, as we have seen, was Steward of the
King's Forest of Essex.   ³ Nos. 13 and 11 above.
⁴ *Record Office MS.* cited by Gairdner, *Rich. III*, pp. 338–9.
⁵ No. 32 below.   ⁶ *Rot. Parl.*, vi, p. 221.
⁷ Anstis, ii, p. 208.
⁸ Nichols, *Wills of Kings and Queens*, p. 347 ; *Excerpt. Hist.*, p. 378.
⁹ *Holinshed*, iii, p. 398 ; *Excerpt. Hist.*, p. 384.

mony.[1] Richard retained his services as Knight of the Body,
and granted him the Castle of Hingham, in Essex, for life.[2]
On Aug. 11, 1484, he, with other commissioners, was sent to
support Richard's attempt to induce the Duke of Brittany to
deliver up, or at least to refuse further shelter to, Henry Tudor
and other Lancastrian refugees, and to arrange certain commercial
matters with the Archduke Maximilian of Austria,[3] while on the
14th of the same month he was appointed Lieutenant of Guisnes,
the important outpost of Calais, with full powers to put in order
its decayed fortifications, in which Tunstall [4] was to assist him.[5]
Richard continued to make use of his diplomatic abilities. In
Oct. 1484 he negotiates with Philip of Austria, Duke of
Burgundy and Count of Flanders, on mercantile questions,[6] and
in Feb. 1485 with the Duke of Brittany about a prolongation
of the truce.[7] In the Bosworth campaign ' Sir Thomas de
Mingumbre ' was with those who ' came to Kynge Richard ',[8]
one of whose principal beneficiaries he was,[9] and, according to
the poem *Bosworth ffeild*, ' Sir Thomas of Mountgomerye ' was
among the leaders who ' sayd Richard shold keepe his croune '.[10]
We may, however, assume that he failed King Richard at the
last, since in the *Device for the Coronation of Henry VII* he and
Borough [11] were nominated to hold the pall over him ; [12] also

[1] ' Wardrobe Account, 1483 ', in *Archaeologia*, i, p. 401.
[2] *Pat. Rolls, 1476–87*, p. 430 : Ap. 26, 1484.
[3] *Lett. & Pap.*, ii, p. 4 ; *Foed.*, xii, p. 231.   [4] No. 42 below.
[5] *Foed., ibid.*   [6] *Ibid.*, p. 249 : Oct. 6.   [7] *Ibid.*, p. 261 : Feb. 20.
[8] *Harl. MS. 542, fol. 34*, quoted by Halsted, ii, p. 568, and by Hutton, p. 209.
[9] See the list of them in Ramsay, ii, p. 534.
[10] *Bp. Percy's Folio MS.*, iii, p. 245, l. 274.   [11] No. 32 below.
[12] *Rutland Papers*, C.S., p. 16.

because he was secured by Henry in the possession of all grants made to him by Edward IV.[1] At the time of Lord Lovel's rising in the North against the Tudor King Montgomery undertook to join the royal muster at Cambridge on July 18–20, 1486, with a contingent of 12 men, ' to awayte uppon my Lord '.[2] On April 4, 1487, a commission of array for Essex against invasion on behalf of Simnel was addressed to Montgomery and others ; [3] he was among the Bannerets who were in attendance at the coronation of Elizabeth of York on St. Catherine's Day that year ; [4] and we read of his being called upon on Dec. 23, 1488, to assist in raising archers in his county of Essex for the expedition for the relief of Brittany in the coming year.[5] In the latter part of March, 1489, it was arranged that the King should stay as his guest on the way to Norwich, though apparently this royal progress was not carried out.[6] Among the Deliveries from the Great Wardrobe that year was, as a gift from the King to Sir Thomas Montgomery for his robes, ' sanguine cloth in grain [7] furred with pure menever and gross menever and silk garter '.[8] These materials were for the surcoat and its lining of a K.G. On the occasion of the creation of Prince

---

[1] *Rot. Parl.*, vi, p. 359.

[2] The attainted Earl of Surrey, who had, however, already been received into the royal favour. (*Household Books of John, Duke of Norfolk & Thos., Earl of Surrey,* pp. 493–4.) This doubtless means 12 men-at-arms.

[3] *Mat. Reign H. VII*, ii, p. 135.   [4] Nov. 25. Leland, *Collect.*, v, p. 230.

[5] *Foed.*, xii, p. 356.   [6] *Paston*, iii, p. 352.

[7] ' Ingrained ' properly means dyed of a fast colour.

[8] *Mat. Reign H. VII*, ii, p. 498. Compare No. 42. The mantle of the Garter was of blue velvet (Ashmole, p. 209) ; the surcoat, originally of woollen cloth, was

Henry [1] as K.B., in Nov. 1494, when a three days' tournament was held at Westminster, Sir Thomas Montgomery was among ' thastates, lordes, bannerettes, and knyghtes ' present,[2] and on Jan. 11 following he ended a life of numerous and varied activities.[3] His will, made July 28, 1489, directs that he be buried ' in the Abbey of Tower-hill,[4] in the Chapel of Our Lady, which I have lately made there '; that the body of his first wife Dame Philippa be removed from Falkbourne to the Tower-hill to be laid by him ; and he appoints Sir Thomas Borough [5] a supervisor of his will.[6] His Garter-plate was still in existence in 1563,[7] and there was formerly in Falkbourne Church a window-portrait of him in a tabard of his arms, of which Anstis [8] gives a cut. He is, however, similarly represented in the still surviving glass at Long Melford in Suffolk.[9] He married (1) Philippa, daughter and heir of John Helion, of Bumstead Helion, Essex, Esquire, and aged fourteen in 28 Hen. VI ; (2) Lora, relict of John Blount, 3rd Baron Mountjoy, of Thurveston,

altered in Edward IV's time to velvet, and its colour changed annually, being successively blue, scarlet, sanguine-in-grain, or white, and later purple was added. (*Ibid.*, pp. 212–13.)

[1] Afterwards Henry VIII.　　　　　　　　[2] *Lett. & Pap.*, i, p. 403.

[3] Beltz, p. clxix ; Anstis, ii, ρ. 208 ; G. E. C., 1st ed., v, p. 399 ; and see *Lett. & Pap.*, ii, p. 61. According to Hazlitt's edition of *Blount's Tenures*, p. 317, his death took place on Jan. 2, 1494, which is evidently wrong.

[4] This was the Cistercian House of St. Mary of Grace near the Tower of London.

[5] No. 32 below.

[6] *Test. Vetust.*, p. 396 ; Nicolas, *Ward. Acc. Ed. IV*, p. 251 ; *Essex Archaeol. Soc. Trans.*, O.S., iii, pp. 168–75.

[7] Anstis, ii, p. 209.　　　　　　　　[8] p. 203.

[9] *Essex A. S. T.*, N.S., xv, p. 42 ; also *Visit. Suff.*, ed. Howard, p. 24.

Derbyshire, and daughter of Sir Edward Berkeley, of Beverston, Gloucestershire ; and left no issue by either wife.[1]

BADGE. A fleur-de-lys gules. Drawn and tricked only in our *MS.*, not described. This is from the coat of Montgomery given above, as in the Long Melford window, where his mother has a mantle of the same.[2] The Montgomery fleur-de-lys is traceable to pre-armorial days, a single lys, not on a shield, forming the device on a seal of John Mundegumri appended to a charter of *c.* 1176.[3]

No. 32. ' Sir Thomas Borough.' Sir Thomas Borough,[4] Knight and Banneret, son and heir of Thomas Borough, of Gainsborough, Esquire, by Elizabeth, daughter and coheir of Sir Henry Percy, of Athol, and of Harthill, Yorks., Knight,[5] was

---

[1] Morant, *Essex*, ii, p. 117 ; *Visit. Essex, 1558*, H.S., i, p. 58 ; *Coll. Top. & Gen.*, vi, p. 154 ; *Lett. Marg. Anjou*, p. 105 ; Alex. Croke, *Geneal. Hist. of Croke Family*, ii, p. 203 ; G. E. C., *loc. cit.*

[2] *Essex A. S. T.*, *ibid.*, p. 43.

[3] *Her. & Gen.*, Pt. XIX, p. 16 ; Ellis, *Antiquities of Heraldry*, p. 195. It may be of interest to note here that *Three fleurs-de-lys or* occur as the principal bearings on the ' flag ' of Sir James Montgomery, of Ireland, in the Great Civil War, probably the last occasion on which personal arms were displayed in the field in this country, most of the ' colours ' used by the Parliamentary and Royalist officers at that time showing *Devises.* See Prestwich, *Respublica*, p. 117, and No. 48 below. Sir James was a Parliamentarian.

[4] Burgh, à Burghe, or à Burgh (as in *Warkworth*, p. 8, and *C. W. R.*, p. 113). On the ' a ' see No. 30 above.

[5] Son of Sir Thomas Percy, who was 2nd son of Henry, 1st Earl of Northumberland. *Glover's Visit. Yks.*, ed. Foster, p. 415 ; *Gen.*, N.S., xii, p. 234 ; *Coll. Top. & Gen.*, v, p. 156 ; vi, p. 89 ; G. E. C., new ed., ii, p. 422, where he is not styled ' Sir '.

aged 24 in 1455.[1] He was the great-great-grandson of Hubert de Burgh, Justiciar and Earl of Kent,[2] and father-in-law of Queen Catherine Parr.[3] 'Thomas Burgh, Esquire,' first appears prominently in 1460, when he is filling the office of Sheriff of Lincolnshire.[4] In a letter of Nov. 6, 1466, to Sir William Plumpton he is described as 'Mr. Borough',[5] though he had been dubbed Knight before the preceding 12th of October, for the will of Thos. Riplingham of that date contains the following passage : 'I will þt a dozen diſhes and as many ſawſers of ſilver, þe whiche were my lord VESSEYS,[6] be deliuered to WILLIAM RILSTON and JOHN FEREBY, to be ſold to my Chamberlein, and to Sir THOMAS BURROW as we were agreed.'[7] He is designated 'Knight', moreover, in the Plea Rolls at Michaelmas, 1466.[8] On Apr. 26, 1467, he was returned as knight of the shire for Lincolnshire,[9] and was partly exempted from the Act of Resumption of 1467–8.[10] In the summer of 1469 he and Sir Thomas Montgomery[11] were, as we have seen, said to have given ill advice to King Edward in dissuading him from taking the field against Clarence and

[1] I. p. m., 11–12 Hen. VII.

[2] Courthope, pp. 39, 498 ; Coll. Top. & Gen., vii, p. 380; and other authorities cited above.

[3] Will of Dame Maude Parr, 1529, in Wills from Doctors' Commons, C.S., pp. 10–11 ; Top. & Gen., iii, p. 354 ; G. E. C., ibid.

[4] Appointed Nov. 7 : List of Sheriffs, p. 79.

[5] Plumpton, p. 17. A Knight, however, was not infrequently called 'Master', and sometimes both titles were accorded him. See, e. g., the examples collected by Dyce in his edition of Skelton, i, p. xxxiii ; ii, p. 178, and Montgomery, p. 57 above.

[6] Vescy's.   [7] Weever, pp. 177–8.

[8] 'Pedigrees from the Plea Rolls', Gen., N.S., xix, p. 35 : Mich. 6 E. IV.

[9] Return Memb. Parl., p. 358.   [10] Rot. Parl., v, p. 581.   [11] No. 31 above.

Warwick,[1] and in the succeeding autumn, when the ' Kingmaker ' found that the country would not tolerate his holding both the rival sovereigns as prisoners at the same time, Borough and Sir William Stanley [2] are believed to have been allowed to assist in Edward's escape from Middleham Castle,[3] and he was a witness to the oath of fealty to him taken by the Earl of Northumberland [4] on his release from the Tower just afterwards.[5]   At the outset of the Lincolnshire insurrection in the following year the supporters of Warwick and Clarence ' droff oute of Lyncolneschyre Sere Thomas à Burghe, a knyght of the Kynges howse, and pullede downe his place, and toke alle his goodes and cataylle that thei myghte fynde '.[6]   This was his manor-house at Gainsborough.   The new manor-house, now known as the ' Old Hall ', and the chief object of interest in the town, is said to have been for the most part put up by his son and successor, but, according to Leland, our Sir Thomas ' made most of the motid manor place by the west end of the chirch yarde '.[7]   In the brilliant march from Ravenspur, during March and April, 1471, which restored the Yorkist King, Borough, with Parr, Montgomery, Harington, and Norris,[8] joined him at Nottingham.[9]   As with Ferrers, Montgomery, and Chamberlain,[10] his interests too were protected in the Act of 1472–3 that conferred the Duchy of

---

[1] Waurin, v, p. 581.   [2] No. 35 below.

[3] Note by J. G. Nichols in ' The Rebellion in Lincolnshire ', *Camd. Misc.*, i, p. 19.   The authority (not given) is Holinshed, iii, p. 293.

[4] No. 12 above.   [5] *Foed.*, xi, p. 649.

[6] *Warkworth*, p. 8, and *C. W. R.*, p. 13 ; *Excerpt. Hist.*, p. 502.

[7] *Itin.*, i, p. 33.   [8] Nos. 30, 31, 43, 45.

[9] Hall, p. 292 ; Holinshed, iii, p. 306.   [10] Nos. 21, 31, 44.

Cornwall on Prince Edward,[1] also in the Act of Resumption of the latter year.[2] His contingent for the first quarter of 1475 numbered 16 men-at-arms and 160 archers, and his pay was £484 11s. 6d., for, although then only a Knight-Bachelor, not yet a Banneret, he received the wages of the latter rank, 4s. a day, ' per fpeciale Warrantum de Privato Sigillo ' ;[3] and for the second quarter the same number of men-at-arms, but his following of archers is not given.[4] We find him among the signatories to Edward's proposals of peace in August,[5] and he is mentioned in the King's will, dated June 20 of that year.[6] On Jan. 5, 1478, he was again returned as knight of the shire for his county ;[7] on Aug. 18 was appointed one of the receivers of the income of the vacant Bishopric of Ely ;[8] and on the last day of the same month crimson cloth of gold was presented to him, as a Knight for the King's Body, from the Royal Wardrobe, for the covering of a brigandine.[9] He was a witness to the confession of John Edward on Aug. 8, 1482,[10] and, like Montgomery, was exempted from the Statute of 1482 'touchyng the reftreynte of exceffive Apparell '.[11] We meet with him among the notables at the coronation of Richard III and his Queen Anne on July 6 in the next year, being presented, as was Montgomery, with cloth of gold and silk for the occasion.[12] At some time after that ceremony he became a Knight of the Garter.[13] With other magnates he

---

[1] Rot. Parl., vi, p. 16.   [2] Ibid., p. 80.   [3] Foed., xi, p. 846.

[4] MS., fol. 2 verso.   [5] Foed., xii, p. 15 : Aug. 13, 1475.

[6] Excerpt. Hist., p. 368.   [7] Return Memb. Parl., p. 364.

[8] Foed., xii, p. 88.   [9] Ward. Acc. E. IV, p. 162. See No. 31 above.

[10] See under No. 31.   [11] Rot. Parl., vi, p. 221.

[12] Archaeologia, i, p. 401 ; Holinshed, iii, p. 398 ; Excerpt. Hist., p. 384.

[13] Beltz, No. 226 ; Anstis, i, p. 220 ; Hope, G. P., lxxxvii.

attended the reception of the Scottish ambassadors in Sept. 1484 ; [1]
and on Feb. 22, 1485, was acting as a commissioner, with
Montgomery and Gunthorpe,[2] to effect a prolongation of the
truce with Francis, Duke of Brittany.[3] Since he was named, in
company with Montgomery, to hold the pall over Henry VII
at his coronation,[4] we may conclude that this soldier, too, did
not stand with Richard at Bosworth Field, though he also had
supported him against Buckingham.[5] Moreover, he was protected under Henry's Act of Resumption of 1485,[6] and accompanied the new King in his First Progress through the country in
March of the succeeding year ; [7] while on the 15th of that month
he and Sir Henry Roos were granted the office of Steward of the
possessions of Edmund, 11th Baron de Roos, attainted, so long as
they remained in the hands of the Crown.[8] He received his final
reward on Sept. 22, 1487, when he was summoned to the Upper
House by writ as 1st Baron Burgh of Gainsborough,[9] but it is
not proved that he ever sat.[10] 'Sir Thomas A Brough' was at
the coronation of Elizabeth of York on Nov. 25, 1487 ; [11] on
Dec. 23, 1488, was assisting in the enlistment of archers for the
coming expedition to Brittany ; [12] in 1489 was an executor to

[1] *Lett. & Pap.*, i, p. 65.   [2] No. 60 below.   [3] *Foed.*, xii, p. 261.
[4] *Rutland Papers*, p. 16.   [5] *Pat. Rolls, 1476–85*, p. 424.
[6] *Rot. Parl.*, vi, p. 377.   [7] Leland, *Collect.*, iv, pp. 186, 191.
[8] *Mat. Reign H. VII*, i, p. 388. Edmund was his brother-in-law.
[9] *Ibid.*, ii, p. 194 ; Dugdale, *Baronage*, ii, p. 288 ; G. E. C., new ed., ii, p. 422.
In the first-named of these authorities, however, we find him still styled ' Knight '
on much later dates : Dec. 15, 1487 (p. 214) ; May 19, 1488 (p. 311) ; June 18,
1488 (p. 326) ; Dec. 23, 1488 (p. 384) ; Feb. 1489 (p. 400) ; Dec. 14, 1490 (p. 554) ;
and also in *Foed.*, xii, p. 448 ; July 7, 1491.
[10] G. E. C., *ibid.*   [11] Leland, *Collect.*, iv, p. 230.   [12] *Foed.*, xii, p. 355.

the will of the Earl of Northumberland ;[1] and on July 7, 1491,
was called upon to help in raising a subsidy in the Parts of
Lindsey for the invasion of France.[2] All offices held by him were
protected by Act of Parliament in 1492.[3] It appears from the
records that he was possessed of a messuage in Calais.[4] He died
on Mar. 18, 1496,[5] and was buried in Gainsborough Church.
'Dominus Thomas Burgh miles ordinis garterii obiit anno
Dom. 1496. Sepultus est in australi parte supremi altaris cum
Margareta domina de Boterax ejus consorte.'[6] His will was
dated Feb. 18 preceding.[7] In it he directs that he be buried in
'my new Chapel [on the S. side] within the Parish Church of
All Saints at Gainsburgh . . . in which I will that a tomb be made
at the North end of the altar . . . with two images or figures
thereon, viz. of me in armour, and of my wife, with our arms,
and the days of our obits ; and I will that the image of me have
my mantle of the Garter, and a garter about my leg '.[8] He
married, between May 1462 and 1464, Margaret, relict of

[1] No. 12 above. *Coll. Top. & Gen.*, ii, p. 65.

[2] *Foed.*, xii, p. 448.   [3] *Rot. Parl.*, vi, p. 454.

[4] *Early Chancery Roll, 441, memb. 5.* P. R. O. ' Quoddam mesnagium in eadem
villa vocatum *a wolle howse* sive *shew howse*, nuper Thome Burghe militis defuncti.'
Westminster, Dec. 7, 1499.

[5] *I. p. m.*, 31 May, 11 H. VII ; G. E. C., new ed., ii, p. 442.

[6] Leland, *Itin.*, i, p. 33 ; v, p. 123.

[7] This may have caused the mistake of Anstis (i, p. 238) and Beltz (p. clxix),
who probably followed him, which places his death on that day.

[8] *Test. Vetust.*, p. 428. It is said that when Gainsborough Church was rebuilt
in 1736–48, the 'image in alabaster' of Sir Thomas Borough was thrown out,
and later discovered buried in the Churchyard ; that it then found its way to the
neighbouring Church of Lea, where it was altered to commemorate some one else,
but has disappeared again since. (*Ex inform.* Sir H. B. Bacon, Bt., and see Stark,
Gainsburgh.)

William, 3rd Baron Botreaux, and daughter of Thomas, 10th Baron de Roos.[1] She died in 1488.[2]

BADGE. 'al [all] the armur of An erme [arm] & the gauntelot.' Simply put, this badge is 'a complete arm-guard with its gauntlet'. If it were not that it is difficult for a medieval pun to be too far-fetched, one would hesitate to suggest here a possible cant on the name of the town of Gainsborough and his own name, i. e. 'Gants-borough'. The same badge appears four times on the standard of his grandson 'Thomas Bourght de Gaynsbourght, Lyncol',[3] afterwards 3rd Baron. A different 'Borowe' badge is given in *Harl. MS. 4632*,[4] *A fleur-de-lys ermine*, taken from the arms of Borough, which were *Azure, 3 fleurs-de-lys ermine*, as on the Garter-plate referred to above.[5]

No. 33. 'Sir Rauffe haſtynges.' Sir Ralph Hastings, of Wansted, Essex,[6] Knight and Banneret, was the third son of Sir Leonard Hastings, of Kirby, Leicestershire, and Burton Hastings, Warwicks, and therefore younger brother of William, Lord Hastings.[7] Edward IV, in the firſt year of his reign, appointed him a King's Esquire for life.[8] These officers were

---

[1] *Ibid.*; and *Glover's Visit. Yorks., loc. cit.*; *Gen.*, vi (1882), p. 141; N.S., xii, p. 234; *Lives of Berkeleys*, i, p. 31.   [2] *I. p. m.*, June 26, 4 H. VII.

[3] *MS. I. 2. Coll. of Arms*, in *Excerpt. Hist.*, p. 332. Reproduced in De Walden, p. 251, where the reference is omitted.   [4] *Coll. Top. & Gen.*, iii, p. 71.

[5] Illustrated also in Hope, *H. for C.*, p. 136; in *Ancestor*, iii, p. 176; and in the glass put up by Borough himself in Newark Church (Dickinson, *Newark*, p. 276).

[6] He and his wife presented to Wansted in 1471, and he again in 1487 (Morant, *Essex*, i, p. 29).

[7] No. 17 above. Father's will in *Test. Vetust.*, p. 280; *Visit. Beds.*, H.S., p. 23.; *Paston*, iii, p. 108; Thoresby's *Ducatus Leodiensis*, i, p. 243.

[8] *Pat. Rolls, 1461–7*, p. 1, July 7; *Rot. Parl.*, v, p. 475.

four in number.[1] At the same time he received, also for life,
the keepership of the ' Lyons, Leoneſſez, and Leopardes ' at
the Tower, with a wage of xii*d*. a day and vi*d*. a day for
the sustentation of each of the beasts.[2] In 1461 he and his
brother William were granted for their lives the Constableship
of the Castle and Forests of Rockingham and the Castle
of Northampton.[3] When Henry VI was captured near Clitheroe,
in July 1465, he was placed in the custody of Ralph Hastings
and others, who escorted him to London.[4] In 1466, and
again in 1471, he was sheriff of Northamptonshire ; [5] and on
May 4[6] of the latter year was created Knight-Bachelor by the
King on the field after the battle of Tewkesbury, and also
a Banneret between that date and the 21st of the same month.[7]
He is said to have been at some time Edward's Master of the
Horse.[8] On Sept. 17, 1472, he was returned as knight of the
shire for Northants,[9] and all his interests, and those of his wife
Anne, were protected in the Act of Resumption of the succeeding
year.[10] On March 21, 1474, he is mentioned as being Knight of
the Body.[11] He was holding the post of Lieutenant of the town
and castle of Guisnes,[12] the most exposed of the outlying forts of
Calais, at any rate before Apr. 26, 1474, for, in a letter of that

[1] Spelman, *Glossarium*, p. 43.

[2] *Rot. Parl.*, v, pp. 475, 533, 590 ; *Pat. Rolls, 1461-7*, pp. 14, 47, 323, 365.

[3] *Pat. Rolls, 1461-7*, p. 13, May 11 ; *Rot. Parl.*, v, p. 534 ; see Clark, *Med. Mil.
Arch.*, ii, p. 443.   [4] *Wil. Wyrc. Ann.*, p. 785.   [5] *List of Sheriffs*, p. 93.

[6] *Ibid.* it is said that he was knighted on May 5.

[7] *A. Wood MS.* F. 11 ; Shaw, ii, pp. 14, 16 ; Metcalfe, pp. 3, 4.

[8] *Coll. Top. & Gen.*, vii, p. 391 ; *Misc. Gen. et Her.*, N.S., iv (1884), p. 258.

[9] *Return Memb. Parl.*, p. 361.   [10] *Rot. Parl.*, vi, p. 81.

[11] *Pat. Rolls, 1467-77*, p. 440.   [12] *Visit. Beds., loc. cit.*

date, it appears that John Paston had been previously requested by Lord Hastings, the Governor of Calais, to cross to France and help his brother, then an invalid, ' in all suche things as concerne the suretie and defense of the Castell of Guysnes during his infirmyties ', while, from the same letter in which this request is referred to, we find that he had recovered.[1] By May 9 following, however, he is again ill, and writes to Paston telling him that he is confined to his bed at Guisnes, and adds some interesting information about the insufficiency of the garrison owing to shortage of money,[2] which seems to have been a chronic condition of things with Calais and its marches in time of peace. From what he says it is clear that the troops there were, as usual, too few, ill paid, and discontented.[3] In the first quarter of 1475 his following consisted of 7 men-at-arms and 100 archers, for which he received £293 9s. 6d., and we learn from the same entry that he was at that time a Knight of the Body to the King ;[4] in the second quarter he brought 8 men-at-arms and the same number of archers as before.[5] There exist two letters, of which the months and days only are known, relating to business matters, from him to George Cely. These were written, one from Calais, the other from Guisnes, during his tenure of command.[6] On

---

[1] *Paston*, iii, p. 108. [2] *Ibid., Suppl.*, p. 146.

[3] This had been, and continued to be, the normal state of affairs at Calais. See, *e. g.*, Sandeman, *Calais under English Rule*, pp. 21–41.

[4] *Foed.*, xi, p. 844. [5] *MS.*, fol. 2 *verso*.

[6] *Cely Papers*, pp. 202–3. The Celys, Richard Cely, and his three sons Richard, Robert, and George, were merchants of the Staple at Calais. The head-quarters of their business was in London, their country-house at Brett's Place, Alveley, near Purfleet in S. Essex. They are mentioned under Nos. 31 above and 39 below. See, too, the letter of Richard III to Hastings as Lieutenant of Guisnes dated June 28 (no year) in Ellis, *Letters*, 2nd Series, i, p. 150.

June 28, 1483, he was discharged of his Lieutenancy. His brother, and superior officer, had been beheaded, apparently on the 20th,[1] and in August, in response to his petition, letters of pardon and confirmation of all lands and offices that he had possessed by the gift of Edward IV, except the Guisnes command, were conceded to him, as well as re-imbursement for his personal expenditure on the fort.[2] Evidently he remained in the royal favour, seeing that from March 4, 1484, to March 11, 1485, he held the Governorship of the Town of Calais, and the Captaincy of Guisnes was restored to him.[3] Yet it is clear that he fell away from Richard at the end, for there is record of a grant to him in Northants on Dec. 6, 1485,[4] and on July 18 in the following year he is mentioned as having previously received grants in Bucks., Berks., and Beds.[5] Again, on Feb. 9, 1489, he is given an annuity of £10 for life, and also the sum of £30 as the salary of the offices of Steward of the Manor and Master of the Game of the Park of Eyton.[6] He had attended the coronation of Elizabeth of York in 1487.[7] In 1495 he died, leaving no male issue, and his wife Anne, daughter of John Tattershall, of Wansted, Essex, survived him.[8] His will,[9] dated

---

[1] *Lett. & Pap.*, i, pp. 15, 16.

[2] *Ibid.*, pp. 46–8. According to Forsyth's *Antiquary's Portfolio*, i, p. 280, this grant of Richard III was dated from the monastery of Gloucester, Aug. 2.

[3] *Early Chancery Roll, 428, memb. 15*; P. R. O.; *Pat. Rolls, 1476–85*, p. 385.

[4] *Mat. Reign H. VII*, i, p. 200.   [5] *Ibid.*, i, p. 506.

[6] *Ibid.*, ii, p. 405.   [7] Leland, *Collect.*, iv, p. 231.

[8] *Coll. Top. & Gen.*, vii, p. 391, where, as in his will, she is called Amy ; *Misc. Gen. et Her.*, *loc. cit.* In *Rot. Parl.*, vi, p. 81, and in *Pat. Rolls*, *loc. cit.*, p. 452, she is named Anne.

[9] *Test. Vetust.*, p. 421.

Sept. 17, and proved Dec. 1, 1495, directs that his body be buried in the Church of St. Bridget, Middlesex, or in the Abbey of Barking, and he leaves to his wife Amy all his manors and lands in Wansted and Woolriche,[1] in Essex and Kent. At Ashby-de-la-Zouch, a Hastings manor, is an alabaster effigy, of late fifteenth century date, which has been doubtfully considered to commemorate him. It is known as 'The Pilgrim monument', because the figure is clad in the 'sclavyne' or pilgrim's robe. It wears the Lancastrian Collar of SS., which was revived by Henry VII.[2]

BADGE. 'Shafront filu[er] wyth 3 Eyftryges [ostrich's] ffedyrs.' The origin of this badge is, so far, a mystery. If his wife was of Talbot or Furnival blood, light might be thrown upon it. In *MS. I. 2. Coll. of Arms* (1510–25) *Seven chamfrons, each adorned with three feathers or* appear as badges on the standard of George Talbot, Earl of Shrewsbury;[3] and in *Cotton MS. Cleopatra. C. v. No. 1* the same nobleman again bears on his standard 'shaffrons gold'. According to *Harl. MS. 1394* the chamfront was a Furnival badge.[4]

---

[1] Woolwich.

[2] An illustration of the slavine may be seen in *The Rows Roll*, No. 22 ; or *Anastatic Drawing Society*, 1857, p. 2, and Pl. VIII ; or *Harl. MS. 4826*, reproduced in Strutt, *Reg. & Eccles. Antiq.*, Pl. XLV ; and, for the word, consult Ducange, *s.v.* ' Sclavina'.

[3] See the reproduction in De Walden, p. 66.

[4] For an excellent example of a chamfront of this period adorned with three feathers see Hewitt's *Ancient Armour*, 1855–60, iii, p. 508, from *Cotton MS. Nero. D. ix, fol. 39, c.* 1480. The plumed horse was a fashion of the time : see the Great Seals of Edward IV, Richard III, and Henry VII. A specimen with one feather is shown in *The Birth, Life, and Death of the Earl of Warwick*, ed. by Dillon and Hope, Pl. XLVIII. This decoration had appeared a century earlier in France: *e.g.* Demay, *Le Costume de Guerre d'après les sceaux*, Pls. XIX, XXV.

No. 34. 'Sir John ffenys.' Sir John Fenys, or Fiennes, Knight and Banneret, was son and heir of Sir Richard Fiennes, declared Baron Dacre (of the South) by patent of Nov. 7, 1458, and who died Nov. 25, 1483, by Joan, granddaughter and heir to Thomas, 6th Baron Dacre.[1] 'Johannes Fenys, miles,' was returned as knight of the shire for Sussex on Apr. 30, 1467, and again on Dec. 24, 1477.[2] He was appointed Sheriff of Surrey and Sussex on Nov. 6, 1470 ;[3] and was one of those who at the restoration of Edward IV swore, on July 3, 1471, to acknowledge his son as heir to the throne.[4] His name does not appear in the Tellers' Roll for the first quarter of 1475 ; in the second quarter he brings 4 men-at-arms, including as usual himself, and 40 archers.[5] He married Alice, daughter and heir of Henry, 5th Baron Fitzhugh, and died in his father's lifetime before Sept. 20, 1483, leaving a son Thomas, a minor aged twelve in 1486, who became, on the death of his grandfather, 2nd (Fiennes) Baron Dacre of the South.[6] The will of Sir John Fiennes's wife, dated Oct. 13, 1485, leaves a portion of her property to ' Thomas, son of Sir John Fynes, Kt.'[7]

BADGE. ' ma[r]tyn ſilu[er].' This is the marten, foumart, weasel, or polecat. An early term for the marten was 'foine' : see Cotgrave, *s. v. Fouïnne* (and *Foine*) : ' The Foyne, wood-

---

[1] Courthope, p. 137 ; G. E. C., new ed., iv, p. 9 (Ped. between pp. 668–9) ; *Coll. Top. & Gen.*, i, p. 300 ; vii, p. 54 ; Poulson, *Hist. of Holderness*, i, p. 226.

[2] *Return Memb. Parl.*, pp. 359, 365.

[3] *List of Sheriffs*, p. 137.   [4] *Foed.*, xi, p. 714.   [5] *MS.*, fol. 3 *recto*.

[6] G. E. C., *loc. cit.* ; *Coll. Top. & Gen.*, *loc. cit.* ; *Visit. Sussex*, H.S., p. 12 ; *Gen.*, N.S., xxxiv, p. 166 ; *Mat. Reign H. VII*, i, p. 31 ; ii, p. 519.

[7] *Test. Vetust.*, p. 390.

Martin, or Beech Martin.' Furs made of its skin were known
as 'foyns', or 'foins'; as in *Pierce the Ploughman*: 'A cote
hap he furred With foyns.'[1] Obviously this badge is a play on
the name, which, so far as I am aware, has not been noticed
before. The word 'foine' is used in blazoning the canting
coat of Martin, of Sussex, in which this animal is a principal
charge.[2]

No. 35. 'Sir Will[*ia*]m ſtanley.' Sir William Stanley, of
Hooton, Cheshire, Knight and Banneret (see *D. N. B.*), was the
younger brother of Lord Stanley.[3] He is not included in the
Tellers' Roll for the first quarter of 1475; in the second quarter
he brought to the muster 2 men-at-arms, that is himself and
another, and 20 archers.[4]

BADGE. 'hart hede ſilu[*er*].' This badge was taken from
his arms: *Argent, on a bend azure three bucks' heads cabossed or.*[5]
It is probably he who is described by this badge as present at
Towton: 'The Grehound[6] and the Hertes Hede þei quyt
hem wele þt day.'[7] It occurs on a seal of his to a Cheshire deed
dated June 12, 1468, at which time he was Sheriff of that county;[8]
also twice on the font[9] in the Church of Holt, Denbighshire, of
which manor he was lord.[10] It is alluded to in *The Song of*

---

[1] Ed. by Skeat, l. 295. See, too, *Prompt. Parv.*, i, p. 168, and note 3.
[2] Papworth, p. 101. See also Spener, *Insignium Theoria*, ii, Pl. 13, and p. 245, *mustela*. [3] No. 18 above. [4] *MS.*, fol. 3 *recto*.
[5] 'Ballard's Roll', *temp.* Ed. IV: *Harl. MS. No. 2076*; Ashmole, p. 713.
[6] Mauleverer? No. 48 below. [7] *Archaeologia*, xxix, p. 346, *init.*
[8] *Ancestor*, ii, p. 139, No. xlvi. [9] *c.* 1485-95.
[10] Illustrated in Dorling's *Leopards of England*, &c., p. 96, and plates facing
p. 94, 96.

Lady Bessy : ' Sir William Stanley made anone / Ten thousand coats readily, / Which were as redde as any blood, / Thereon the hart's head was set full high.' [1]   And ' Sir William Standley ten thowsand coates / In an howres warnyng readye to bee, / They were read as any blode, / There the hartes head is sett full hye '.[2] He is referred to by his badge also in *The Rose of England* : [3] ' & then came in the harts head ; / a worthy sight itt was to see, / they Iacketts that were of white & redd / how they Laid about them lustilye.' ' A hert's hede silver ' was used as a crest by Stanley of ' Hutton ' ; [4] and ' The helme of Stanley is a hart, silver '. [5]   The buck's head charge in the arms is supposed to have been adopted by the House of Stanley as allusive to the Forestership of the Wirral.[6]

No. 36. ' Sir Robert Tailboffe of Kyme.'   Sir Robert Talboys,[7] of S. Kyme, Lincolnshire, Knight and Banneret, aged 40 on Feb. 4, 1491,[8] was the son and heir of Sir William Talboys, titular Earl of Kyme, by Elizabeth, daughter of William, 1st Baron Bonville.[9] Sir William was the somewhat turbulent Lancastrian who, in 1450, had been sent to the Tower and fined the then heavy sum of £3,000 for attempting to assassinate Lord Cromwell ; [10] who, later, was one of the refugees in Edin-

---

[1] Version I, p. 33.   [2] Version II, p. 70.
[3] ll. 113–16 ; *Bp. Percy's Folio MS.*, iii, p. 194.
[4] ' Wall's Crests ', *Ancestor*, xi, p. 183.
[5] *Lansdowne MS. 858, fol. 22 b.*   [6] *Coll. Top. & Gen.*, viii, p. 1.
[7] Tailbosse, or Tailbois.   [8] *Lincs. Pedigrees*, H.S., iii, p. 946.
[9] *Coll. Top. & Gen.*, ii, p. 194.
[10] *Wil. Wyrc. Ann.*, p. 766 ; *Rot. Parl.*, v, p. 200 ; and see *Paston*, i, pp. 96–8. Lord Cromwell was the builder of Tattershall Castle.

burgh with Queen Margaret ; [1] and who, in the end, was caught
'in a cole pyt' with his pockets full of the wages that he should
have paid to the Queen's soldiers, beheaded at Newcastle after
the defeat of his party at Hexham [2] and attainted.[3] He styled
himself 'Earl of Kyme', and this title is accorded to him by
Warkworth,[4] while Gregory [5] writes of him with scant respect
as merely 'thys Taylbosse'. The Croyland Chronicle,[6] however,
speaks well of him as a staunch supporter of the Abbey Church
there. Some of his forfeited possessions were given to Sir Thomas
Borough.[7] In 1472 this attainder was reversed, and the estates were
restored to his son Robert of our Roll, who had joined the Yorkist
party,[8] and on Sept. 21 that year was returned as knight of the
shire for the county of Lincoln.[9] Sir Robert's name does not
appear in the Tellers' Roll for the first quarter of 1475, but in
the second quarter, as we see, he brings 12 men-at-arms and
80 archers.[10] On Jan. 5, 1478, he was again returned as knight
of the shire for his county,[11] and in 1480 served as Sheriff.[12] Three
years later he is in the list of those who attended the coronation
of Richard III,[13] to whom obviously he did not adhere at the

[1] *Paston*, ii, p. 46 : Aug. 30, 1461.
[2] *Wil. Wyrc. Ann.*, p. 782 ; *Warkworth*, p. 4 ; and *C. W. R.*, p. 106 ; *Greg.
Chron.*, p. 226 ; *Three 15 Cent. Chron.*, p. 179, where, as in the *Croyland Chronicle*,
p. 522, he is described as 'armiger' only.
[3] *Rot. Parl.*, v, pp. 477, 480 ; *I. p. m.* 4 E. IV, vol. iv, p. 327, No. 49.
[4] *Loc. cit.*   [5] *Loc. cit.*   [6] *Loc. cit.*   [7] No. 32 above.
[8] *Rot. Parl.*, vi, p. 18 ; *Lincs. Peds.*, *loc. cit.* ; *Coll. Top. & Gen.*, *loc. cit* ; *Gen.*,
1878, p. 51.   [9] *Return Memb. Parl.*, p. 361.   [10] *MS.*, fol. 3 *recto.*
[11] *Return Memb. Parl.*, p. 364, where he is still styled 'armiger', which must
be an error.   [12] Appointed Nov. 5 : *List of Sheriffs*, p. 79.
[13] *Excerpt. Hist.*, p. 384.

last, for he accompanied Henry VII to the North on his progres
through the country in March of the year after Bosworth.[1] It i
on record that upon May 19, 1488, he was appointed a commissioner of sewers in Lincolnshire,[2] that on Dec. 23 following h
was one of the county magnates called upon to enlist archer
for the Breton expedition,[3] and that on July 7, 1491, he wa
assisting to raise the Lincolnshire share of the subsidy to mee
the cost of the invasion of France in the succeeding year.[4] H
died on Jan. 31, 1495, and was buried at Kyme.[5] By his will,
dated Nov. 16, 1494, he directs that he be buried in the Priory
of Kyme, on the N. side of the choir, ' and there I will hav
a tomb with a picture of me, and another of my wife '.[7] She wa
Elizabeth, daughter of Sir John Heron, Knight, by Elizabeth
daughter of Sir William Heron, of Ford Castle, Northumberland
Knight.[8] We sometimes find him described as ' Lord of Kym
and Redisdale ', and he so styles himself in his will. On th
S. front of the small border pele-castle of Elsdon, Northumber
land, now used as the rectory, is a shield of the arms of Umfravill
and the inscription ' R. D. d[e] rede ' upon a separate stone belov
them. The estate of Redesdale, as well as that of Kyme, ha
descended to Sir Robert Talboys through the Umfravilles, hi
great-grandmother Eleanor being the heiress to both. I hav
only a drawing of this achievement, but, judging from that, th

[1] Leland, *Collect.*, iv, p. 186.   [2] *Mat. Reign H. VII*, ii, p. 311.
[3] *Foed.*, xii, p. 355.   [4] *Ibid.*, p. 447.
[5] *Lincs. Peds.*, *loc. cit.*, where, if *Test. Vetust.* is right, the dates are inaccurate.
[6] *Test. Vetust.*, p. 420. Proved June 19, 1495.
[7] Kyme was a Priory of Austin Canons, founded by Philip de Kyme, 1177–94
[8] *Lincs. Peds.*, *loc. cit.*; *Gen.*, ii, p. 51.

whole seems to be of late fifteenth-century date, in which case it may refer to our man, ' Robertus Dominus de Rede ', and his claim through the Umfravilles.[1]

BADGE. 'the whyt Boull.' 'A Bull passant argent' appears to have been used as a crest by Tailboys of Kettleby, Lincs.[2] Beyond this I have been able to find nothing. No memorial of Sir Robert survives at Kyme.

No. 37. ' Sir John Radeclyff ffitzwat[er].' Sir John Ratcliffe Fitzwalter, of Attleborough, Norfolk, Knight and Banneret, son and heir of Sir John Ratcliffe, K.G., by Elizabeth, daughter and sole heir of Walter, 7th Baron Fitzwalter, was born on Jan. 1, 1452 [3] (see *D. N. B.*). He is not in the Tellers' Roll for the first quarter of 1475 ; for the second quarter his contingent musters 6 men-at-arms and 70 archers.[4]

BADGE. garbrale filu[er].' This is drawn in the *MS.* as a heart-shaped elbow-piece, with its straps and buckle, and a large wing on each side. A Fitzwalter crest was a winged heart,[5] and that might well have been the origin of this form of the badge. For a heart-shaped coudière of this period see that given in Hope's *Heraldry for Craftsmen*, p. 186.[6] In the French campaign of 1513 his son and successor, Robert, used as one of the badges on his standard ' an elbow gard . . . gold ' ; [7] and on his standard in *MS. I. 2. Coll. of Arms* [8] three ' garbralles argent, with gold

---

[1] For the rather complicated descent see G. E. C., 1st ed., iv, pp. 424–5 ; and *Gen.*, N.S., xxvi, pp. 193–211.   [2] Burke.

[3] G. E. C., new ed., v, p. 723 ; Courthope, p. 199.

[4] *MS.*, fol. 3 *recto*.   [5] Burke.

[6] Referred to under No. 24 above.   [7] *Cotton MS. Cleopatra C. v.*

[8] *Excerpt. Hist.*, p. 325.

buckles ',[1] but these last are of an altogether different and much more ordinary pattern, are without the wings, and moreover are not only elbow-guards, but arm-guards also, combining vambrace and rerebrace. The attendant motto there is *Je Garderay*.[2]

No. 38. ' Sir Thomas howard.' Sir Thomas Howard, Knight and Banneret, son and heir of John, 1st (Howard) Duke of Norfolk,[3] by his wife Catherine, daughter of William, Baron Moleyns, was born in 1443 (see *D. N. B.*). In the first quarter of the 1475 expedition this ' lusty and noble young gentleman ' [4] brought 6 men-at-arms and 60 archers, and was paid £177 9*s.* ; [5] for the second quarter the same number of men-at-arms but only 40 archers.[6] It was he who later won Flodden Field for Henry VIII, and in consequence, the Dukedom of Norfolk for himself.

BADGE. ' falet filu[*er*].' The drawing is a very conventional representation of a sallet, a fashion of head-piece then of com-

---

[1] Figured in De Walden, p. 212.

[2] As to the word *garbralle*, ' gar ', a curtailment of ' garde ', combined with ' bralle ', a corrupt abbreviation of ' brachelle ', is perhaps its explanation. ' Brachelle =brassart, armure de bras ' (Lacombe, p. 239, and *Suppl.*, p. 69). Godefroy gives a form ' braçuel ' =arm-armour. Thus we have here an equivalent to the familiar *gardebras* or *bracer*, though the drawing in our *MS.* shows only an elbow-guard.

[3] The Lord Howard of this Roll, No. 20.

[4] Polydore Vergil, C.S., p. 190 : the ' florens & illustris adolescens ' of the Leyden edition, p. 695.

[5] *Foed.*, xi, p. 844, where he is styled not *miles*, but *armiger pro corpore Domini Regis*.

[6] *MS.*, fol. 3 *recto.* Doyle (ii, p. 589, and iii, p. 477) says that he led in 1475 two hundred archers, but gives no authority for this unlikely number.

paratively recent adoption in England, and of which there were
various forms. This is not one of the familiar Howard badges.

No. 39. 'Sir humffrey Talbot.' Sir Humphrey Talbot,
Knight and Banneret, was a younger son of John, 1st (Talbot)
Earl of Shrewsbury, 'the English Achilles', by his second wife
Margaret, eldest daughter of Richard, 5th (Beauchamp) Earl
of Warwick.[1] He served as a captain under John Mowbray,
Duke of Norfolk,[2] at the latter's siege of Caistor in August and
September, 1469, and was then already a Knight.[3] To the army
of invasion in France in 1475 he contributed for the first
quarter 10 men-at-arms and 100 archers, receiving in payment
£298 0s. 6d., and from the same Tellers' Roll we learn that he
was then a Knight of the Royal Body, but he is not described
there as a Banneret ;[4] for the second quarter, by then at any rate
a Banneret, his following was the same.[5] There is a rather pleasing
little record in *Testamenta Vetusta* :[6] John Wenlock, perhaps
his steward, in his will, dated Oct. 31, and proved Dec. 10, 1477,
bequeaths 'to my master, Sir Humphrey Talbot, a standing
cup of gold', and appoints him one of his executors. He was
returned as knight of the shire for Berks on Dec. 24 in the same
year,[7] and in 1479 was Sheriff of Oxon. and Berks.[8] We meet
with 'Sir Umfry Tawbot' in the *Cely Papers*[9] as buying a horse
in 1480 from George Cely at Calais, 'with which he whos welle
content'. In that year he received the grant of a house in Calais

[1] Stow, i, p. 337 ; Hunter, *Hallamshire*, p. 48 ; *Lives of Berkeleys*, ii, p. 72.
[2] No. 8 above.   [3] *Paston*, ii, p. 369 ; *Will. Worc. Itin.*, p. 322.
[4] *Foed.*, xi, p. 845. He had been a Knight of the Body as early as Sept. 3, 1473
(*Pat. Rolls*, 1467–77, pp. 396–7).   [5] *MS.*, fol. 3 *recto*.   [6] p. 343.
[7] *Return Memb. Parl.*, p. 363.
[8] Appointed Nov. 5. *List of Sheriffs*, p. 108.   [9] p. 46.

together with an annuity of £40.[1]   A memorandum of June
28, 1483, orders that he is to continue in his office of Marshal
of Calais,[2] and some six months later a captured Breton ship was
brought into the harbour there and presented to him by the
King.[3]   In July of this year he was acting, with Sir Richard
Tunstall [4] and others, as a commissioner to treat with those sent
by the French King about certain questions touching the Calais
frontier.[5]   It seems fairly clear from *The Song of Lady Bessy*,[6]
and from his subsequent history, that he did not support
Richard III at Bosworth.   In Feb. 1486 he received from
Henry VII the re-grant of his house in Calais ; [7] and on April 25
following a licence was granted ' dilecto et fideli nostro Humfrido
Talbot militi marescallo villae nostrae Calesiae, quod ipse, cum
sex personis in comitiva sua ', should go on a pilgrimage to
Rome.[8]   On Dec. 15 of the same year he was engaged in the
arrangement of commercial matters with Maximilian, King of
the Romans.[9]   In 1489, while still Marshal of Calais, he was
present at the battle of Dixmude on June 13, when he was left
with six score archers ' at the water [10] of Gravelyng for a stale [11]
and to keep the passage '.[12]   October, 1492, found him [13]

[1] *Pat. Rolls, 1476–85*, p. 417 : June 10.

[2] *Lett. & Pap.*, i, p. 14.   For a list of the officials of Calais and the authorities for
it see Plummer's *Fortescue*, p. 229.   [3] Gairdner, *Rich. III*, p. 150, and note 2.

[4] No. 40 below.   [5] *Foed.*, xii, pp. 195–6 : July 16, 1483.   [6] Cited below.

[7] *Mat. Reign H. VII*, i, pp. 321, 340 : Feb. 28 and March 4.

[8] *Ibid.*, i, p. 415.   [9] *Foed.*, xii, p. 320.   [10] Ditch.

[11] Ambush.   Compare ' stealth '.   For the word used in the sense of ' decoy '
or ' bait ', see Shak., *Temp.*, iv, 187 : ' For stale to catch these thieves '.   Also
Tam. Shr., III, i, 90.

[12] Leland, *Collect.*, iv, p. 247 ; Hall, p. 445 ; Holinshed, iii, p. 494.   Consult
the map of the marches of Calais in *Chron. Cal.* ; also *Archaeologia*, liii, p. 289 ;
and see the *Journal of Kg. Ed. VI*, pp. 30–1.   [13] Like No. 55 below.

mong the Nobles, Knights, and Gentlemen who rode to meet
he French ambassadors in the matter of the treaty of that year, by
which it was privately agreed by Charles VIII that Edward IV's
nnuity of 1475 should be paid to Henry VII.[1] Next month,
s there was peace with France, a royal licence was again granted
o him to make a pilgrimage, this time to Jerusalem, 'aliaque
oca ad quae votum fecerit', with six soldiers of Calais in his
rain, leaving a sufficient deputy in his office of Marshal of the
own during his absence. Upon his return he was to re-occupy
hat post.[2] On March 5, 1493, he was commissioned, with two
thers, to admit to the Order of the Garter Alphonso, Duke of
Calabria.[3] This investment took place at Suessa on May 19
ollowing, the Duke succeeding to the stall vacated by the death
f Sir John Savage [4] at the siege of Boulogne in the preceding
October.[5] Soon after, in the same year, Talbot died, leaving
o issue. In his will,[6] dated Feb. 18, 1492, he describes himself
s Marshal of the town of Calais, and mentions his sister Elizabeth,
Duchess of Norfolk,[7] and his wife as both then living. The
atter, Jane, or Joan, daughter and coheir of John Champernoun,
f Devon, Esquire, died in 1505.[8]

BADGE. ' Renynghonde filu[er] on fhau[l]d[er] a mollet.'
This ' running hound ' was the talbot, the well-known punning
adge of his house, and the mullet is his cadency mark, as, at
his date, third surviving son. His father, slain at Châtillon in

---

[1] *Lett. & Pap.*, ii, p. 291.

[2] *Foed.*, xii, p. 505 : Nov. 28, 1492.

[3] *Ibid.*, pp. 517, 528.

[4] No. 51 below. Beltz, p. clxix.

[5] Polydore, Leyden, 1651, p. 744.

[6] *Test. Vetust.*, p. 409. The date of the proving there given is obviously wrong.

[7] Wife of No. 8 above.

[8] *Pat. Rolls, 1476–85*, p. 243 ; *Test. Vetust.*, p. 471 ; see Stow, i, p. 337.

1453, is alluded to by this badge about 1449 : ' Talbott oure goode dogge ; ' [1] and again in 1450 : ' Talbott oure gentille dogge.' [2] So, too, our man's eldest brother, the 2nd (Talbot) Earl of Shrewsbury, in the poem on the battle of Northampton, where he fell, July 10, 1460 : ' Talbot ontrew was the. oon Dogges name.' [3] Sir Gilbert Talbot, Sir Humphrey's nephew, is similarly referred to in *Lady Bessy* : King Richard is made to say that none of the Talbots shall ' run him by ' ; [4] and, again, Sir Gilbert Talbot has ' ten thousand doggs / In one hour's warning for to be '. [5] In like manner it is said in line iii of *The Rose of England*, also of Sir Gilbert, who commanded Henry's right at Bosworth : ' the Talbott he bitt wonderous sore.' [6] In the French expedition of 1513 Sir Gilbert bore, as one of the badges on his standard, ' A Talbot passant sylver with a cressent [7] apon his shulder for a difference '. [8] In *Harl. MS. 4632* [9] the Talbot badge is given as *A Talbot passant argent*. Talbots appear also as supporters on the seal of John, 1st (Talbot) Earl of Shrewsbury, as Baron Talbot and Furnival, in 1406. [10] The talbot occurs, too, as a crest of the House : ' Talbot of Baschawe [11] beryth to his crest a hounde silver passant.' [12]

No. 40. ' Sir Thomas gray.' Sir Thomas Grey, Knight and Banneret. The difficulty of identifying a Grey of this period

---

[1] *Polit. Poems*, R.S., ii, p. 222.   [2] *Ibid.*, p. 224.
[3] *Archaeologia*, xxix, p. 335.   [4] Version I, p. 7.
[5] *Ibid.*, p. 33, and Version II, p. 70.   [6] *Bp. Percy's Fol. MS.*, p. 194.
[7] Because he was the second son of the Earl of Shrewsbury killed at Northampton.
[8] *Cotton MS. Cleop. C. v.*   [9] *Coll. Top. & Gen.*, iii, p. 67.
[10] Given in Hope, *G. P.*, li, and in his *H. for C.*, pp. 203–5. He was not created E. of Shrewsbury till 1442.   [11] Bashall, near Clitheroe, Yorks.
[12] ' Wall's Crests ' : *Ancestor*, xi, p. 180.

below the rank of Baron and bearing a Christian name shared by others is, in this instance, greatly diminished by the badge given in the *MS.*, which makes it fairly clear that our Captain here was one of the Greys of Northumberland. This apparently narrows the choice to two Thomas Greys with preference, for a reason presently to be shown, to Sir Thomas Grey, 2nd son of Sir Ralph Grey, of Heaton, Wark, and Chillingham, by Elizabeth, daughter of William, 4th Baron Fitzhugh, of Ravensworth in Richmondshire.[1] Sir Ralph Grey, elder brother of Sir Thomas, had been degraded from knighthood and executed in 1464,[2] and as Ralph's son Thomas was in 1475 a minor aged eighteen or nineteen, and was not created a Banneret till 22 Edward IV,[3] this youth may be disregarded. His uncle Sir Thomas was thus at this time the head of the family.[4] There was a Sir Thomas Grey, of Horton in Glendale, who in point of age would fit in here, but the Greys of Horton were a cadet branch of the Greys of Heaton, and the considerable following brought to the muster seems to indicate that our leader was the temporary head of the House of Heaton. There is no commander of his name in the Tellers' Roll for the first quarter of 1475; in the second quarter Sir Thomas Grey brings 8 men-at-arms and 80 archers.[5] Among a large number of entries in the records referring to Sir Thomas Greys of this period some with probability, but not one with absolute certainty, can be said to relate to our man, and I have,

---

[1] G. E. C., new ed., v, Ped. between pp. 668–9; Raine, *N. Durham*, p. 329.

[2] See under No. 29 above.

[3] March 4, 1482—March 3, 1483. Raine, *op. cit.*, p. 328.

[4] *Ibid.*, p. 326; *Coll. Top. & Gen.*, i, pp. 303, 406–7.

[5] *MS.*, fol. 3 *recto*.

therefore, considered it safer to omit them all, but I think that his identity has been established. Sir Thomas married (1) Alice daughter of Edward, 1st (Nevill) Baron Abergavenny, (2) Katherine Sampton.[1]

BADGE. 'íkalyng lader íilu[er].' A scaling-ladder was the well-known crest of Grey of Northumberland, and this, as well as the badge, was probably a play on the surname. M.E. grē = 'a step, stair (*gradus*)' : O.F. gré = 'rung of a ladder'.[2] 'I have . . . appointed six greces [steps] to be before the high altare' occurs in the will of Henry VI.[3] I do not know that this has been suggested before. It may be added that *Barry of six argent and azure* was a regular Grey coat, which strongly suggests a ladder.[4]

No. 41. 'Sir John Arundell.' Here again the badge determines the House, and shows that this is not one of the Arundel of the south-west. Sir John Arundel, Knight and Banneret was the fourth son of William, 9th (Fitzalan) Earl of Arundel by Joan, daughter of Richard Nevill, Earl of Salisbury, and brother of Thomas Fitzalan, who, in 1487, succeeded as 10th (Fitzalan) Earl of Arundel.[5] It was possibly he who was created a K.B. at the coronation of Elizabeth, Queen of Edward IV on Ascension Day,[6] 1465.[7] From the Tellers' Roll we see

---

[1] 'Sed sine liberis obijt' : *Visit. Salop.*, H.S., p. 107 ; Raine, *op. cit.*, p. 329

[2] Stratmann, p. 306 ; *Prompt. Parv.*, i, pp. 208–9 ; Godefroy.

[3] Nichols, *Wills of K. and Q.*, p. 297.

[4] Papworth, p. 52 ; and the Early Rolls of Arms, *passim*.

[5] *Lett. & Pap.*, i, p. 403 ; *Coll. Top. & Gen.*, i, p. 300; G. E. C., new ed., p. 249 ; Dallaway, *Hist. of Sussex*, ii, p. 148.

[6] May 26.   [7] *Wil. Wyrc. Ann.*, p. 784.

that he brought to the army for the first quarter of 1475 2 men-at-arms, that is one besides himself, and 20 archers, and that his remuneration was £61 8s. 6d.; [1] for the second quarter he brought the same.[2] At the funeral of Edward IV, in April 1483, he was one of the watchers by the body, 'without the herse', and also made an offering to the corpse.[3] From the accession of Henry VII onwards we are faced with a difficulty, that of disentangling him from a Sir John Arundel 'of the West', whose family had been Lancastrians. Both were present at the Westminster Tournament of Nov. 1494, and are distinguished in the list as 'Sir John Arundell, baneret, broder to therll of Arundell', and 'Sir John Arundell of the West contre'.[4] The same doubt arises in the case of other records and entries, where there is no such discrimination, and which must therefore remain unused here. Judging from the counties named, however, the following should relate to our man. Sir John Arundel was appointed on Dec. 23, 1488, a commissioner for Sussex and Surrey to raise archers for the expedition to Brittany,[5] and on Aug. 21 in the following year was included among the commissioners of Peace and of Oyer and Terminer for the former county.[6]

BADGE. 'an Akkorn.' As pointed out, any doubt about this soldier being a member of the Fitzalan family is set at rest by his badge. On the standard of his brother the Earl gold acorns and oak leaves appear repeatedly,[7] and on the effigy of his mother is the Yorkist Collar of Suns and Roses linked together

---

[1] *Foed.*, xi, p. 847.   [2] *MS.*, fol. 3 *recto*.   [3] *Lett. & Pap.*, i, pp. 8, 10.
[4] *Ibid.*, p. 403.   [5] *Foed.*, xii, p. 356; *Mat. Reign H. VII*, ii, pp. 385, 387.
[6] *Ibid.*, p. 477.
[7] *MS. I. 2. Coll. of Arms*, in *Excerpt. Hist.*, p. 317; De Walden, p. 175.

by oak-leaves.[1] The oak-leaves are found at any rate as far back as the times of Brian, 1st Baron Fitzalan of Bedale, who died in 1306,[2] for a female figure on the monument to him at Bedale wears a fillet composed of them round her head.[3] This badge, in the form of a sprig of oak with acorns, appears as part of the crest of Fitzalan on one of the Elizabethan Roundels described and illustrated in *Archaeologia*, lxx, p. 59, and Pl. II, No. 2. Dallaway [4] gives a cut of the crest of Sir John's father: an acorn between two oak leaves.

No. 42. 'Sir Rychard Dunstalle.' Sir Richard Tunstall,[5] Knight and Banneret, was son and heir of Sir Thomas Tunstall, of Thurland Castle [6] and Tunstall, Lancashire, Knight, by Eleanor, daughter of Henry, 3rd Baron Fitzhugh, of Ravensworth, Richmondshire.[7] He was appointed by Henry VI one of the four Esquires of the King's Body on Sept. 3, 1452, with an income of 40 marks, and was already a Knight in 1455, and in receipt of a life-annuity of £40, which was bestowed on him because 'the said Richard made unto us the first comfortable

---

[1] Stothard, *Mon. Eff.*, Pls. 136–7; also in Hope, *H. for C.*, p. 280.

[2] G. E. C., new ed., v, p. 641. [3] Blore, *Mon. Rem.*, No. 3.

[4] *Op. cit.*, ii, p. 149. See also *ibid.*, pp. 196–7.

[5] Or Dunstall. The latter form is also found in *Wriothesley's Chronicle* (*A°*. 1536, C.S., i, p. 34), and 'Donnestal' appears in Waurin (v, p. 344). His name was misread in our *MS.* by Planché (*Pursuivant*, p. 186) as 'Dunstable', an error which has been repeated by copyists from that book.

[6] Near Hornby, a fortified mansion, leave to crenellate which was granted to Sir Thomas Tunstall, Sir Richard's grandfather, in 1404. (Whitaker, *Richmondshire*, ii, p. 271; Turner and Parker, *Dom. Arch.*, iii, pp. 217, 421.)

[7] G. E. C., new ed., v, Ped. between pp. 668–9. He was therefore first cousin to Sir Thomas Grey, No. 40 above.

relation and notice that oure moſt entierly belovyd wyf the Quene
was with child, to oure moſt finguler confolation, and to all oure
true liege people grete joy and comfort '.[1] Till about the middle
of 1468 Sir Richard Tunstall was a prominent Lancastrian.
During the last three years of Henry VI's reign he held office as
Master of the Mint,[2] and was Warden of the Exchange in the
27th, 31st, and 36th years [3] of that King.[4] We firft come across
him in a military capacity as being present at Henry's victory at
Wakefield on Dec. 31, 1460, and defeat at the Second Battle of
St. Albans on Feb. 17, 1461. This is shown by the Act of
Attainder referred to presently. On March 13 following, just
before Towton Field, he was ordered by Henry to summon to
arms on the Royal behalf all loyal men of the Knaresborough
diſtrict.[5] After Towton, March 29, he and his son Thomas were
attainted by Edward IV,[6] and in 1462 he was reported by a spy
to be one of the refugees with Queen Margaret in Scotland.[7]
A letter of September that year mistakenly states that he had been
taken and beheaded by the Yorkists,[8] but in the same correspondence he is spoken of as alive and active in November, and we
read that ' Syr Wylliam Tunstale [9] is tak with the garyson of
Bamborowth, and is lyke to be hedyd, and by the menys of Sir
Rychard Tunstale is owne brodyr '.[10] About Christmastide

[1] *Pat. Rolls, 1452–61*, p. 18; *Rot. Parl.*, v, p. 318. As, however, this was
nearly eight years after the King's marriage, the son, when born, was regarded by
many, besides the Yorkists, as spurious.

[2] Ruding, i, p. 33 (where ' 39 ' is misprinted ' 49 ').

[3] Sept. 1, 1448—Aug. 31, 1449 ; 1452–3 ; 1457–8.

[4] *Ibid.*, i, p. 58 ; ii, p. 144.   [5] *Plumpton*, p. lxvii.

[6] *Rot. Parl.*, v, p. 477, &c. ; *Wil. Wyrc. Ann.*, p. 778.

[7] *Three 15 Cent. Chron.*, p. 158 ; *Archaeologia*, xxix, p. 134.

[8] *Patson*, ii, p. 111.   [9] A Yorkist throughout.   [10] *Paston*, ii, p. 120.

Sir Richard ' Dunstalle ' was at Dunstanburgh Castle,[1] then besieged by Scrope [2] and other Yorkist leaders. Upon its surrender on Dec. 27 he seems to have got away to Alnwick, at this time also beleaguered, and escaped with the Scotch relieving force across the border on the day it fell, Jan. 6, 1463.[3] By the end of that year ' Kinge Edward was possessed of alle Englonde, except a castelle in Northe Walles called Harlake, whiche Sere Richard Tunstalle kepte '; [4] but he was in the field again in the ensuing spring, for we find him present with the Lancastrian force defeated on April 25 at Hedgeley Moor.[5] At one time during Henry's wanderings, either before this, after Towton, or after Hexham, on May 14, 1464,[6] where also Tunstall fought, the ex-King was carried off to safety by him and took refuge in Thurland Castle,[7] in return for which, as Tunstall was already attaint, his Thurland estates were given by Edward to Sir James Harington.[8] At some subsequent date he returned to Harlech,[9] since at the surrender of ' that castylle ... so stronge that men sayde that hyt was impossybylle unto any man to gete hyt, but poyntment [10] hit

[1] *Three 15 Cent. Chron.*, p. 159 ; *Excerpt. Hist.*, p. 365.   [2] No. 19 above.

[3] *Wil. Wyrc. Ann.*, p. 780. But the evidence is conflicting.

[4] *Warkworth*, C.S., p. 3 ; *C. W. R.*, p. 105.

[5] *Three 15 Cent. Chron.*, p. 178.   [6] Hall, p. 260.

[7] Waurin, v, p. 344 ; *Wil. Wyrc. Ann.*, p. 785, says that Henry was ' captured by Tunstall, but escaped '. This must be a mistake.

[8] No. 43 below. *Foed.*, xi, p. 548 : July 29, 1465. *I. p. m.* 6 E. IV, vol. iv, p. 333, No. 45, where Tunstall is entered as ' attinctus ', gives a list of his lands in Lancs., Yorks., and Westmorland.

[9] Leland, *Collect.*, ii, p. 499.

[10] Appointment, *i. e.* agreement. Compare Fabyan, p. 163 : ' A peace or apoyntment was concluded atweene the ii kynges and them.'

was gotyn ',[1] he was captured and sent to the Tower,[2] the date given being Aug. 14, 1468. This conflicts with an entry in *Foedera* [3] that on Nov. 30, 1467, he was associated with Lord Howard,[4] both 'dilecti et fideles Regis', as a commissioner to treat with the French King. However, it is clear that about this time he was taken into favour by Edward.[5] Indeed, we find him in 1470 again Master of the Mint,[6] while by 1473 he had earned from his new sovereign the reversal of his attainder.[7] Sir Richard 'Townstall' brought for the first quarter in 1475 ten men-at-arms and 100 archers, and received for this service £298 0s. 6d. ;[8] in the second quarter his contingent was the same ;[9] and on August 13 he appears as a signatory to Edward's proposals to Louis.[10] Obviously he had by then become a trusted adherent of the Yorkist King. This is shown, too, by the commissionerships confided to him in the succeeding years to treat with the French diplomats on various matters in 1477 and 1478.[11] In June, 1483, he was occupying the post of Deputy of the Castle of Calais under Sir Humphrey Talbot,[12] and on July 16 he, Talbot, and others, were acting as commissioners to deal with the French representatives about questions concerning the Pale.[13] Next, to more than crown his recovery of position,

---

[1] *Greg. Chron.*, p. 237.

[2] *Wil. Wyrc. Ann.*, p. 791 ; *Three 15 Cent. Chron.*, p. 182.

[3] xi, p. 591.   [4] No. 20 above.

[5] *Three 15 Cent. Chron.*, p. 182. In the *Pat. Rolls, 1467-77*, pp. 97, 271, his pardon is dated variously as Oct. 22, 1468, and July 4, 1471.   [6] Ruding, i, p. 279.

[7] *Rot. Parl.*, vi, p. 47.   [8] *Foed.*, xi, p. 845.   [9] *MS.*, fol. 3 *recto.*

[10] *Foed.*, xii, p. 15.   [11] *Ibid.*, xii, pp. 45-8, 50-1, 53, 61-4, 90.

[12] No. 39 above. A letter of instructions to Tunstall there is recorded in *Grants of Ed. V*, p. 2.   [13] *Foed.*, xii, pp. 195-6.

in or about the same year Richard III made him a Knight of
the Garter;[1] succeeding to the stall vacated by the death of
Sir William Parr.[2] In 1484 he is still in office at Calais, for we
read of his being nominated on Aug. 14 to assist Montgomery[3]
in rectifying the decayed fortifications of Guisnes.[4] Presumably
he did not adhere to King Richard at the last, seeing that on
June 18, 1486, a grant was made to 'the beloved Knight'
Richard Tunstall of an annuity for life of £100 out of the
customs and subsidies of the port of Kingston-on-Hull; and on
Oct. 26 following a mandate was issued to the officials of that
port to pay to Tunstall all arrears of the annuity regularly in
future.[5] Upon the former of these two dates he also received the
grant for life of the office of Steward of the lordship of Kendal, &c.[6]
On Aug. 18 in the same year, by the irony of fate, he was commissioned, with another, to administer the oath of allegiance to
Sir James Harington,[7] his sometime supplanter at Thurland,[8]
while later that year, 'propter prudentiam singularem, fidem[9]
& gravitatem', he was one of the 'clari viri' selected by
Henry VII as his councillors.[10] It was apparently at this period
that he was holding the post of Steward of the Honour of Pontefract.[11] There is record of a grant on March 20, 1487, to Sir
Richard Tunstall, 'King's Counsellor' and a Knight for the

---

[1] Beltz, No. 277; Anstis, i, p. 220; Hope, *G.P.*, lxxxviii.
[2] No. 30 above.   [3] No. 31 above.   [4] *Foed.*, xii, p. 231.
[5] *Mat. Reign H. VII*, ii, p. 45.   [6] *Ibid.*, i, p. 464.   [7] No. 43 below.
[8] *Lett. & Pap.*, ii, p. 369; *Mat. Reign H. VII*, i, p. 541.
[9] Compare the saying 'The Trusty Tunstalls'. There is a list of such family
epitheta in Lower's *Patronymica Britannica*, p. xxxviii.   [10] Polydore, p. 719.
[11] *Archaeol. Institute, York Vol.*, 1848, pp. 21, 22; May 16; *Plumpton*, pp. 52,
55, 59. In two of the letters he addresses Sir Robert Plumpton as cousin.

King's Body, of an annuity of £117 3s. 4d., on surrender of the previous grant of £100, payable, as before, out of the customs of Hull,[1] and on Aug. 28 following there was another grant to this ' King's Counsellor ', and yet another of the next presentation to the living of South Somercotes, Lincolnshire.[2]   On St. Catherine's Day that year he was among the Bannerets in attendance at the coronation of Elizabeth of York.[3]   In connexion with Simnel's rebellion, he and others received from the King on May 1, 1487, money and instructions to assist the city of York ' in caas that the Kynges enymes approche thiddre '.[4]   February 11, 1488, brought with it a grant in survivorship to Sir Richard Tunstall and Thomas Grafton, merchant of the Staple of Calais, of ' the office called Sandgill,[5] within the lordships of Mark and Oye, which is 7d. on every cart of merchandize or marketable goods coming to or leaving the town of Calais '.[6]   This year, being ' vir aetate & prudentia gravis ', he was sent as an envoy to try to effect a reconciliation between Charles VIII of France and Francis, Duke of Brittany ;[7]

[1] *Mat. Reign H. VII*, ii, p. 132.

[2] *Ibid.*, ii, p. 188.   [3] Leland, *Collect.*, iv, p. 230.

[4] ' Original Documents ; Simnel's Rebellion ', in *Arch. Inst. Yk. Vol.*, 1848, pp. 15, 19, &c.

[5] This seems to be a variant form of ' Sandgelt ', which is mentioned in the *Chronicle of Calais* (p. 103 : *Proc. of July 13, 1527*) in connexion with ' Wharfgelt ' and other harbour dues, and apparently meant a toll payable by users of the harbour to defray the cost of keeping it free from sand.   Tunstall and Grafton, then, would have the collecting of this toll.

[6] *Mat. Reign H. VII*, ii, p. 242.   Mark and Oye were Royal lordships, or manors, lying between Calais and Gravelines.   As is well known, merchants passing to and from Calais and Flanders had to travel by the road between the sea-shore and the Castles of Mark and Oye and to pay certain tolls and dues.

[7] Polydore, p. 732.   See, too, Bacon, *Hist. Hen. VII*, p. 48, and *Foed.*, xii, p. 337.

and next year he was left by the King to settle things in Yorkshire after the suppression of the disturbances which had resulted in the assassination of the Earl of Northumberland.[1] Apparently from a fiscal point of view he was unsuccessful, for he had been appointed ' ad Subfidium levandum, cujus ne Dodrantem quidem remifit ' ;[2] still he was retained there as one of the three Northern magnates[3] entrusted with the rule of the disorderly Northumbrian counties during the minority of the son of the murdered Earl.[4] On May 14, 1491, one John Paynter was charged before the Lord Mayor of York of having said that the late Earl of Northumberland, who had been killed by the ' plebs rudis ',[5] driven ' stark mad and wode '[6] by the attempt to raise the subsidy referred to, had died a traitor to Henry VII, and uttered other calumnies. Somewhat to the distaste of the municipal authorities, the case was settled by Tunstall as the King's representative in the North.[7] Easter, 1489, was kept by the King at Hertford, and with the other Knights of the Garter present at the Court was Tunstall.[8] Among the deliveries from the Royal Wardrobe that year a similar gift is recorded as made to him from the King for his robes as a K.G. as was made to Montgomery at the same time.[9] Shortly before his death, which occurred at the end of 1491, or early in 1492,[10] he was assisting to raise money in Yorkshire for the French expedition of the latter

[1] No. 12 above : Ap. 28, 1489. Polydore, p. 735.

[2] Bacon, *H. VII*, Latin Version, p. 121 ; Eng. Version, p. 69.

[3] No. 38 above being another of them.   [4] Leland, *Collect.*, iv, p. 246.

[5] Polydore, p. 735.   [6] Skelton's ' Elegy ' : *Percy's Reliques*, i, p. 104.

[7] Davies, *York Records*, pp. 220–4.

[8] Leland, *Collect., loc. cit.*   [9] See under No. 31 above.

[10] Beltz, clxix.

year.[1] On Nov. 5, 1491, he had been appointed Sheriff of that
county, but did not account, evidently owing to his death. His
successor was nominated on May 1, 1492, and rendered his
account from Michaelmas, 1491.[2] Tunstall's wife was Elizabeth,
daughter of Sir William Franke.[3]

The substance of the Indenture made Aug. 20, 1474, between
Edward IV and Sir Richard Tunstall for the purposes of the
expedition of 1475 will have its interest here. The latter is to
furnish for the war in France for one year 10 spears (he, as was
customary, being reckoned in) and 100 archers, himself for
2s. per day,[4] each of the other spears at 1s. per day, and ' Rewardes of *vi d. by the Day for everich of the said other speres* ',
and 6d. per day for each archer. ' Of which Wages and Rewardes,
as well for him as for everich of his Retinue, the said *Richard*
shall be Paid, for the first quarter of the seid whole Yere, at
Westminster, the last day of January next comyng, by the handes
of the Treforer of England for the tyme being.' He shall be
told when and where to muster : the said year's service to begin
on the day of mustering. Payment for the second quarter of
the year is to be made to Tunstall after the commissioners of
the King have viewed his muster for that quarter. And for the
rest of the said year's service ' on the yonder syde of the See ' he
is to be paid monthly in English money, or other money current
there to the value of English money, by the Treasurer of the

---

[1] *Foed.*, xii, p. 464 : Dec. 6, 1491.   [2] *List of Sheriffs*, p. 162.
[3] *Dugdale's Visit. Yorks.*, in *Gen.*, N.S., xx, p. 133.
[4] This was a Knight's pay, that of a Banneret being 4s. ; hence it seems that
at the date of this indenture he had not yet attained to the latter rank. These
indentures were on parchment, therefore many survive ; but muster-rolls, being
on paper, were perishable.

King's Wars for the time being. Payment is to be made to him within eight days after the end of each month, and if that is not done Tunstall will be quit and discharged of these indentures. He is to muster with his retinue from time to time to be viewed as often as the King may require. The King is to find the shipping for transport to France, and also to provide for the re-shipment home, for Tunstall and his following, horses, ' harneis ', and food. If at any of the above musters beyond the sea Tunstall's numbers are short, except through death or sickness, evidence of which is required, the wages and rewards are to be reduced in proportion, and any such money paid in advance is to be refunded by him. As to spoil, one-third of Tunstall's personal booty is to go to the King, as well as one-third of the third of the booty of his retinue which is by custom due to Tunstall from them. Such booty is to comprise everything : prisoners, goods, &c. That the thirds are fair thirds in value is to be certified on oath by Tunstall.[1] The names and the rank of prisoners, and the nature, quantity, and value of booty are to be reported within eight days, if possible, to the Constable, or the Marshal, on pain of forfeiture of the whole. If Tunstall captures the French King, or his son, or any commander acting as commander-in-chief in the place of such, the prisoner is to become the prisoner of the English King, who will make reasonable agreement for them with the captor.

If any land, or real estate generally, happen to fall to Tunstall by descent or otherwise in England while he is in the King's service, such lands, &c., are not, in default of homage, fealty,

---

[1] If the leader found a soldier his ' mount ', he took half the plunder, if a soldier provided his own horse, the leader took only a third. (*Fifth Report of Commission on Hist. MSS.*, 30; and *Tenth Report*, Pt. IV, p. 226.)

or any other service, to be retained by the escheators, &c., but the said homage, &c., is to stand over till Tunstall's return to England. He, and his followers also, while in the field, are to have Letters of Protection under the Great Seal against civil processes at home, and he is to certify under the seal of his arms which members of his contingent require this protection, and such certificates are to be given to the Keeper of the Privy Seal.[1]

BADGE. ' the whytt Coke.' This badge is the same as the crest on Tunstall's Garter-plate.[2] Among the Knights of the Bath made at the coronation of Anne Boleyn at Westminster, May 31, 1533, was Sir Richard's great-grandson, Sir Marmaduke Tunstall, whose crest was *A cock argent, combed and beaked or*, *wattled gules*.[3] In Wall's *Book of Crests* 'Tunstal beryth to his crest a cocke geules'.[4] Cuthbert Tunstall,[5] when Bishop of Durham,[6] used cocks as supporters.[7]

No. 43. ' Sir James haryngton.' Sir James Harington, of Brierley, Yorks., Knight, was the second son of Sir Thomas Harington, of Hornby and Brierley, Knight, by Elizabeth, daughter and coheir of Thomas, Baron Dacre. His father, and his elder brother Sir John Harington, both fell on the Yorkist

---

[1] *Foed.*, xi, pp. 817–19. The indenture made with Tunstall's grandfather, Sir Thomas Tunstall, on Apr. 29, 3 Hen. V, is in *Foed.*, ix, p. 233, and a translation from the French original was printed by Nicolas, *Battle of Agincourt*, 1827, p. xxxi.

[2] Hope, *G. P.*, lxxxviii.

[3] *Cotton MS. Claudius C. iii*, cited by Metcalfe, p. 65.

[4] *A°*. 1530. *Ancestor*, xii, p. 64. If correct, presumably a differencing tincture.

[5] The question of his legitimacy does not concern us here. See on this Leland, *Itin.*, ii, p. 16, and Whitaker, *Richmondshire*, p. 271.

[6] 1530–59.

[7] Longstaffe, ' Old Official Heraldry of Durham ', in *Her. & Gen.*, viii.

side at the Lancastrian victory of Wakefield, Dec. 30, 1460.[1]
Apparently Sir James took a leading part in the arrest of Henry VI
near Waddington Hall, Yorkshire, in July 1465, since he was
rewarded for his services on that occasion with the Tunstall
estates [2] at Thurland, Lonsdale, and Kendal ; [3] and £66 13s. 4d.
was paid him ' for costs and charges for taking Henry, late de
facto et non de jure King of England '.[4] His great-grandson,
Sir John Harington, the Elizabethan wit, alludes to this in a letter
of 1609 to Prince Henry : ' My ancestor Sir James Haryngton
did once take prisoner, with his party, this poor Prince ; for which
the House of York did graunt him a parcel of lands in the northern
counties, and which he was fool enough to lose again after the
battle of Bosworth.' [5] One of this writer's epigrams is very
apposite to the times of the War of the Roses : ' Treason dothe
never prosper. What 's the reason ? / Why, if it prosper, none
dare call it Treason.' [6] The year 1466 found Sir James Harington
holding the office of Sheriff of his county ; [7] and he is probably
the ' Jacobus Haryngton, miles ', returned as knight of the shire
for Lancs. on May 4, 1467, and again on Jan. 12, 1478.[8] In
the Act of Resumption of 1467–8 he is specially exempted as
regards the grant of the Tunstall estates and other gifts.[9] In

---

[1] Actually his father died of his wounds on the day after the battle. *Visit.
Chesh.*, *1580*, H.S., p. 140 ; Hunter, *S. Yorks.*, ii, p. 402 ; Whitaker, *Richmondshire*,
ii, p. 252 ; *Coll. Top. & Gen.*, i, p. 302 ; *Greg. Chron.*, p. 210 ; *Eng. Chron.*, p. 107 ;
Misc. Gen. et Her., N.S., iii, p. 236.

[2] See under No. 42 above.

[3] *Foed.*, xi, p. 548 ; *Pat. Rolls*, *1461–7*, pp. 445, 460 ; and compare *Rot. Parl.*,
v, p. 584.

[4] *Devon, Issues*, p. 489.   [5] *Nugae Antiquae*, i, p. 385.   [6] *Ibid.*

[7] Appointed Nov. 5 : *List of Sheriffs*, p. 162 ; *Plumpton*, p. 17.

[8] *Return Memb. Parl.*, pp. 358, 364.   [9] *Rot. Parl.*, v, pp. 584, 608.

Edward's historic march from Ravenspur Harington and Sir William Parr,[1] 'two good knights', joined him at Nottingham.[2] In 18 Ed. IV he was Seneschal of the Honour of Pontefract.[3] His name does not appear in the Tellers' Roll for the first quarter of 1475, in which year he was again Sheriff of Yorkshire ;[4] in the second quarter his contingent numbers 12 men-at-arms and 100 archers.[5] What occasioned the following civility we do not know. In March 1478 ' 16*d*. was paid for 1 gallon of red wine, and one pottell [6] of sweet wine bought and given to James Harington, Knight . . . by order of the major '.[7] In 1480 a licence was granted to ' James Haryngton, Knight of the Body ' and his heirs to build walls and towers around and within his manors of Farleton, Lancs., and ' Brerely ', Yorks., and to crenellate them ;[8] in the summer of the same year he was ordered to assist in raising troops in the West Riding to resist the Scotch invasion then threatened ;[9] and in July 1482 he was one of the commanders of the left wing of the English army which took Edinburgh.[10] He is mentioned also in May of that year as an arbiter, together with the Duke of Gloucester, the Earl of Northumberland, Sir William Parr,[11] and others, in the matter of a certain

---

[1] No. 30 above. See also Nos. 31, 32, 45.

[2] Fleetwood, *Arrival of Kg. Ed. IV*, C.S., p. 7 ; and in *C.W.R.*, p. 46 ; Holinshed, iii, p. 306 ; Waurin, v, p. 649.

[3] March 4, 1478—March 3, 1479 ; Hunter, *S. Yorks.*, ii, p. 402.

[4] Appointed Nov. 5 : *List of Sheriffs*, p. 162. [5] *MS.*, fol. 3 *verso*.

[6] A measure of two quarts.

[7] Mayor [of York]. Davies, *York Records*, p. 71.

[8] *Pat. Rolls, 1476–85*, p. 150.

[9] *Foed.*, xii, p. 118 : June 20. [10] Hall, p. 331.

[11] Nos. 7, 12, 30 above.

Plumpton property ;[1] and on Nov. 4 following was appointed a Vice-Constable of England.[2] He was in attendance at the coronation of Richard III, to whom he was Clerk of the Council,[3] and fought for him at Bosworth,[4] in consequence of which he was attainted in the first Parliament of Henry VII,[5] and was named among the adherents of the late King whose lands and goods were to be ' enquired into '.[6] In Aug. 1486 he took the oath of allegiance to Henry, which was administered to him by Sir Richard Tunstall,[7] and on the 22nd of that month was granted a general pardon.[8] This pardon, however, did not include remission of forfeiture, for on March 4, 1489, all lordships and manors forfeited by him, including Brierley, were granted to Sir Edward Stanley, a Knight for the King's Body.[9] His will had been made in 1483.[10] He seems to have been still living in 1497, for he is mentioned in the will of his kinswoman Jane, Lady Pilkington, dated Jan. 2 that year. She leaves him for life her moiety of Balderston, since he had ' no livelod '.[11] He

---

[1] *Plumpton*, p. lxxxix.   [2] *Foed.*, xii, p. 169.

[3] *Ashmole MS. 863, p. 437*; *Excerpt. Hist.*, p. 384; Holinshed, iii, p. 398.

[4] *Harl. MS. 542, f. 34*, printed in Hutton, pp. 204 *et seq.*; ' Poem of Bosworth ffeild ', in *Bp. Percy's Folio MS.*, l. 332, where he is termed ' sad at assay ', *i. e.* steadfast under test.

[5] *Rot. Parl.*, vi, pp. 275–6; *Plumpton*, p. 48; *Harl. MS.*, *loc. cit.* The Sir Robert Harington who paid a similar penalty at the same time was his younger brother.   [6] *Mat. Reign H. VII*, i, p. 536: Aug. 7, 1486.

[7] No. 42 above. *Lett. & Pap.*, ii, p. 369; *Mat. Reign H. VII*, i, p. 541.

[8] *Ibid.*, p. 540.   [9] *Ibid.*, ii, p. 422.

[10] *Misc. Gen. et Her.*, N.S., iii, p. 237, where is a list and valuation of his forfeited lands, and an account of their regrant to his family by Henry VIII and Elizabeth.

[11] Whitaker, *Whalley*, ii, pp. 357–8; and his *Richmondshire*, *loc. cit.* A letter

married Joan, daughter and heir of John Nevill, of Wymersley, Yorks., Althorpe, Lincs., and Oversley, Warwicks., and relict of Sir (?) William Gascoigne, of Gawthorpe, &c., Yorkshire, great-grandson of the celebrated Lord Chief Justice Gascoigne.[1]

BADGE. ' Lyonp[ar]tes hed filu[er].' ' Or ' is added as a correction. The head is drawn erased. This must mean a ' lionpard's ', *i. e.* a ' leopard's ' head. *Gules, three leopards' heads argent*, was a Nevill coat, and we may therefore suppose that this badge was connected with his wife's family or with that of his grandmother Margaret Nevill. Wall [2] gives the crest of Harington of Hornby as ' A leopard's head sable, &c.'

No. 44. 'Sir Robert Chamberleyn.' Sir Robert Chamberlain, of Gedding, Suffolk, Barking, Essex, and Barnham-Broom, Norfolk, Knight, was the son and heir of Sir Roger Chamberlain by Margaret, daughter and heir of John Martin.[3] He held a command under the Duke of Norfolk [4] in the expedition to Scotland of 1462,[5] and Edward IV, when off Cromer, on his way to Ravenspur in March 1471, put him and a Sir Gilbert Debenham on land to see how those parts were affected towards him. Both being East Anglians, they would be suitable persons

in *Nugae Antiquae*, ii, p. 253, says that he was slain at Bosworth : clearly a mistake.

[1] Foster, *Yorks. Pedigrees, s. n.* Nevile of Chevet ; *Glover's Visit. Yks.*, ed. by Foster, p. 384 ; Whitaker, *Richmondshire, loc. cit.* ; *Coll. Top. & Gen.*, i, p. 302. If *Visit. Chesh., loc. cit.*, be correct, he seems to have had two wives : the one there mentioned is . . . daughter and heir of . . . Urswicke.

[2] *Ancestor*, xi, p. 181.

[3] *Visit. Norf.*, H.S., p. 71 ; *Visit. Cambs.*, H.S., p. 41 ; Blomefield, ii, pp. 288, 380 ; vi, p. 40 ; Morant, *Essex*, ii, p. 261 ; *Rot. Parl.*, vi, p. 455.

[4] No. 8 above.   [5] *Paston*, ii, p. 121.

for such a mission.[1] In 1472 he was returned as knight of the shire for Suffolk,[2] and his interests also, like those of others in this Roll, were protected in the Act of 1472–3 which conferred the Duchy of Cornwall on Prince Edward.[3] He is not in the Tellers' Roll for the first quarter of 1475, but in the second quarter he brought 12 men-at-arms and 100 archers.[4] Not many other details of him and his career seem to be on record, but he was Knight of the Body in 1476, and is mentioned in a letter of Aug. 25, 1478, where Sir John Paston writes of him as ' my cousin ' ;[5] and in the *Household Books of John, Duke of Norfolk*, occur a couple of entries : ' Item, paid, the same day [6] at Sir Robard Chamberleynes place for burding [7] of iij men be iij wekes, at xiij*d*. a man the weke,—summa vij*s*.,' [8] and ' Item, to my Lady Chamberleynes man for brynging of wyn—iiij*d*.' [9] In 1485 he was holding office as Sheriff of Anglesea.[10] Early in 1491 he got into serious trouble. He was attainted by Parliament, without trial, for treasonable correspondence with the French King,[11] took sanctuary at St. Cuthbert's, Hartlepool, the franchises of which, however, were not respected,[12] and in June of that year was beheaded : ' Thys yere sir Robert Chamberlyne lorde [*sic*] be-heddyd.'[13] Again, ' Also in March was sir Robert Chamberlen, Knyght, Rayned and adjugged at Stratford of the

---

[1] Fleetwood, p. 2, and in *C. W. R.*, p. 37 ; Waurin, v, p. 641 ; Holinshed, iii, p. 303. [2] *Return Memb. Parl.*, p. 362.

[3] *Rot. Parl.*, vi, p. 16. [4] *MS.*, fol. 3 *verso*.

[5] *Pat. Rolls, 1467–77*, p. 569, May 28 ; *Paston*, iii, p. 235.

[6] Tuesday, May 19, 1483. [7] Boarding. [8] Roxburghe Club, p. 393.

[9] *Ibid.*, p. 449 : Aug. 22 following. [10] *Pat. Rolls, 1476–85*, p. 509.

[11] *Rot. Parl.*, vi, p. 455. [12] *Lett. & Pap.*, i, pp. 98–100.

[13] *Chron. of Grey Friars*, R.S., ii, p. 181 ; and in *C.S.*, p. 25.

Bowe, and then brought vnto the Tower. And from thens he and other ij were drawen from Westmynster vnto the Tower hyll; where the ij persons were saued, and he was beheded '.[1] He married Elizabeth, daughter and coheir of Sir John Fitz Ralph, of Little Ellingham, Norfolk, Knight.[2]

BADGE. ' ffryrs gerdill Azur.' Is there in this Friar's Girdle an indirect play upon the name Chamberlain ? The habits of Friars, as of Monks, were commonly of ' cameline ', or ' chameline ',[3] a material made of camel's hair, ' de setis camelorum ', as the old Rule said. The girdle was of the same, and *camelus* in L.L. meant a cord, or rope, of camel's hair. Camel's hair girdles are still used in the East of Europe. The crest and supporters of the arms on the monument to Sir William Chamberlain, K.G.,[4] in East Harling Church, Norfolk, are supplied by the camelopard,[5] probably also a cant on the surname. The crest is a camelopard's head couped.

No. 45. ' Sir Will[ia]m Norys.' Sir William Norris,[6] of Bray, Ockwells, and Yattendon, Berks., Knight, was son and heir of John Norris [7] by his first wife Alice, daughter and coheir

---

[1] *Chron. Lond.*, p. 195 ; also in *Six Town Chronicles*, p. 171. He is referred to in Warbeck's Proclamation of July 1497, printed in Henry's *History*, xii, App. I, p. 387. See, too, Pollard, *Hen. VII*, i, p. 150, note. As Busch remarks (i, p. 419), Bacon, in writing his version (Eng. ed., p. 154; Lat., p. 256), evidently ' worked from memory with the help of a few notes, and principally of his imagination '.

[2] *Visit. Norf., Visit. Cambs.*, Blomefield, and Morant, *ut supra* ; *Her. & Gen.*, viii, p. 439.   [3] L.L. *Camelinum*, &c.   [4] Died 1462.

[5] Farrer, *Church Heraldry of Norfolk*, p. 42 ; *Coll. Top. & Gen.*, iv, p. 364.

[6] Or ' Norreys '.

[7] ' Squyer ', as he describes himself in his will (given in full in Kerry's *Hundred of Bray*, p. 116), and ' esquire ' in that of his wife Margaret the Duchess of Norfolk,

of Richard Merbury [1] of Yattendon.[2] On Nov. 21, 1459, he
was returned as knight of the shire for Berks.,[3] was created
Knight Bachelor at the Yorkist victory of Northampton, July 10,
next year,[4] and took part in the expedition to Scotland of 1462,[5]
while the years 1468, 1481, and 1486, saw him Sheriff of Oxon.
and Berkshire.[6] During the short-lived restoration of Henry VI
he seems to have wavered in his allegiance to his own party, for
he received a verbal pardon from Edward IV on April 8, 1471,[7]
and was one of the Yorkist leaders who joined him at Nottingham[8]
when on his march from Ravenspur.[9] His name is not in the
Tellers' Roll for the first quarter of 1475 : in the second quarter
his retinue was 12 men-at-arms and 100 archers.[10] In 1483 he is
mentioned as being Knight for the Body to Edward IV,[11] and as
having attended the coronation of Richard III.[12] In the succeed-

cited below, also 'armiger' in *I. p. m.*, 6 Ed. IV, p. 337, No. 45, *A°.* 1467; not,
as is often stated, a Knight. He was the builder, between 1446 and 1466, of the
existing well-known manor-house at Ockwells : see *Archaeologia*, lvi, Pt. 2.

   [1] Or ' Merbrook '.

   [2] *Visit. Berks.*, H.S., ii, p. 185 ; Kerry, *op. cit.*, pp. 116–20 ; *Archaeologia*,
loc. cit., pp. 331, 334. Sir William's father married, as his third wife, Margaret,
daughter of Sir John Chedworth, Kt. ; and she married later Sir John Howard,
1st (Howard) Duke of Norfolk (G. E. C., 1st ed., vi, pp. 47–8), and occurs below.
All three wives are mentioned in John Norris's will.

   [3] *Return Memb. Parl.*, p. 352.   [4] Shaw, ii, p. 12 ; Metcalfe, p. 2.

   [5] *Three 15 Cent. Chron.*, p. 157.

   [6] Appointed upon each occasion on Nov. 5 : *List of Sheriffs*, p. 108.

   [7] *Pat. Rolls, 1467–77*, p. 241 ; *Stonor Letters*, i, p. 118.

   [8] See Nos. 30, 31, 32, 43 above.

   [9] *Warkworth*, p. 14, and in *C. W. R.*, p. 122 ; Leland, *Collect.*, ii, p. 504.

   [10] *MS.*, fol. 3 *verso*.

   [11] Lee, *Hist. of the Church of Thame*, pp. 441–2 ; Money, *Hist. of Newbury*,
pp. 185–8.   [12] *Excerpt. Hist.*, p. 384 ; Holinshed, iii, p. 398.

ing year he was attainted for participation in Buckingham's
rebellion against Richard. He had been one of the leading men
in the Berkshire rising connected with that movement, and,
by Proclamation of Oct. 23, a reward of 500 marks in money
and £40 in land was offered for his capture.[1] He was not caught,
and the attainder was reversed in the first year of Henry VII,[2]
from whom he received important grants and offices on Sept. 23,
1485, and July 5, 1486, the latter being of the manor of Reden-
hall, Norfolk, forfeited by William Catesby.[3] All grants to him
were excepted from Henry's Act of Resumption of 1485.[4]
Among these was the Wardenship of the Forest of Wychwood.[5]
On Jan. 4, 1486, he had been appointed a commissioner to
administer oaths not to aid or protect felons [6] in any way or join
in unlawful assemblies, &c.[7] He held a command in Henry's
army at the battle of Stoke, June 9, 1487,[8] was among the
Knights present at the coronation of Elizabeth of York on Nov. 25,[9]
and in 1488 is recorded as being ' Bailiff for the Queen ' for the
manor and hundred of Bray.[10] On Dec. 23 of that year he was
called upon to help in raising bowmen in Oxon. and Berks.
for the Breton expedition,[11] and was one of the leaders against
Perkin Warbeck when the latter landed in Cornwall in Sept.
1497.[12] In 1495 he had succeeded to certain additional estates

---

[1] *Rot. Parl.*, vi, pp. 245 *et seq.* ; *Foed.*, xii, p. 204 ; *Pat. Rolls, 1476–85*, pp.
471–2, 487.   [2] *Rot. Parl.*, vi, p. 273.

[3] *Mat. Reign H. VII*, i, pp. 43, 482 ; Blomefield, v, p. 368.

[4] *Rot. Parl.*, vi, p. 358.   [5] *Ibid.*   [6] *i. e.* the King's enemies.

[7] *Foed.*, xii, p. 280 ; *Mat. Reign H. VII*, i, p. 243.

[8] Kerry, *op. cit.*, p. 114.   [9] Leland, *Collect.*, iv, p. 231.

[10] Kerry, *op. cit.*, p. 6.   [11] *Foed.*, xii, p. 357 ; *Mat. Reign H. VII*, ii, p. 386.

[12] Polydore, p. 766.

in Berkshire on the death of his stepmother, Margaret, Duchess of Norfolk, and [1] is mentioned as holding other lands there in 1489, 1492, and 1493.[2] The will of the Duchess, proved Dec. 3, 1494, mentions her husband John Norris, ' Esquire '.[3] In 1503 ' two refonable Aides ' were demanded by the King, one for the expenses of the Knighting of Prince Arthur, the other for those of the marriage of the Princess Margaret to James IV of Scotland, and at the head of the list of the commissioners for raising the Berkshire quota is the name of Sir William Norris.[4] He died, seized of Ockwells, in 1507.[5] His wives were (1) Isabel,[6] daughter and coheir of Sir Edmond Inglesthorpe, Knight, and relict of John Nevill, Marquis of Montacute ; [7] (2) Joan, daughter of John de Vere, 12th Earl of Oxford ; [8] (3) Anne,[9] daughter of John Horne, Alderman of London, and relict of Sir John Harcourt.[10]

BADGE. ' Blake Rawyn hede Rafyd.' This badge of a *Black Raven's head erased* is taken from the coat of Norris. The arms of John Norris, father of Sir William, as shown in the glass at Ockwells, were *Argent, a chevron between three ravens'*

---

[1] See Note 2 on p. 102 above ; Kerry, *op. cit.*, pp. 114, 148.   [2] *Ibid.*

[3] *Test. Vetust.*, p. 404.   [4] *Rot. Parl.*, vi, pp. 532, 541.

[5] Kerry, *op. cit.*, p. 114.   [6] Kerry, p. 115, says Alice . . .

[7] *Pat. Rolls, 1476–85*, pp. 63, 192, 487 ; *Lives of the Berkeleys*, iii, p. 114 ; Blomefield, vii, pp. 128, 517. According to *Visit. Berks., 1532*, H.S., i, p. 10, ' one of the dovght[rs] and heyre to the lorde Marcus Montagu by whome he had no yssue '. According to *Visit. Berks., 1665–6*, H.S., ii, p. 185, ' . . . dau. & coh. to John Nevill Marques Mountacute.'   [8] Kerry, *op. cit.*, p. 115.

[9] Joane, according to *Misc. Gen. & Hen.*, 5 Series, ii, p. 184.

[10] *Visit. Berks., 1665–6*, ii, p. 185. The Henry Norris, Esquire of the King's Body to Henry VIII, who was executed on May 15, 1536, for alleged intimacy with Queen Anne Boleyn, was his grandson.

heads erased sable : his crest was *A raven rising proper* ; [1] and Sir Edward Norris, our man's son, bore the same. [2] In ' A Fifteenth Century Book of Arms ' those of a John Norrys of Berkshire are recorded as ' Silver, a cheveron sable between iij ravyn hedys rased of sabyll with three crescents upon the cheveron ' for a difference. [3] In Wall's Crests ' Norys beryth to his crest a crowe sable, &c.' [4] The raven is explained by the fact that the Norris arms given above were originally the canting coat of Ravenscroft, which was adopted by Sir William's great-great-grandfather, John Norris, of Bray and Ockwells, when he married Millicent, daughter and heir of . . . Ravenscroft, of Cotton End, Beds., and Hardingstone, Northants, Esquire, and relinquished those of his own house. [5]

No. 46. ' Sir John harlwyn.' This was doubtless Sir John Harlewin, of Sidmouth, Devon, Knight, who was knighted by Edward IV. [6] Ascerton, in the parish of Sidmouth, was bought about 1422 by a John Harlewin of Sidmouth. [7] He is not in the

---

[1] Reproduced in *Archaeologia*, lvi, pt. 2, p. 331, and pl. xviii (1).

[2] See List of Knights made by Hen. VII after the battle of Stoke, June 9, 1487, in the *Cotton MS.* printed in Leland's *Collect.*, iv, p. 214 ; also *Paston, Suppl.*, p. 157.

[3] *Ancestor*, v, p. 175.   [4] *Ibid.*, xi, p. 184.

[5] *Visit. Berks.*, *1665–6*, ii, pp. 184–5 ; *Gen.*, iv, p. 227 ; *Top. & Gen.*, ii, p. 362. Sir William's father, above mentioned, had used an entirely different badge : a *conduit* (*Polit. Poems*, ii, p. 222; and *Excerpt. Hist.*, p. 162). Was this object a pun on Raven and the French *Ravin*, a conduit, or water-passage ?

[6] Tristram Risdon, *Chorographical Description of Devon*, p. 34. The family was established in Devonshire at any rate by Henry VI's reign, and was still there when Risdon wrote. A ' Johannes Harlewyn, armiger ', died 4 Ed. IV (Mar. 4, 1464—Mar. 3, 1465) seized of lands in that county, at Taddesford, Langeford, and Exeter : *I. p. m.*, vol. iv, p. 474, No. 4.

[7] *Ex inform.* Mr. H. Tapley-Soper, of University College, Exeter ; also

Tellers' Roll for the first quarter of 1475 ; for the second quarter he brought 3 men-at-arms and 50 archers.[1]

BADGE. 'Blake farezyn hede Cope.' *A black Saracen's head couped.*

No. 47. 'Sir John fferrers'. Sir John Ferrers, of Walton-on-Trent, Derbyshire, Knight, who is shown by his badge to be of the Ferrers of Groby, Leicestershire, was the son and heir of Sir Thomas Ferrers, of Tamworth, Staffs., by Anne, daughter of Leonard Hastings, of Kirby.[2] He may have been the Sir John Ferrers who was knighted in the field at Tewkesbury on May 4, 1471.[3] In the Tellers' Roll for the first quarter of 1475 his contingent is given as one man-at-arms besides himself and 20 archers, for which he received £61 8s. 6d. ;[4] in the second quarter it was men-at-arms the same, but archers only 15.[5] On Dec. 11, 1477, he was returned as knight of the shire for Stafford.[6] He was still living in 6 Hen. VII,[7] but predeceased his father, who died in 1498, and his wife was Maud, daughter and coheir of Sir John Stanley, of Elford, Staffs., Knight. She was dead by June 1, 1490.[8]

Vivian, *Visit. Devon.*, p. 443. In Hutchinson's *MS.* ' Hist. of Sidmouth' is a pedigree of Harlewyn, the earlier portion of which has been published in *Notes & Queries* (3 S., ix, 215), but from the part relating to our period one generation at least is missing. [1] *MS.*, fol. 3 *verso.*

[2] *Visit. Warwicks.*, H.S., p. 165 ; *Coll. Top. & Gen.*, viii, pp. 267, 341 ; G. E. C., new ed., v, p. 632.

[3] *Paston*, iii, p. 9 ; Shaw, ii, p. 15.   [4] *Foed.*, xi, p. 844.
[5] *MS.*, fol. 3 *verso.*   [6] *Return Memb. Parl.*, p. 364.
[7] Aug. 22, 1490—Aug. 21, 1491.

[8] Authorities under note 4 above; also ' Chetwynd Chartulary ', in *Collect. Hist. Staffs.*, ' Wm. Salt Archaeol. Soc.' (1891), xii, pp. 265, 330, 333.

BADGE. '. . . filu[er] paffant a mafkell gold.' There is some omission before ' silver '. Probably we are to read ' A unicorn passant silver, charged on the shoulder with a mascle gold ', for a difference. The badge of the Marquis of Dorset [1] was *A Unicorn ermine couchant on a sun or*.[2] The ' maskell ' is from the coat of Ferrers of Groby, which was ' Gules, seven voided lozengys of gold '. These arms of Ferrers of Groby are found at least as far back as the Siege of Carlaverock [3] and the Baron's Letter.[4] The standard of Sir Edward Ferrys, *c.* 1510–25,[5] was ' Vert, a unicorn courant ermine, charged on the shoulder with a crescent sable between six mascles or ', and four more mascles also appear on the same standard.[6] In Wall's Crests [7] ' Ferrers of Groby beryth to his crest an unicorne ermyns '. The seven mascles came with the De Quincy arms, which were adopted by Ferrers with the Groby inheritance, when William de Ferrers married Margaret, coheir of the former house. Etymologically, the word ' mascle ' seems to be the O.F. *macle*, the mesh [8] of a net,[9] which we find in the well-known Harrington (herring-net) ' knot '. It may, however, be a play on the name Quincy : a *quinconce* arrangement : [10] If these points are united by lines, a row of mascles is the result : ⬦⬦⬦ Thus we easily

---

[1] No. 11 above.   [2] *Coll. Top. & Gen.*, iii, p. 66.

[3] Nicolas, *Siege of Carlaverock*, pp. 48, 273 ; and Wright's edition, pp. 20, 21.

[4] *Ancestor*, vii, p. 252.   [5] MS. I. 2. *Coll. of Arms*, in *Excerpt. Hist.*, p. 337.

[6] In some of the early Rolls of Arms mascles are called ' pierced lozenges ', ' false lozenges ', or simply ' lozenges '.   [7] *Ancestor*, xi, p. 187.

[8] M.E. ' maske, of a nette. *Macula* '. *Prompt. Parv.*, ii, p. 329.

[9] Godefroy ; Ducange, &c.

[10] Such as was used in planting trees. Cotgrave, *s. v.*

get to the seven mascles of the Ferrers which fit the heater-shield. The word is familiar to us in the Latin *quincunx*, a noted Roman military formation.[1]

No. 48. 'Sir John maleuerer.' Sir John Mauleverer, Knight, was the son and heir of John Mauleverer, of Allerton Mauleverer, Yorkshire, Esquire, by Isabel, daughter of Sir John Markenfield.[2] He was created Knight Bachelor at the battle of Wakefield, Dec. 30, 1460, 'by the handes of' the 3rd (Percy) Earl of Northumberland,[3] and seems to have been present at Towton.[4] A letter addressed to him by John Nevill, Earl of Northumberland, dated Dec. 7, 1465 (?), shows that he was about this time holding office under that nobleman, then Warden and Commissary-General of the East Marches towards Scotland.[5] At the feast on the occasion of the 'intronization' of George Nevill, Archbishop of York, in June, 1465, he acted as 'Panter'.[6] He is mentioned several

---

[1] *e. g.* Ælian, *De Instruendis Aciebus*, p. 325. It also had the same arboricultural meaning. The medieval captain used the works of the classical writers on field-tactics and siege-craft. For example, Geoffrey of Anjou, only a generation earlier than Roger, the first De Quincy Earl of Winchester to bear 'fausse losengez', was found studying the *De Re Militari* of Vegetius at his siege of the Castle of Montreuil-Bellay in 1151 (*Hist. Gaufr. Ducis*, Marchegay, pp. 286–7); and the same writer is quoted by Lydgate, *Troy Book*, 'After the doctrine of Vygecius', Prolog., l. 89. Among the books of Edward IV was a MS. translation into English of the *De Re Militari*, on which see Plummer's *Fortescue*, pp. 175–6. According to *Gen.*, N.S., x, p. 91, De Quincy was originally of Cuinchy, between Béthune and la Bassée, on the frontier of Artois and Flanders.

[2] *Glover's Visit. Yorks.*, p. 67; *Plumpton*, pp. 46–7; Thoresby, *Duc. Leod.*, i, p. 191.　　　　[3] Shaw, ii, p. 12; Metcalfe, p. 2.

[4] 'Verses on the Battle of Towton': see under his badge below.

[5] *Plumpton*, p. 25; Nicholson, *Leges Marchiarum*, p. 44; Doyle, ii, p. 650.

[6] Leland, *Collect.*, vi, p. 3, where the duties of this official are specified at con-

other times in the Plumpton correspondence : among these on
Dec. 5, 1469, as having a difference with Sir William
Plumpton,[1] and in connexion with a marriage jointure of
Dec. 15, 1471.[2] For the first quarter of the 1475 expedition
his retinue numbered 2 men-at-arms, besides himself, and
30 archers, in payment for which he received £81 ;[3] his
numbers in the second quarter were the same.[4] He is not in
the list of those who joined Richard III at Bosworth,[5] but his
son Sir Thomas is. The latter, however, received a general
pardon on Nov. 19, 1485, with remission of forfeiture,[6] and was
in the train of the Earl of Northumberland,[7] the deserter of
Richard at the battle, to welcome the new King on his visit
to Yorkshire.[8] Sir John Mauleverer married Alison, daughter
of John Banks, of Newton-in-Craven and Whixley.[9]

BADGE. 'whytt greyhonde [c]urrant.' In the line 'The
Grehound and þe Hertes Hede,[10] þei quyt hem well þᵗ day',
from the 'Verses on the Battle of Towton'[11] we seem to see the
badge of Sir John Mauleverer. It is taken from the charges in
the arms of his house, *Three leverers, or greyhounds, courant in
pale argent*,[12] 'levrier'[13] being a pun on the latter part of the
surname. The greyhound was also used as a Mauleverer crest. In
Glover's Visitation of Yorkshire[14] is an outline of a seal of Sir

siderable length and in much detail. See, too, Round, *The King's Serjeants*,
p. 212.

[1] p. 23. [2] p. lxxxiv. [3] *Foed.*, xi, p. 844. [4] *MS.*, fol. 3 *verso*.
[5] *Harl. MS. 542, fol. 34.* [6] *Mat. Reign H. VII*, i, p. 168 ; ii, p. 320.
[7] No. 12 above. [8] *Cotton MS.* printed in Leland, *Collect.*, iv, p. 186.
[9] *Glover's Visit. Yorks.*, *loc. cit.* ; Thoresby, *loc. cit.* ; *Yonge's Visit. Yorks.*, p. 54 ;
Plumpton, loc. cit. [10] See No. 35 above. [11] *Archaeologia*, xxix, p. 346.
[12] The tincture of the field is variously given.
[13] *Canis leporarius*, a 'hare-hound '. [14] Ed. by Foster, p. 83.

Alnath Mauleverer,[1] grandfather of our Sir John, which shows this greyhound crest. 'Maliverer beryth to his crest a greyhond;'[2] and Sir John's nephew, another 'Sir Halnath Maleverer' used as a crest *A greyhound statant argent, collared and ringed* for a difference.[3]

No. 49. 'Sir lawrence Raynford.' Sir Laurence Rainford,[4] of Rainford Hall, Lancashire,[5] Bradfield, Essex, and 'Brokesbourne', Herts., was the son and heir of Sir William Rainford,

---

[1] 3 Hen. IV: Sept. 30, 1401—Sept. 29, 1402.

[2] 'Wall's Crests': *Ancestor*, xi, p. 189.

[3] *Cotton MS. Claudius C.* iii. In *Harl. MS. 4632*, printed in *Coll. Top. & Gen.*, iii, p. 75, a variant of this Mauleverer badge, 'A greyhound current gules, collared and ringed or', is wrongly attributed to Malore, unless the user himself was guilty of the error of believing that the names were connected. (There is an entry in Burke's *General Armory* which may point to this, if it is not a mistake in that work.) They are, however, quite distinct, Mauleverer being local, from Maulévrier, near Yvetot in Normandy, whereas Mallóry (the stress is on the 'o') is a nickname from O. F. *maleüré*, for *male auguratus*. (See Professor Weekley's *Romance of Names*, p. 139; the same writer's *Surnames*, p. 213; and Godefroy.) It may be worth adding here (as in the case of No. 31 above) that the banner of Col. Mauleverer, who, in 1642, commanded a regiment of horse in the Parliament army, bore 'Sable; three hare hounds currant Argent, collared . . .' (Prestwich, *Respublica*, p. 112), while his cornet, or flag as a company-commander, like those of most officers on either side in the Great Civil War, displayed an unheraldic *devise*, influenced probably by the Emblem Literature. Specimens of the sheets illustrating these colours are in the possession of the editor; there are copies also in the Bodleian (Sutherland Clarendon). If Col. Mauleverer was a direct descendant of our man, he would apparently be his great-great-great-grandson William, younger brother of Sir Thomas Mauleverer who was created a Baronet on Aug. 2, 1641. But he may have been of the Potter-Newton branch.

[4] Or Rainsford.

[5] Rain[s]ford is a chapelry in the parish of Prescot, S. Lancs.

Knight, by Eleanor, daughter and heir of Edward [1] de ' Broxesbourne ', and ' widow to . . . merbury '.[2] Laurence Rainford, then still an Esquire, was captured at Kyriel's defeat of Formigny, Apr. 15, 1450.[3] Whether he escaped or was ransomed we do not know, but in the following June he was in the garrison at the siege of Caen, from which the defenders marched out on its surrender to the French.[4] In 1453 he was associated with Astley and Montgomery [5] in the Iyalton *v.* Norreys Appeal of Battle, as counsellor to the former.[6] The year 1465 found him Sheriff of Essex and Herts.,[7] and he was created a Knight Bachelor before Easter, 1466.[8] In June of the following year he acted as one of the three counsellors [9] of Lord Scales [10] in his duel with the Bastard of Burgundy; [11] and in the succeeding September a son of his, ' Filius Laurencii Raynford, militis ' [12] was among those sent to demand the surrender of Caistor to the Duke of Norfolk.[13] He served again as Sheriff, this time of Wilts., in 1469.[14] He is not in the Tellers' Roll for the first quarter of

[1] Or Edmund.

[2] Alfred Ransford, *The Origin of the Ransfords*; *Visit. Essex, 1558,* H.S., i, p. 96; *Gen.,* 1878, p. 105.

[3] *Will. Worc. Collections,* p. 360. I can find no other Laurence Rainford in the family during this period, and have therefore assumed that this and the following entries and notices down to 1489 relate to our man, whom the dates all suit.

[4] *Ibid.,* p. 631.   [5] Nos. 29, 31 above.

[6] *Proc. Privy Coun.,* vi, pp. 129, 139.

[7] Appointed Nov. 5 : *List of Sheriffs,* p. 45.

[8] *Ibid.,* and Shaw, ii, p. 14.   [9] Nos. 15 and 29 above were the other two.

[10] No. 13 above.   [11] *Excerpt. Hist.,* p. 202.

[12] Whether John or Edward is not stated.

[13] No. 8 above. *Will. Worc. Itin.,* p. 322.

[14] Appointed Nov. 5 : *List of Sheriffs,* p. 153.

1475 ; in the second quarter he brings 12 men-at-arms, himself counted in, and 60 archers.[1] In 1480 he conveyed the Order of the Garter to Hercules d'Este, Duke of Modena and Ferrara ; [2] and was himself thrice 'named' for that dignity : by Sir John Astley, on Feb. 10, 1480, again by him on Sept. 15, 1482, and on Apr. 22, 1485, by Sir Thomas Montgomery and Astley,[3] but got no further. He was one of the witnesses to the confession of John Edward on Aug. 8, 1482.[4] On Apr. 7, 1487, a Commission of Array for Essex is addressed to him and others for guarding against invasion by the supporters of Simnel ; [5] and on Aug. 21, two years later, a Commission of Peace and of Oyer and Terminer for that county.[6] His will was dated 1490,[7] and proved on Nov. 6 of that year. In it he directs that he be buried in the Abbey of St. John the Baptist of Colchester, in the Chapel of St. Mary, next the tomb of Sir William Hunte, late Abbot of the said Abbey, which was done. He leaves 'to my wife Anne an annual rent of 20 marks . . ., but if my said wife says or does anything contrary to this my will she shall be wholly excluded from this rent for all time to come and this especially on account of her very great ingratitude shown me in my heavy sickness'.[8] He married (1) Elizabeth Fiennes, daughter of James, 1st Baron Saye and Sele, and relict of Alex. Iden, sometime Sheriff of Kent ; (2) Anne, daughter of Henry, 2nd

---

[1] *MS.*, fol. 3 *verso.*

[2] *State Papers.* Brown, 'Venetian Archives', 1557–8, R.S. : Copy of letter from the Duke to Edward IV. The Duke succeeded to the stall vacated by the death of Charles the Bold (Beltz, p. clxvi).   [3] Anstis, i, pp. 207, 212, &c.

[4] See under No. 31 above.   [5] *Mat. Reign H. VII*, ii, p. 135.

[6] *Ibid.*, p. 478.   [7] Ransford, *ibid.*

[8] Communicated by Mr. Alfred Ransford ; and see *Gen.*, N.S., xxii, p. 29.

(Percy) Earl of Northumberland, and relict of Sir Thomas Hungerford.[1] Anne died on July 5, 1522, ' at an extreme old age ', and was buried in St. Michael's Chapel in the Church of St. Michael, Westminster.[2]

BADGE. '1 . . . filu[er].' This badge is not drawn. It was doubtless a lys from the arms of Rainford of Bradfield, Essex : *Gules, a chevron engrailed between three fleurs-de-lys argent.*[3]

No. 50. ' Syr Nycolas langford.' Sir Nicholas Langford, of Langford, Derbyshire, Knight, was son and heir of Sir Nicholas Langford, Knight, by Margaret, daughter of Sir Edmund Appleby, Knight.[4] He was knighted on May 4, 1471, on the field after Tewkesbury,[5] and a ' Nicholaus Longford, miles ' was returned as knight of the shire for Derby on Sept. 24, 1472.[6] He brought to the muster for the first quarter of 1475 6 men-at-arms and 60 archers, his pay being £179 14s. 6d. ;[7] for the second quarter 8 men-at-arms and archers as before.[8] When Henry VII made his first Progress to the North in March 1486, Langford was in his train.[9] He married Joan, daughter of Sir Lawrence Warren of Poynton, Cheshire, Knight.[10]

[1] Hotspur's son.
[2] Dallaway, *Sussex*, ii, p. 306 ; Ransford, p. 5 ; *Pat. Rolls, 1452–61*, p. 506 ; *1476–85*, p. 171.　　　　　　　　　　　　　[3] Papworth, p. 421, col. 1.
[4] *Visit. Derbyshire*, in *Gen.*, N.S., viii, pp. 17, 18 ; *Rot. Parl.*, v, p. 456 ; *Langford Charters*, ' 1470, Conveyance to Nicholas Longford, esq., son & heir of Nicholas Longford, kt.' (communicated by Mr. J. S. Ryder, of Chesterfield).
[5] Shaw, ii, p. 15.
[6] *Return Memb. Parl.*, p. 360. This, however, may have been his father who was still living in 1470, as is shown by Note 4 above, and who, in fact, did not die till 1483 (*I. p. m..*, 21 E. IV, vol. iv, p. 407, No. 52 ; *Coll. Top. & Gen.*, i, pp. 347–8.
[7] *Foed.*, xi, p. 845.　　　　　　　[8] *MS.*, fol. 3 *verso.*
[9] Leland, *Collect.*, iv, p. 186.　　　[10] *Visit. Derb., loc. cit.*

Badge. 'ij whyngges filu[er].' These were probably shoveller's wings from the crest of Langford. This crest, with three wings is seen on the effigy attributed to his father in Long-ford Church.[1]

No. 51. ' Sir John Sauage.' Sir John Savage, Junior, Knight, was the son and heir of Sir John Savage, of Clifton,[2] Cheshire, K.B., by Katherine, sister to Thomas, 2nd Baron Stanley[3] (see *D. N. B.*). He took to France in the first quarter of 1475 3 men-at-arms, that is two besides himself, and 30 archers, and received in payment £91 ;[4] and in the second quarter his contingent numbered the same.[5]

Badge. 'Vnycorne hede Rafyd filu[er].' Sir John Savage is referred to in *The Rose of England*[6] by this badge as being at Bosworth : ' soe well the vnicorne did him quite.' Richard Savage, of Nottinghamshire, bore, as badge, on his standard in the expedition to France of 1513 ' A Unicorne's hed sylver with a differance '.[7] The Savage crest was the same : ' Savaige bereth to his crest an unicornes heede silver hor.[8] or and mane verd, &c.'[9] The crest of Sir Humphrey Savage, knighted by Henry VII at the battle of Stoke, June 9, 1487, was *A Unicorn's head erased argent armed or.*[10] Thomas Savage, brother of our Sir John, used, when Archbishop of York,[11] two unicorns as supporters.[12]

[1] See, too, Papworth, p. 296.

[2] Afterwards called Rock Savage.

[3] No. 18 above. See *Lady Bessy*, Version I, pp. 8, 14, 37 ;. Version II, pp. 45, 74 ; *Archaeologia*, xxxiii, p. 66.   [4] *Foed.*, xi, p. 844.   [5] *MS.*, fol. 3 *verso*.

[6] p. 194, l. 112.   [7] *Cotton MS. Cleop. C. v.*   [8] Horn.

[9] ' Wall's Crests ': *Ancestor*, xi, p. 181.   [10] *Cotton MS. Claudius C. iii.*

[11] 1501–7.

[12] Bedford, *Blazon of Episcopacy*, p. 137 ; Purey-Cust, *Heraldry of York Minster*, p. 379.

No. 52. ' Sir James Radcleffe.' Sir James Radcliffe, Knight, was the second son of Sir John Radcliffe, of Attleborough, Norfolk, K.G.,[1] by Katherine, daughter and coheir of Sir Edward Burnell, of Billingford, &c., Norfolk, Knight, and was therefore uncle of No. 37 above.[2] In August, 1469, while still an Esquire, he was among those with the Duke of Norfolk [3] at the siege of Caistor.[4] His name is not in the Tellers' Roll for the first quarter of 1475 ; in the second quarter his contribution to the force was one man-at-arms, that is himself, and 12 archers.[5] A grant is recorded on July 27, 1479, of an annuity of £20 ' to the King's Knight James Radclyf, one of the King's carvers ', and on Nov. 5, 1479, he was appointed Sheriff of Worcestershire.[6] ' I think that . . . Sir Jamys Radclyff, and other of myn aqueyntance whyche wayte most upon the Kyng, and lye nyghtly in hys chamber, wyll put to ther good wyllys.' So wrote John Paston to his mother in Nov. 1479.[7] In the following year he, and Sir Edward Widville, the Queen's brother, escorted Margaret, Duchess of Burgundy, wife of Charles the Bold, across the sea on her visit to her brother the King of England, when each of these knights had of the King's ' yift . . . a yerde of velvet purpulle and a yerde of blue velvet for theire jackettes to be made of '.[8] In April, 1483, he bore the Banner of Our Lady at the funeral of Edward IV,[9] and in 1485 and 1486 he is mentioned as being Lieutenant of the

[1] Who died in 1441 (*I. p. m.*, 19 Hen. VI, vol. iv, p. 204, No. 33).
[2] Foster, *Yorks. Pedigrees, s. n.*, Radcliffe.   [3] No. 8 above.
[4] *Wm. Worc. Itin.*, p. 322.   [5] *MS.*, fol. 3 *verso*.
[6] *Pat. Rolls, 1476–85*, p. 159 ; *List of Sheriffs*, p. 158.
[7] *Paston*, iii, p. 262.   [8] Nicolas, *Ward. Acc. Ed. IV*, p. 165.
[9] *Lett. & Pap.*, i, p. 5 ; *Archaeologia*, i, p. 350.

Tower.[1] His wife was Katherine, daughter of George Nevill, Baron Latimer,[2] and relict of Sir Oliver Dudley.[3]

BADGE. None given.

No. 53. 'Sir Will[ia]m Truffell.' Sir William Trussell, of Coblesdon [4] and Acton Trussell, Staffs., and Wayborn, Norfolk,[5] Knight, was son and heir of Sir Thomas [6] Trussell by Elizabeth, daughter and heir of William [7] Burley, Esquire.[8] He was perhaps the William Trussell who was one of the Yeomen of the Crown in 1467–8.[9] 'Willielmus Trussell, miles' was returned as knight of the shire for Leicestershire on Sept. 17, 1472.[10] In 11 Ed. IV,[11] being then 'Valet de Chambre' to the King, he was granted the custody of his private Palace at Westminster for life, and became Knight of the Body before 1475.[12] To the muster in that year he brought for the first quarter 6 men-at-arms, himself accounted for one, and 60 archers, his payment being £179 14s. 6d.;[13] and in the second quarter the same strength as before.[14] Later

[1] *Mat. Reign H. VII*, i, pp. 207, 232.   [2] Who died in 1469.

[3] *Coll. Top. & Gen.*, i, p. 301 ; Foster, *Yks. Peds.*, *loc. cit.*

[4] *Aliter* Cublesdon, now Kibblestone.

[5] He was possessed also of manors in Berks., Essex, Leicestershire, Northants, and Warwicks.

[6] According to some authorities William, but Thomas is shown to be right by *Pat. Rolls, 1467–77*, p. 306.   [7] Some authorities say John.

[8] Dugdale, *Warwicks.*, i, p. 715 ; 'Chetwynd Chartulary', p. 316 ; *Dodsworth MS.*, Bodl., 11, p. 314 ; *I. p. m.*, 3 E. IV, vol. iv, p. 320, No. 16 ; 'Pedigrees from Plea Rolls', *Gen.*, N.S., xviii, p. 186, 28 Hen. VI ; Blomefield, under Wayborn.

[9] *Rot. Parl.*, v, p. 594.   [10] *Return Memb. Parl.*, p. 361.

[11] Mar. 4, 1471—Mar. 3, 1472.

[12] *Pat. Rolls, 1476–85*, p. 275 ; Dugdale, *op. cit.*, p. 717.

[13] *Foed.*, xi, p. 846.   [14] *MS.*, fol. 3 *verso*.

in that twelvemonth he was serving as Sheriff of Warwicks.
and Leicestershire ; [1] and on New Year's Day, 1478, was again
returned as knight of the shire for the latter county.[2] He died
in 20 Ed. IV.[3] At the time of his death he held the manor of
Kelington, in Essex, of the Prior and Convent of Pritwell,
by socage rent of 30s., as well as that of Wenington.[4] His wife
was Margaret, daughter of . . . Kene.[5] On Feb. 3, 1487, is
recorded a grant to Elizabeth, Queen of Henry VII, of an
annuity of £100 out of the profits and revenues of lordships and
possessions lately belonging to William Trussell, Kt., during
the minority of Edward his son and heir.[6] This Edward
'Trussell, the Knyght's son', is mentioned as dining with John
Paston in June, 1469.[7]

BADGE. ' Blake as hede Rafid & bout the nek Croune gold.'
It seems likely that this badge commemorates Trussell's descent
from the marriage [8] of his ancestor Sir William Trussell, of
Coblesden, with Maud, daughter and coheir of Sir Warine de
Meynwaryn,[9] for an ass's head out of a crest-coronet was the
crest of the Mainwarings.[10] It appears also as the Trussell crest
in *Visit. Warwicks., 1619* ; [11] and on the official seal, dated
1660, of Edward Trussell, Esquire, Sheriff of Hants, is a castle
(not upon a shield) ensigned with a wreath, and, as crest, out of

[1] Appointed Nov. 5 : *List of Sheriffs*, p. 146 ; Dugdale, *ibid.* ; *Pat. Rolls,
1476–85*, p. 13.   [2] *Return Memb. Parl.*, p. 364.

[3] Mar. 4, 1480—Mar. 3, 1481. *I. p. m.*, vol. iv, p. 402, No. 83 ; and Dugdale,
op. cit., p. 715.

[4] Morant, *Essex*, i, p. 84.   [5] Blomefield, under Wayborn.
[6] *Mat. Reign H. VII*, ii, pp. 116, 149.   [7] *Paston*, ii, p. 358.
[8] *c.* 30 Ed. I : 1301–2.   [9] Blomefield, *loc. cit.*
[10] 'Wall's Crests' : *Ancestor*, xi, p. 182.   [11] H.S., p. 92.

a mural crown an ass's head.[1] It is not often that one may cite Gerard Leigh seriously, but he may be right in his explanation of how the ass came to be used in any way in heraldry, concluding 'the Affe not to bee vnworthie to be borne in armes' because it was the only animal ever ridden by Christ.[2] This was possibly a tradition.

No. 54. 'Sir Rychard Brandon.' Sir Richard Brandon, Knight, was, as his badge shows, of the Brandons of East Anglia, but I have failed to identify him.[3] There was a Sir Robert Brandon, a prominent man at this period, and our *MS.* may have mistaken the Christian name, but one has no right to assume this. His name does not appear in the Tellers' Roll for the first quarter of 1475 : in our *MS.*[4] he is entered as a solitary man-at-arms, and brought no archers, unless the record is incomplete.

Badge. 'lyon hede Rafyd gold.' Sir Charles Brandon, Viscount Lisle,[5] afterwards Duke of Suffolk, bore, as badges, on his standard *Six lions' heads erased gold, guttée de larmes crowned silver and red*.[6] He had also, at the time of his knighting,[7] used, as crest, *A lion's head erased or, guttée de larmes, ducally crowned per pale gules and argent*.[8] The origin of the bi-coloured crown

---

[1] *Her. & Gen.*, iv, p. 224.   [2] *Accedence of Armorie*, fol. 55 verso.

[3] Mr. Walter Rye tells me that he knows of no Sir Richard Brandon, but adds that there does not exist a good pedigree of the Brandons. Both Molinet and Haynin give a Sir William Brandon only, possibly the father of the 1st Brandon Duke of Suffolk. A Richard Brandon, of Cromer, was buried in the Chapel of St. Nicholas in Cromer Church, 1484 (Blomefield, viii, p. 107), but he is not styled a knight.   [4] Fol. 3 *verso.*   [5] 1513–23.

[6] *MS. I. 2. Coll. of Arms.* Reproduced in De Walden, p. 255.

[7] Mar. 20, 1512.   [8] *Cotton MS. Claudius C. iii.*

is to be found in the arms : his father, Sir William Brandon, who was killed by Richard III at Bosworth, bore ' dargent et de gulz berre [1] a ung lyon dor corone du champe '.[2]

No. 55. ' Sir Rychard Corbett.' Sir Richard Corbet, of Moreton Corbet and Shawbury, Shropshire, Knight, son and heir of Sir Roger Corbet by Elizabeth, daughter and heir of Thomas Hopton,[3] was aged ' 19 and more ' in 1467, at the time of his father's death.[4] According to Sir Clements Markham,[5] he was knighted after Tewkesbury, May 4, 1471. On Feb. 26, 1474, a commission was issued to Richard Corbet, Knight, and others, to array the King's lieges of the county of Hereford against certain rebels.[6] To the muster for the first quarter of the following year he brought 3 men-at-arms, and 20 archers, and was paid £68 5s. ; [7] in the second quarter his men-at-arms still numbered three, but no archers are mentioned in the Roll.[8] That he was trusted by Richard III is clear, for in the first year of that King's reign a commission was issued to Richard Corbet, Kt., and others, to assess certain subsidies and appoint collectors of the same in his county ; [9] and next year he was

[1] Barry. [2] *Harl. MS. 78, f. 31.* Quoted in Gairdner, *Richard III*, p. 364.
[3] *Visit. Salop.*, H.S., pp. 135, 256. His mother's third husband was No. 35 above.
[4] *Pat. Rolls, 1467-77*, pp. 95, 444. G. E. C., new ed., v, p. 88 ; *I. p. m.*, 7 E. IV, vol. iv, p. 339, No. 17 ; A. E. C., *The Family of Corbet*, Pedigree, p. 261.
[5] *Richard III*, p. 77, but no authority is stated. The *Paston* list (iii, pp. 9, 10) gives only a Sir Robert Corbet, and there is no Sir Richard in either Shaw or Metcalfe. *The Family of Corbet, loc. cit.*, merely says that he was ' knighted by 1473 '.
[6] *Pat. Rolls, 1467-77*, p. 429.
[7] *Foed.*, xi, p. 846.   [8] *MS.*, fol. 3 *verso.*
[9] *Pat. Rolls, 1476-85*, p. 396.

in the commission of array issued in December to inquire into treasons.[1]   At the coming of Henry Tudor he joined him at Shrewsbury, took the oath of allegiance to the adventurer, and is said to have collected 800 men, with whom he marched to Bosworth.[2]   A petition by him to Henry VII for some return for his services has been published.[3]   On Dec. 23, 1488, Sir Richard was a commissioner for Shropshire to raise archers for the expedition to Brittany,[4] and served as a leader under Sir Robert Willoughby with the force sent there to avenge the defeat and death of Sir Edward Widville.[5]   He was one of the forty Knights entertained at the Royal board at Greenwich, where the Court was kept during Christmas, 1489, owing to the prevalence of measles in London.[6]   In Henry VII's French invasion of 1492 he indentured for a year with one man-at-arms, that is himself, having his custrel and page,[7] 4 mounted archers and 12 archers on foot ;[8] and at the subsequent reception of the French ambassadors that year he was one of those in the King's entourage.[9]   He married Elizabeth Ferrers, daughter of Walter Devereux, Baron Ferrers of Chartley,[10] and died on Dec. 6, 1492.[11]

BADGE.   None given.

[1] *Pat. Rolls, 1476–85*, p. 491.   [2] Blakeway, quoted in *Fam. Corbet*.
[3] *Fam. Corbet*, from Nichols, *Hist. Leic.*
[4] *Mat. Reign H. VII*, ii, p. 386.   [5] Polydore, p. 734 ; Hall, p. 442.
[6] Leland, *Collect.*, iv, p. 254.   See under No. 51 above.
[7] *Foed.*, xii, pp. 478–9.   The pay for these two attendants would be 1s. 6d. per day each.
[8] The pay for these men was 6d. per day apiece, whether on horse or on foot. *Ibid.*, p. 480.   [9] *Lett. & Pap.*, ii, p. 292.   See under No. 39 above.
[10] No. 21 above.   *Visit. Salop.*, H.S., p. 136 ; *Misc. Gen. & Her.*, i, p. 7 (1868) ; *Fam. Corbet, loc. cit.*   [11] G. E. C., *loc. cit.*

No. 56. ' Sir John Crokke.' This was Sir John Croker, of Lineham, S. Devonshire, Knight,[1] whose mother was daughter and heir of . . . Bonvile.[2] ' John Crokker ' of Devon was one of the local personages ordered in March and April, 1470, to do their best to arrest Clarence and Warwick,[3] and ' John Crokere ' was made knight at Tewkesbury on May 4 the following year.[4] In a letter of Sept. 28 ensuing Sir John Paston writes,[5] ' Sir Thomas Fulfforthe escaped owte of Westminster [6] and with an C sperys, as men seye, and is in to Devenshyr ; and ther he hathe strekyn off Sir John Crokkers hed,[7] and kylt an other knyght off the Corteneys, as men seye '. His name is not included in the Tellers' Roll for the first quarter of 1475 ; in the second quarter he provided 6 men-at-arms but no archers.[8] It is said [9] that an augmentation to his canting crest, *A Raven proper*, was granted to him by Louis XI in that year. What the augmentation was, or why it was given, is not stated, nor is any authority adduced. According to Burke,[10] Edward IV granted him at the same time for crest *A drinking-cup or, with three fleurs-de-lys of the same issuing therefrom, and charged with a rose*, in allusion to his position as cup- and standard-bearer to the King in this expedition. Prince and Risdon are presumably the authorities

[1] The family was originally of Crocker's Hele and Crokern Tor (near Dartmoor Prison), the place of assembly of the Stannary Court from 1305 to 1749 (Pole, *Description of Devon*, p. 379 ; Taylor, *Words and Places*, p. 206).

[2] Tristram Risdon, p. 194.   [3] *Foed.*, xi, pp. 655–6.

[4] *Paston*, iii, p. 10 ; Shaw, ii, p. 15 ; Metcalfe, p. 3.   [5] iii, pp. 17–18.

[6] Where he had been in Sanctuary : *ibid.*, p. 15.

[7] This, of course, was a mistake, unless Croker's father was also Sir John and was still living, the statement relating to the latter.   [8] *MS.*, fol. 3 *verso*.

[9] *Her. & Gen.*, viii, pp. 377–8.   [10] *General Armory.*

for the statement.[1] He was not wholly guiltless of the turbulent
ways of his period, for ' John Crocker, of Lyneham, Kt., John
Crocker, of Lyneham, gentleman,[2] and three others, were sued [3]
by John Fortescu, Armiger, for breaking into his closes and houses
at Ermyngton and Rattre [4] and taking twenty horses and ten
cows belonging to him '.[5] On Dec. 23, 1488, Croker was called
upon to assist in raising archers in Devonshire for the coming
campaign in Brittany ; [6] and ' Joannes Crokerus ' was prominent
among those who helped to put down the Warbeck rebellion
of 1497, and assisted in the repulse of Perkin's attack upon Exeter
on Sept. 18.[7] He died on May 18, 1508, as is shown by the
inscription on his brass in Yealhampton [8] Church,[9] where he is
buried : ' Hic jacet Johannes Croker miles quondam ciphorarius
ac signifer illustrissimi regis Edwardi quarti qui obiit 18 Maii
anno Domini millesimo quingentesimo octavo.'[10] Judging from
a grant of March 10, 1486, the office of standard-bearer to the
King carried with it a salary of £40 a year.[11] He married
Elizabeth, daughter of Sir Richard Fortescue, of Punsbourne,
Herts., and Winston,[12] Devon, and relict of (1) . . . Elliott,

---

[1] Prince, *Worthies of Devon*, p. 271 ; Risdon, *op. cit.*, p. 194. It is repeated in
Burke's *Hist. of Commoners, s. n.* Croker, and in Foster's *Pedigree of Croker of Lineham*,
appended to *A Genealogical Account of the Fox Family* [p. 24].   [2] His son ?

[3] At Michaelmas, 19 Ed. IV (1479).   [4] Both in S. Devon.

[5] ' Pedigrees from the Plea Rolls ' : *Gen.*, N.S., xx, p. 88. John Fortescue was
perhaps his brother-in-law : see below.

[6] *Foed.*, xii, p. 357 ; *Mat. Reign H. VII*, ii, pp. 384–6.

[7] Polydore, p. 766 ; *Halliwell's Letters*, i, p. 183 ; *Harl. Misc.*, vi, p. 586.

[8] *Aliter* Yealmpton.   [9] The Parish Church of Lineham.

[10] Prince, *op. cit.*, p. 273 ; Haines, ii, p. 49.

[11] *Mat. Reign H. VII*, i, p. 382.   [12] Or Windsor.

(2) John Wood.[1]   According to Risdon [2] he married . . .,
daughter of . . . Champernon ; presumably another wife.

BADGE.   None given.

No. 57. 'Sir fimond mounford.'   Sir Simon Mountfort, of
Hampton-in-Arden and Coleshill, Warwickshire, Knight, was
originally the second son, but eventually the son and heir, of
Sir Baldwin Mountfort, Knight, by Joan, sister (or daughter)
of Sir Richard Vernon, Knight.[3] A 'Simon Mountfort, armiger',
is mentioned in a legal instrument of 33 Hen. VI,[4] and may very
well have been our man, as I have not found this Christian name
in the Norfolk Mountforts of the time.   He received knighthood
in the first year of Edward IV,[5] and we read that ' Sir Simon
Montfort' and others were sued for lands and tenements in
Toneworth, at Hilary, 4 Ed. IV, when the plaintiff secured the
verdict.[6] In the 9th year of the same King [7] he was appointed
to the Lieutenancy of the Isle of Wight and Carisbrooke Castle
under Anthony, Lord Scales ; [8] on March 7, 1470, was one
of the Warwickshire notables called upon to raise men in that
county against the King's enemies ; [9] and in the following year
was serving as Sheriff of Warwicks. and Leicestershire.[10]   Accord-

---

[1] *Visit. Essex,* H.S., Pt. II, p. 571 (the pedigree on pp. 33–5 appears to be
inaccurate) ; *Her. & Gen.,* viii, p. 379 ; *Stonor Letters,* i, p. xxi, where a brother-in-
law, Sir John Fortescue, of Punsbourne, is mentioned.   [2] p. 194.

[3] Sir Baldwin, who died 14 Ed. IV, became a priest in the last year of Henry VI's
reign, and gave Hampton to Simon.   Robert, the elder son, had died 9 Ed. IV.
Dugdale, *Warwicks.,* pp. 1008–11 ; *Visit. Essex, 1558,* H.S., i, pp. 84–5 ; *Visit.
Essex, 1612,* H.S., i, p. 256 ; *Rot. Parl.,* vi, p. 503 ; *Pat. Rolls, 1461–7,* p. 51.

[4] ' Chetwynd Chartulary ', *op. cit.,* xii, p. 323.   [5] Dugdale, *loc. cit.*

[6] ' Pedigrees from the Plea Rolls ' : *Gen.,* N.S., xix, p. 30.   [7] 1469–70.

[8] No. 13 above. Dugdale, *loc. cit.*   [9] *Foed.,* xi, pp. 652–3.

[10] Appointed Apr. 11 : *List of Sheriffs,* p. 146.

K 2

ing to Dugdale,[1] he was created a Banneret on May 24, that year, but he is not so described in our *MS.* of four years later. He is absent from the Tellers' Roll for the first quarter of 1475, and in the second quarter appears without any following.[2] Dugdale, however, tells us [3] that he was retained to serve in France in this expedition for one year with 5 spears, ' himself accounted ', and 60 archers, receiving 2*s.* per day for himself, 1*s.* 6*d.* per day each for the other 4 spears, and 6*d.* for each archer, and was to have one-third of any booty taken by himself or any of his retinue.[4]   On Jan. 5, 1478, ' Simon Mountfort, miles ' was returned as knight of the shire for Warwicks,[5] and a grant of Dec. 26, 1485, is recorded by which he received for life the office of Steward of the Lordship of Castle Bromeche,[6] Warwickshire. A special commission of jail delivery for the King's prison at Warwick was addressed to him and others on March 2, 1488, and again in 1489 ; [7] and he was one of those ordered on Dec. 23 of the former year to raise archers in his county for the next year's Breton campaign.[8]   In Hilary Term, 1494, ' Simon Montfort, Kt.', was summoned to answer Humphrey Seymour and Ann his wife to warrant the manor of Monkspathe and land in Molyngton, co. Warwick, and land in Hidate Bartram, co. Gloucester.[9]   He performed numerous other public functions and held many lesser appointments till his fall in 1494, when he was accused of complicity in the Warbeck plots.[10]   The actual offence named was that he had treasonably sent £30 to Perkin

---

[1] *Op. cit.*, p. 1011.   [2] *MS.*, fol. 3 *verso.*

[3] *Loc. cit.*   [4] See the Tunstall indenture above.

[5] *Return Memb. Parl.*, p. 365.   [6] Bromwich. *Mat. Reign H. VII*, i, p. 222.

[7] *Ibid.*, ii, pp. 264, 481, 483.   [8] *Foed.*, xii, p. 357.

[9] ' Pedigrees from Plea Rolls ' : *Gen.*, N.S., xxv, p. 90.   Result not stated.

[10] See Nos. 35 and 37 above.

by Henry his younger son. His trial was held in the Guildhall : he did not deny the charge, was drawn through the city, hanged and quartered at Tyburn, and attainted.[1] His wife was Anne, daughter to Sir Richard Verney, of Herts., Knight.[2]

BADGE. ' flourdelys goulys.' This looks as though there were some actual, or supposed, connexion with the Montfords of Feltwell, Norfolk, who bore *Argent* (or *Or*) *three fleurs-de-lys gules*.[3]

No. 58. ' mr Dodeley Dean of the Kynges chapell.' William Dudley, *alias* Sutton, third son of John, 4th (Sutton) Baron Dudley, had been Dean of Windsor since Dec. 4, 1473 (see *D. N. B.*). He is in the Tellers' Roll for the first quarter of 1475, his remuneration being given as 2*s.* a day, the total payment for the 91 days amounting to £9 2*s.* ;[4] in the second quarter his pay is doubled, and is the same as that of a baron.[5]

BADGE. ' A grat Sylu[er].' In *Harl. MS. 4632*[6] *A grating formed by four perpendicular and three transverse bars or* is given as a badge of Dudley. It appears on the reverse of the jetton (struck before 1460) of the Dean's father.[7] In *Promptorium*

---

[1] *Wriothesley's Chron.*, i, p. 3 ; *Chron. of Grey Friars*, p. 181 ; *Arnold's Chron.*, p. xxxix ; *Six Town Chron.*, pp. 164–5, 172 ; *Chronicles of London*, pp. 203–7 ; Polydore, p. 750 ; *Rot. Parl.*, vi, p. 503 ; Bacon, p. 131 ; Dugdale, p. 1012. It is referred to in Warbeck's Proclamation (*Harl. Misc.*, vi, p. 562). See under No. 44 above.

[2] *Visit. Essex, 1558*, H.S., p. 85. Mountfort's attainder was reversed in Feb. 1504, and his son and heir Thomas restored. (*Rot. Parl.*, vi, p. 526 ; *Statutes of the Realm*, ii, p. 669.)   [3] Papworth, pp. 850–1 ; Blomefield, ii, p. 196.

[4] *Foed.*, xi, p. 848.

[5] *MS.*, fol. 4 *recto*. Dudley eventually became Bishop of Durham. The Dean and Chaplains of the King's Chapel, and other Chaplains, had been in the retinue of Henry V in the Agincourt campaign : see Nicolas, *Battle of Agincourt*, 1833, p. 389.   [6] *Coll. Top. & Gen.*, iii, p. 67.

[7] *Medallic Illustrations of British History*, i, p. 15, No. 5. Edward, 5th (Sutton)

Parvulorum[1] ' grate ' is defined as ' trelys wyndowe ... Cancellus'. It is perhaps seen in the fretty lining of the *infulae* on Dudley's privy seal when Bishop of Durham shown by Surtees.[2] Is it possible that this badge was founded on the old Sumery, or Somerie, coat of *Azure, fretty argent*[3] (in French blazon *treillissé*), the Someries being ancestors of the Suttons ?

No. 59. ' mr perife Courteney.' Piers Courtenay third son of Sir Philip Courtenay, of Powderham, near Exeter, Knight,[4] had been Dean of the Royal Chapel of St. Stephen's, Westminster, since 1472 (see *D. N. B.*). He is not in the Tellers' Roll for the first quarter of 1475 ; our *MS.* tells us that in the second quarter his remuneration was the same as that of the Dean of Windsor, 4*s.* per day.[5]

BADGE. ' A scant[6] Antony Crofe Azur.' Courtenay had held the Mastership of St. Anthony's Free Chapel and Hospital in London, which he resigned in 1474.[7] This doubtless explains his badge, for the Tau Cross was an emblem of St. Anthony.[8]

Baron Dudley (1492–1531) is said in Mrs. Palliser's *Historic Devices,* 1870 (p. 337), to have used this badge, and an illustration of it, in the form of the grating of a window, is given ; but, as usual, she cites no authority.

[1] i, p. 207.

[2] *Hist. Durham*, i, Seals, Pl. V, 7 ; also *Archaeologia*, lxxii, Pl. IV, No. 5.

[3] As in, *e. g.*, the Dering and Planché Rolls of Arms : *Reliquary*, 1876–8 ; and *Gen.*, N.S., v, p. 178, No. 658.

[4] By More (*Rich. III*, pp. 96, 98), and by Polydore (Lat. ed., p. 700 ; Eng. ed., pp. 199–200), he is wrongly called brother of the Earl of Devon. That would be Edward Courtenay, cr. Earl of Devon by Hen. VII on Oct. 26, 1485. (See Courthope, pp. 158–9.)　　　　　　　　　　　　[5] *MS.*, fol. 4 *recto*.

[6] Error for ' seant '.　　　　　　　　　[7] *Monumenta Vetusta*, vol. iii.

[8] For the tincture of this Cross see Ashmole, p. 62 ; Tanner, *Notitia Monastica*, Pl. III, No. 107.

On the Courtenay Mantelpiece in the Hall of the Episcopal
Palace at Exeter, of which see Piers was Bishop from 1478 to
1487, the Tau Cross occurs eight times without, and six times
with, St. Anthony's other emblem of a bell suspended to it.[1]
The Tau Cross also appears thrice without the bell on the stone
armorial panel formerly in the Bishop's Palace at Winchester, to
which see Courtenay was preferred in 1487, and now in the house
of the Master of the Hospital of St. Cross there.   It is also to be
seen in the glass at Doddiscombsleigh Church, and, with the bell, on
the 15th-cent. rood-screen at Kenton, Devon.[2]   On Jan. 27, 1886,
the body of ' venerabilis Pater Petrus episcopus . . . flos militiae
patriae suae '[3] was exhumed : his skeleton measured 5 ft. 10 in.[4]

   No. 60. ' mr John gounthrope.'   John Gunthorp, at the time
of the present expedition, had been Dean of Wells since Jan. 19,
1473 (see *D. N. B.*).   In the Tellers' Roll for the first quarter
of 1475 he is entered as ' Decanus de Welles & Elimosnarius
Domini Regis ', and his stipend was 2s. per day, the total
payment to him being £9 2s., ' pro Attendentiis suis super
Personam Regiam in Servitio suo Guerrae ultra mare '.   His
retinue consisted of 1 man-at-arms, Thomas Ustwayte, Gent., and
12 archers, for which he further received £34 2s. 6d.[5]   In the
second quarter his personal emolument was doubled, as in the case
of Deans Dudley and Courtenay, and no following is given.[6]

---

   [1] Husenbeth, *Emblems of Saints*, p. 14 ; see, too, Gibbs and Halliday, *The
Courtenay Mantelpiece at Exeter* ; also Hope, *H. for C.*, p. 177 and fig. 94.
   [2] *Arch. Journal*, June 1913, p. 170, Pl. VI ; and *ex inform.* Mr. G. M^cN.
Rushforth.
   [3] As the *Croyland Chronicle*, p. 574, describes him.   [4] *Gen.*, N.S., iii, p. 189.
   [5] *Foed.*, xi, p. 847.   [6] *MS.*, fol. 4 *recto.*

BADGE. ' A ſawter gold ou[er] the ſawter A lyon hede raſed ſilu[er].' The saltire is no doubt the cross of St. Andrew, to whom the Cathedral Church of Wells was dedicated, while the lion's head erased is taken from the arms of Gunthorp's family : *Gules, a bend compony argent and azure between two lions' heads erased of the second.*[1] His rebus, a *gun* (cannon), and a scroll that bore the motto ' Virtuti parent omnia ',[2] remains on the oriel window put up by him in the Deanery at Wells,[3] and the gun appears no less than 103 times on the wing of the Deanery which he built.

No. 61. ' mr gartier Smyrte.' Garter King of Arms in 1475 was John Smert,[4] who had been promoted from Guienne Herald to that office by Henry VI on Apr. 3, 1450,[5] and reappointed by Edward IV on March 1, 1462, with a stipend of £40 a year.[6] He is mentioned in the *Issue Roll* of Michaelmas, 1453, as having received on Feb. 19 preceding, £6 13s. 4d. in payment for certain official services ; [7] his name appears, too, in the letter of Oct. 10, 1459, sent to Henry VI by York, Warwick, and Salisbury, after the Yorkist victory of Blore Heath, on Sept. 23 of

---

[1] This coat is found in several different forms at Wells (*Ex inform.* The Very Rev. the Dean of Wells, Dr. J. Armitage Robinson).

[2] Sallust, *Cat.*, 2, 7.   [3] See Hope, *H. for C.*, p. 192 and fig. 111.

[4] Ashmole, pp. 253-4 ; Weever, p. 419 ; Noble, p. 60 ; Dallaway, *Enquiries into Heraldry*, Appendix LIV. The surname is merely a variant of Smart, as the arms and records both show. (See *Gen.*, N.S., xxvi, p. 57.) His name is spelt ' Smart ' in ' Ped. from the De Banco Rolls ', 2 H. VII ; *Gen.*, N.S., xxii, p. 93.

[5] *Foed.*, xi, p. 263 ; Edmondson, i, p. 103 ; Anstis, ii, pp. 318, 348 ; *Gen.*, N.S., vii, p. 185.

[6] *Foed.*, xi, p. 488. The date on the *Pat. Rolls, 1461–7*, p. 72, is Sept. 4.

[7] Devon, *Issues*, p. 477.

that year,[1] and also in a record of payments of arrears to heralds dated Sept. 7, 1460.[2] His fee of £40 a year is specially exempted from the Acts of Resumption of 1464 and 1467–8.[3] In 1470 he was sent by Edward IV to order Clarence and Warwick to attend and answer the accusation of treason against them.[4] We read that in Oct. 1472, Mr. Garter Smert was suffering from ' an Impediment in his tonge ', wherefore on a state occasion of that time ' Mr. Norroy [5] cryed yᵉ larges in . . . the hall ' for him.[6] Neither his name nor that of any heraldic officer is entered in the Tellers' Roll for the first quarter of 1475 ; in the second quarter his pay is that of a Baron, 4s. a day.[7] Comines [8] says that Garter was a native of Normandy. He seems, however, to have made a twofold mistake here, for the evidence tends to show that it was not Garter but Ireland King of Arms who met Louis XI at Beauvais with Edward's defiance,[9] and Ireland at that time was Thomas Ashwell.[10] The earliest official grant of arms known is one by Garter Smert, dated Sept. 24, 1456, to the Tallow Chandlers Company of London.[11] Smert's prede-

---

[1] *Eng. Chron.*, p. 81.   [2] *Foed.*, xi, p. 467 ; *Pat. Rolls, 1452–61*, p. 637.

[3] *Rot. Parl.*, v, pp. 530, 609.   [4] *Ibid.*, vi, p. 233.   [5] No. 65 below.

[6] ' Record of Bluemantle the Pursuivant ', in Kingsford's *Eng. Hist. Lit. in the 15th Cent.*, p. 384.

[7] *MS.*, fol. 4 *recto* ; and see Anstis, ii, p. 354. Accounts of the fees of heraldic officials in the 15th cent. have been printed in *Hearne's Cur. Disc.*, i, pp. 148–50 ; Dallaway, *op. cit.*, pp. 142–8 ; Leland, *Collect.*, iii, p. 234.

[8] Ed. by Dupont, i, p. 338.

[9] ' Letter of Francesco Rovero ', *Dépêches Milanaises*, i, p. 206.

[10] Noble, p. 63.

[11] *Her. & Gen.*, i, p. 120. Sir J. B. Paul has given a description of it in his *Heraldry in Relation to Scottish Hist. and Art*, p. 204. It was shown at the *Her. Exhib. Burl. Ho.*, Cat., p. 60.

cessor had been Sir William Brugge,[1] the first to hold the title of Garter,[2] and whose daughter, Katharine, was Smert's first wife.[3] Brugge died before March 20, 1449 ;[4] a representation of him from *MS. Ashmole, 764*, is reproduced here.[5] Smert died before July 16, 1478, on which date his successor was appointed.[6] At one time he seems to have been living in the parish of St. Bride's, Fleet Street, where we learn from the ' De Banco Rolls ' that his house had a garden.[7] In *Miscellanea Genealogica et Heraldica*[8] is an illustration of Smert's signature in 1456. The Kings of Arms wore their crowns on great occasions, as, *e. g.*, at the duel between Lord Scales[9] and the Bastard of Burgundy : ' at ev[er]y corner [of the barriers] a Kyng of Armes crownyd '.[10]

BADGE. ' A Brode Arowe hed Blake Armyned.' This badge is taken from the coat of Smert, or Smart : *Argent, a chevron between three pheons sable*,[11] but differenced. ' Armyned ' here can only mean ' Counter-ermine ', as the older, and better, phrase was, or ' Ermines ', as the moderns call it : that is a black fur with white ermine spots. This fur was not known to early armory, and Upton, writing before August, 1436, seems uncertain of its existence : ' Sunt tamen quidam qui ymaginati funt contrarium (*i. e.* to ermine), quafi fi SCUTUM ESSET DE

[1] *Aliter* Bruges, or Del Brug.
[2] Ashmole, p. 252 ; Edmondson, i, p. 105 ; Weever, p. 419.
[3] Anstis, ii, p. 354.   [4] *Ibid.*, p. 344 ; Noble, p. 60.
[5] See Frontispiece. A travesty of it appeared in Dallaway, *op. cit.*, p. 124.
[6] Noble, *ibid.*
[7] *Gen.*, N.S., xxii, p. 93. The year-date there given must be an error.
[8] 4 Ser., v, p. 123.   [9] No. 13 above, and see under No. 29.
[10] *Excerpt. Hist.*, p. 203. See, too, Anstis, i, p. 460.
[11] Anstis, ii, p. 355 ; Guillim, p. 334 ; *Gen.*, N.S., vii, pp. 185, 191.

Nigro Colore Totaliter Factum, Parvis Maculis Albis Conspersum, ut hic [*Drawing*]. Et bene volo quod talia Arma portentur.'[1] In Blount's Manuscript English version, referred to above, the passage runs : 'Howbeyt there be fome whiche imagine the contrary of the faid Armes,[2] thinking that the felde fholde be hole blacke And ffpekkyld wyth lytell whyte fpottes, As here [*Drawing*]. And I Deny not but foche Armes maye be borne.' Counter-ermine is not mentioned in Upton's earlier work the *Tractatus de Armis*, written soon after 1394, under the pseudonym of ' Johannes de Bado Aureo ', that is John of Guildford.[3]

No. 62. 'mr of the Ordenance pykes v[i]z John fturgyn.' John Sturgeon, Esquire, was apparently a Hertfordshire man. In the Act of Resumption of 1467–8 exemption is made in favour of a grant for life to ' John Sturgeon ', of the manor of Goddes-bury in Herts., and other lands and tenements in the same county, of the yearly value of £12, which had been granted to him in 1463 ;[4] and the interests of ' John Sturgeon Esquire ', one of the Ushers of the King's Chamber, are protected also in the similar Act of 1473.[5] On Jan. 21, that year, John Sturgeon, Esquire, ' one of the gentlemen ushers of the King's Chamber ' was appointed to take carpenters, plumbers, and others for the works of the ordnance.[6] On March 30, 1474, he and another had been ordered to raise 13 men-at-arms and 1,000 archers as a reinforcement for the Duke of Burgundy.[7] In our *MS.*

---

[1] *De Studio Militari*, p. 167.   [2] *i. e.* of ermine.

[3] Archbishop Laud's copy is in the possession of the editor. ' Bado ' is for ' Vado '.   [4] *Rot. Parl.*, v, p. 588 ; *Pat. Rolls, 1461–7*, p. 296, Dec. 1.

[5] *Rot. Parl.*, vi, p. 83.   [6] *Pat. Rolls, 1467–77*, p. 365.

[7] *Foed.*, xi, p. 791, where he is styled ' armiger '.

Sturgeon is described as Master of the Ordnance Pikes, that is commander of the pikemen who guarded the artillery,[1] but he was much more than this. We learn from Rymer [2] that he was himself Master of the Ordnance, and also head and paymaster of the transport, with four subordinate officers under him at 1s. a day apiece. Under each of the latter were 6 'Charyotmen' at 8d., and 30 'Carters' at 6d., a day apiece. These payments exactly absorb the £364 allowed him for the first quarter of the expedition. His personal pay, therefore, we learn only from our MS.[3] It was 5s. 8d.[4] a day, only a shilling less than that of an Earl, testimony to the importance attached to his post.[5] These were his wages when on service. In time of peace his stipend was 2s. daily, with allowances of 6d. a day for a clerk, and the same for a yeoman.[6] This appointment was often held by men of knightly rank, as by Sir Richard Guylforde, 'The Pilgrim', in 1485,[7] and Sir Simon Norton in 1513.[8] Indeed, as early as nearly half a century before this a Master of the King's Ordnance is recorded as receiving the high wage of 100 marks a year.[9] By the end of the fifteenth century every

[1] Such protection was necessary, because, owing to its slow service, primitive field ordnance would otherwise be liable to capture between discharges. (See, e. g., Arch. Journ., 1911, p. 83 ; Monstrelet, ii, p. 519.) For the same reason pikemen were needed in the early days of portable firearms to protect the musketeers.

[2] Foed., xi, p. 844. (Omitted in the edition by Holmes.)   [3] Fol. 4 recto.

[4] This is so unusual a sum that one almost suspects an error in the MS. for 6s. 8d.

[5] In like manner ' Les grands maîtres de l'artillerie des armées françaises depuis Louis XI furent des hommes d'une haute valeur '. (Viollet-le-Duc, Dict. Mob. Fr., vi, p. 415.)   [6] Pat. Rolls, 1476–85, p. 76.

[7] Rot. Parl., vi, p. 364 ; Collins, Baronetage, v, p. 2.

[8] Cotton MS. Cleopatra C. v.

[9] £66 13s. 4d. : Proc. Priv. Coun., iv, p. 31 : March 8, 1430.

expedition of importance was equipped with artillery and its attendant vehicles. Little, nevertheless, as a rule, is told us by the contemporary writers [1] about the efficacy of gunnery in our battles, Châtillon and the skirmish of Lose Coat Field excepted. We may therefore conclude that, whatever value it possessed for siege-work, as yet it did not materially contribute towards deciding the issue of an action in the field. Sturgeon's activities were not confined to military matters. On Nov. 5, 1467, he was appointed Sheriff of Cornwall,[2] and was one of the persons in that county commanded to do their utmost to arrest Clarence and Warwick in 1470.[3] 'Johannes Sturgeon, armiger' is returned as knight of the shire for Herts. on Sept. 24, 1472, and again on Dec. 11, 1477 ; [4] and he serves as Sheriff of the same county and Essex in 1473, 1479, and 1483.[5] There is recorded a grant to him for life, on July 22, 1486, of an annuity of £20 ; [6] and that he was a person of local importance is further seen from the issue, on June 14, 1489, of a commission of Peace and of Oyer and Terminer for Hertfordshire to John Sturgeon and others.[7] In the Church of New Bigging 'An old defaced Tomb remains according to Tradition erected for John Sturgeon, Sheriff of the two Counties [8] in the 2ᵈ· of Richard III. The Infcription and Arms were upon a Stone againft the Wall '.[9]

---

[1] Comines's account of the battle of Fornova is an exception (Bk. VIII, chs.10–12) ; and on the clever way in which it was used at Marignano see Oman, ii, p. 279.

[2] *List of Sheriffs*, p. 22.   [3] *Foed.*, xi, p. 656 : Ap. 15.

[4] *Return Memb. Parl.*, pp. 361, 364.

[5] *List of Sheriffs*, p. 45. He had surrendered his post of Master of the Ordnance by May 18, 1482. (*Pat. Rolls, 1476–85*, p. 299.)

[6] *Mat. Reign H. VII*, i, p. 515.   [7] *Ibid.*, ii, p. 477.   [8] Essex and Herts.

[9] Salmon, *Herts.*, p. 164. I have been unable to trace this monument.

No. 63. ' mr of˙ the Kynges Tenttes Rychard garnet.'
Richard Garnet, ' brother and heire of Thomas Garnet Squyer,
tenant in chief, nowe dede ', is protected in his grants by the
Resumption Act of 1473, and received licence to succeed to his
brother's possessions on July 13, 1477.[1] He is entered in the
Tellers' Roll for the first quarter of 1475 as *Serviens Pavilionum
Regis*, where his pay is given as 4*s.* per day, the same as that
of a Baron or a Banneret. He brings two *valetti* at 1*s.*, and
22 more at 6*d.* a day, each, his total receipt being £77 7*s.*[2]
In the second quarter he receives only 3*s.* 4*d.* a day, and nothing
is said about his following.[3] Garnet's Indenture with the King
for this expedition has been printed by Rymer,[4] dated Nov. 20,
1474. It is worth giving here : ' This Indenture made between
the *King* oure Soveraigne Lord Edward the IVth of the one Part,
and his Trufty and Wel beloved Richard Garnet Squyer, Serjant
of his Tents, on the other Party, WITNESSETH that the fame
Richard is Retained and Beleft [5] towards the fame our Soveraigne
Lord, to doe him Service of Werre in his Duchye of Normandy
and in his Reaume of Fraunce, for an hole Yere as a Man of Arms
at his Spere, with xxiv Yemen well and fufficiently Habiled,
Armed, and Arraied as it apperteyneth taking Wages for Him-
felfe iv*s.* by the Day,[6] for ii of the faid Yemen either of them
xii*d.* by the Day, and for every of the Remanent vi*d.* by the Day,

[1] *Rot. Parl.*, vi, p. 88 ; *Pat. Rolls, 1476–85*, p. 77 ; *I. p. m.*, 11 E. IV, vol. iv, p. 351.

[2] *Foed.*, xi, p. 848. His appointment as Serjeant of the King's Pavilions dated
from July 20, 1461. (*Pat. Rolls, 1461–7*, pp. 125, 358.)

[3] *MS.*, fol. 4 *recto*.   [4] *Foed.*, xi, p. 819.   [5] Chosen, *i. e.* appointed.

[6] This remarkably high pay for an Esquire is doubtless accounted for by the
special position he held as regards the royal person, and, judging by his wage given
below, was, like Sturgeon's, enhanced owing to his being on active service.

Of which Wages, as well as for him as for everiche of his Retinue, the said *Richard* shall be paid, the first Quarter of the said hole Yere, at Westminster, the last Day of January next comyng, by the Hands of the Treforer of England for the tyme being *&c. ut in aliis Indenturis.*' There is record of a grant in Richard III's reign to Garnet, ' for his good service', of the office of ' pavillioner' and serjeant of the King's tents for life, with wages of 12*d.* per diem for himself, and 4*d.* per diem for a yeoman under him, and 100*s.* yearly for a house to lay the tents in; 46*s.* 8*d.* for his robes, and 13*s.* 4*d.* for his yeoman's robes; to be taken from the issues of the lordships of Wrotell,[1] Havering, Boyton, Hadleigh, and Rochford, in Essex, and the lordships of Tunbridge, Penshurst, Middleton, and Marden, in Kent, by the hands of the receivers.[2] Garnet died in the second year of Richard III.[3]

' M[*emoran*]d[*um*] fcurers.' These scourers, or scouts, received 12*d.* a day each.[4]

No. 64. 'Clarenfceux.' Clarencieux King of Arms at this date was William Hawkeslowe,[5] whose wage in the expedition was at the rate of 28*d.* per day.[6] He was ' lately deceased' in 16 Ed. IV,[7] 'having been drowned in the Spanish seas in 1476, and was buried at St. Mary, Somerset, on May 7th that year'.[8] He ended his life in great debt and poverty, and the King ordered that some provision should be made for his widow and

---

[1] Now Writtle.   [2] *Pat. Rolls, 1476–85,* p. 443.

[3] *I. p. m.,* vol. iv, p. 419, No. 12; where he is entered as still ' armiger', and as seized of property in Southwark and South Lambeth.   [4] *MS.,* fol. 4 *recto.*

[5] Edmondson, i, p. 99; Noble, p. 62; Dallaway, *App.,* p. liv.

[6] *MS.,* fol. 4 *recto.*   [7] 1476–7.

[8] Anstis, ii, p. 380; *Gen.,* iv (1880), p. 127.

children.[1] For his signature see *Miscellanea Genealogica et Heraldica*, and also for his seal and counter-seal.[2]

No. 65. 'Noroy.' Norroy King of Arms was then Thomas Holme, of Walden, Essex.[3] On Sept. 1, 1462, when 'Windsor Herald Marshal of Arms', he was granted the lands in Kent forfeited by the rebellion of Robert Merefyn.[4] His pay in the expedition of 1475 was the same as that of Clarencieux, 28*d.* per day.[5] In 16 Ed. IV[6] he was promoted by the King to be Clarencieux in the place of Hawkeslowe deceased.[7] 'Thomas Clarencewe Heraldus, Rex Armorum', was appointed on July 5, 1480, one of the officials to arrange an alliance with Christian I, King of Denmark and Scandinavia,[8] and on March 29, 1482, 'Thomas Holme, *aliàs dictus Clarencew, unus noſtrorum Regum Armorum*', was nominated for life one of the ' Milites Pauperes '[9] in the Royal College of Windsor, where he was allotted a house and garden within the precincts of the Castle in the room of a Poor Knight deceased.[10] Edmondson[11] records a protest by Sir Thomas

[1] Anstis, ii, p. 380.

[2] 4 Ser., v, pp. 121, 271. For some grants of arms by him see *Visit. Cornwall*, H.S., p. 275 ; *Gen.*, iv (1880), p. 127 ; *ibid.*, N.S., xxvi, p. 254 ; *Her. & Gen.*, i, p. 120 ; *Misc. Gen. et Her.*, N.S., i (1874), p. 29 ; *ibid.*, 3 Ser., iv, p. 117 ; *ibid.*, 4 Ser., v, p. 267 ; *Visit. Worc.*, H.S., p. 16 ; *Ancestor*, viii, p. 125 (but ? date) ; *Her. Exhib. Burl. Ho.*, p. 61.

[3] Edmondson, i, p. 93 ; Noble, p. 62 ; Ashmole, p. 161, where his name is spelt ' Hulme ' ; *Pat. Rolls*, *1452–61*, p. 512.

[4] Anstis, ii, p. 467. ' Myrfyn of Kent ' : *Paston*, ii, p. 46 ; *Wil. Wyrc. Ann.*, p. 782.   [5] *MS.*, fol. 4 *recto*.   [6] 1476–7.

[7] Edmondson, *loc. cit.* Confirmed by Richard III, Feb. 17, 1484, with £20 a year and livery of his robes. (*Pat. Rolls*, *1476–85*, p. 389.)

[8] *Foed.*, xii, p. 121.   [9] *Aliter* ' Alms-Knights '.

[10] *Foed.*, xii, p. 154. The Alms-Knights' lodgings were in the Lower Bailey to the right of the Great Gate : see Hollar's drawing in *Arch. Journ.*, 1913, p. 191.

[11] i, pp. 101–2.

Holme, made in 22 Ed. IV,[1] against Ireland King of Arms for granting arms in the South of England, which was under the jurisdiction of Clarencieux. We see from these last two authorities that by this time he had been knighted. In April, 1483, he officiated at the funeral of Edward IV.[2] We meet with him again in Rymer in an official capacity under the date Jan. 1484;[3] and later in the same year in the letters of Richard III concerning the Incorporation of the Heralds.[4] He resigned his post on Jan. 4, 1485, but was restored by Henry VII in his second year.[5] In 1489 he is again engaged in negotiations with the King of Denmark, now John.[6] He made his will in 1493[7] and Noble[8] gives that as the year of his death. He married twice: (1) Christiane, relict of John Garland, of Walden, Essex, merchant, (2) Elizabeth . . .[9] For his signature in 1482 see *Miscellanea Genealogica et Heraldica*.[10] Was he an ancestor of Randle Holme? The Holmes were an 'heraldic family', as Moule expresses it.[11]

[1] 1482–3.

[2] *Lett. & Pap.*, i, p. 9, where there is a mistake in the note, corrected above.

[3] *Foed.*, xii, p. 210.   [4] *Ibid.*, p. 215: March 2.

[5] Edmondson, i, p. 90; Noble, pp. 60, 62, 86; *Gen.*, i, p. 2.

[6] *Foed.*, xii, p. 373: Aug. 6.   [7] Anstis, ii, p. 380.   [8] p. 86.

[9] Anstis, *loc. cit.*; *Pat. Rolls, 1452–61*, p. 522; *1461–7*, p. 509.

[10] 4 Ser. v, p. 122.

[11] *Bibl. Her.*, pp. 240–2; consult, too, Lower, *Curiosities of Heraldry*, pp. 271–2, and *Hist. Soc. of Lancs. and Chesh.*, 1849, pp. 86 et seq. For some grants of arms by him, see *Misc. Gen. et Her.*, 2 Ser. iv, p. 145; 3 Ser. i, p. 1; 4 Ser. iii, p. 273; 4 Ser. v, pp. 268–9; *Gen.*, N.S., xvii, p. 273; *Her. & Gen.*, i, pp. 80, 121; *Proc. Soc. Antiq.*, Ser. 2, xvi, p. 343; *Tonge's Visit. Yks.*, Surtees Soc., 41, App., p. xxxviii; *Visit. Beds.*, H.S., p. 77; *Visit. Berks.*, H.S., ii, p. 195; *Visit. Bucks.*, H.S., p. 53; *Visit. Warwicks.*, H.S., p. 155; *Ancestor*, viii, pp. 125–6; *Her. Exhib. Burl. Ho.*, p. 61; Stow, i, p. 182.

No. 66. ' marche.' March King of Arms at this time was John Ferrant.[1] The title is commonly supposed to have been taken from Edward IV's Earldom of March and Ferrant to have been the first holder of it,[2] but it seems to have existed in the reign of Richard II.[3] His pay was the same as that of his brother Kings of Arms, 28*d.* per day.[4] March's jurisdiction ran in Devonshire, Cornwall, Cheshire, and Wales.[5]

' Heralld ſ[er]geauntz at Armes.' . . . ' purſ[er]u[a]nts.' Nothing, of course, can be said about the identity of any Herald, Serjeant-at-arms, or Pursuivant, as no names are entered in our *MS.*,[6] and the Tellers' Roll for the first quarter of 1475 makes no mention even of any such officers. The wages of Heralds and Serjeants-at-arms were, we see, the same, 2*s.*, that of Pursuivants 1*s.* 6*d.* per day.[7] The little Corps of *Servientes ad arma* is said to have been formed by Richard I, in imitation of Philip Augustus,[8] when in the East, to protect himself from assassination by the emissaries of the ' Old Man of the Mountain '.[9] Originally there were 24 members, later 30,[10] and at first sons of

---

[1] Noble, p. 64 ; Weever, p. 421 ; Dallaway, App., p. lv.

[2] Noble, *ibid.*   [3] See on this Edmondson, i, pp. 95–6.   [4] *MS.*, fol. 4 *recto.*

[5] This seems to suggest the Welsh Marches as the origin of the name.

[6] Fol. 4 *recto.*

[7] In the case of Serjeants ' clothyng perteynyng to the ſeid office ' was allowed (*Rot. Parl.*, v, pp. 187, 199, &c.). When not on service a Serjeant received 1*s.* a day (*ibid.*, pp. 320, 474, &c.).   [8] Ducange, *s. v.* ' Servientes armorum '.

[9] Grose, *Mil. Antiq.*, i, p. 173.

[10] In 1455 they numbered 21, and it was decided then to appoint no more till they were reduced to the number of Henry Vth's time (*Rot. Parl.*, v, p. 320). The King's Serjeants in the Agincourt campaign mustered either 7 or 8 : the authorities differ (Nicolas, *Agincourt*, 1827, p. 104). In 1461 there seem to have

Knights alone were eligible, afterwards those of simple gentlemen were admitted. Their duties were to attend the person of the King and preserve his privacy, whence their other name of [H]ostiarii armorum,[1] to superintend the arrest of traitors,[2] and assist at their trials. At home some of them were told off to perform similar functions in connexion with the two Houses of Parliament, and certain of the high officers of State.[3] According to Guillim,[4] a person under arrest by a Serjeant-at-arms was immune for the time being from any other arrest, and it is natural to suppose that this was the case in the earlier times dealt with here. In a record of March 13, 1427, ten marks[5] were to be paid to a Serjeant-at-arms who was to convey certain hostages of the King of Scotland from the Tower to the North.[6] This tells us another of the occupations of these officers. The symbol of the authority of a *Serviens ad arma* was his silver, or silver-gilt mace.[7] A cut of a Serjeant-at-arms of about 1420, with his mace, is given in Hewitt,[8] from an incised slab at St. Denis ; and the brass of a ' serviens Henrici Quinti ', of that year exists at Wandsworth.[9] Another brass in which the Serjeants' mace is

been only four (*Rot. Parl.*, v, p. 474, and Note 7 below) ; while in the Act of Resumption of 1467-8 twenty-one are named (*Rot. Parl.*, v, pp. 593-4).

[1] Ducange. ' Huissiers '.

[2] *Lady Bessy* says (Version I, p. 15) of Gilbert Talbot ' Their durst no sarjant him arreast, / He is called so perlous of his body '.   [3] Cowel, *Interpreter, s. v.*

[4] p. 28.   [5] £6 13s. 4d.   [6] *Proc. Priv. Coun.*, iii, p. 265.

[7] See Cowel, *loc. cit.* ; Taylor, *Glory of Regality*, pp. 158-9 ; Grose, *op. cit.*, i, pp. 173-5, who says that in Edward IV's time their number was reduced to four.

[8] iii, p. 405.

[9] *Surrey Archaeol. Collect.*, x, p. 293 ; xxxiii, p. 18 ; Haines, ii, p. 205 ; Manning and Bray, *Hist. Surrey*, iii, p. 353.

well shown is that at Broxbourne to John Borrell, 1531.[1] There
are other English brasses of these officials, but they do not show
the maces. Two illustrations from *MSS.* in which they do appear
will be found in Strutt's *Regal and Ecclesiastical Antiquities,*[2]
temp. Henry V and Henry VI respectively. Other examples
may be seen in Montfaucon.[3]

No. 67. ' Will[ia]m Warde.'   On Dec. 8, 1474, a William
Warde, doubtless the same person, was appointed to stimulate
and superintend the making and collecting of, and the paying
for, good and sufficient bows and arrows for this campaign, in
the counties of Dorset, Somerset, Devon, and Cornwall.[4] From
the Tellers' Roll for the first quarter of 1475 we learn, what our
MS. does not tell us, the capacity in which he served in France.
He was in charge ' xxxv Hominum Laboratorum vocatorum
Manyonerers,[5] Casters of Dyks and Trenchis & aliorum Operum
necessariorum in eadem Ordinat[*ione*] '.   These were paid 6*d.*,
and his own wage was 12*d.* per day, his total receipt being
£84 3*s.* 6*d.*[6] The relatively high pay given to these ' manyonerers ',

---

[1] Haines, i, p. 126 ; ii, p. 80 ; Beaumont, *Anc. Mem. Brasses,* p. 130.

[2] Plates XL, XLIII.   [3] *Op. cit.,* i, Pl. XCV ; ii, Pls. CCXXI–II, CCXXVI.

[4] *Foed.,* xi, p. 839 ; *Pat. Rolls, 1467–77,* pp. 462, 492.

[5] Of the meaning of this word there is no doubt, but the word itself does not
occur in any of the dictionaries.   The L.L. form it represents apparently would be
manuonerarius (*manus* and *onus*), but the form as given in Ducange is *manuoperarius*
(*manus* and *opus*).   The English word here used, however, may be either a blunder
or a corruption.

[6] *Foed.,* xi, p. 847.   (Incomplete in the edition by Holmes.)   Molinet says
(i, p. 141) that the English brought with them a novel engine of war after the
fashion of a great plough, drawn by more than fifty horses, for making straight away
deep and broad trenches.

and their small number, would suggest that they were really fore-
men-engineers, under whose skilled direction manual labourers
would be hired to work. Warde's daily wages in the second
quarter were the same,[1] being that of an Esquire. In the list of
those who adhered throughout to Richard III is a Sir William
Warde, who may have been this man ; [2] and ' Sir William Ward,
alwayes that was wight ' was one of the leaders who ' said Richard
shold keepe his crowne '.[3] As, unlike Roose below, ' Sir William
Warde ' seems to disappear from the records after that time,
this may be so. On the other hand a ' William Warde the elder,
Esquier ', is protected in Henry VII's Resumption Act of 1485.[4]

No. 68. ' Edmond Gregory.' Gregory is not in the Tellers'
Roll for the first quarter, but, from his being associated with
Warde in our *MS.*,[5] and receiving the same pay, we may fairly
conclude that he performed similar duties. His identity I have
been unable to establish.

No. 69. ' Comptroller of the Ordonance Will[ia]m roofe.'
According to the Tellers' Roll for the first quarter of 1475
' Willelmus Roffe Contrarotulator Ordinationum Regis ' brings
2 men-at-arms, himself reckoned in, and 10 archers, his daily
pay being 4s., as much as that of a Baron, and his total receipt
£47 15s. 6d.[6] In our *MS.*[7] nothing is said about any retinue, but
his personal wage is the same. In connexion with this expedition
Rosse was commissioned to take carpenters called whelers and

---

[1] *MS.*, fol. 4 *recto.*
[2] *Harl. MS. 542, f. 34.* Printed by Hutton, p. 209, and by Halsted, ii, p. 568.
[3] ' Bosworth ffeilde ', *Bp. Percy's Fol. MS.*, iii, p. 245.
[4] *Rot. Parl.*, vi, p. 361.   [5] Fol. 4 *recto.*
[6] *Foed.*, xi, p. 847.   [7] Fol. 4 *recto.*

cartwrights and other carpenters, joiners, stonecutters, smiths, plumbers, shipwrights, coopers, sawyers, fletchers, chariotmen, horseharness makers, and other workmen within the realm of England and the town and marches of Calais, and elsewhere under the King's obedience, for the works of the King's ordnance, and bombards, cannons, culverins, fowlers (apparently guns of forged, not cast, iron), serpentines (long guns, supposed to have increased range), and other cannon, powder, sulphur, saltpetre, stone, iron, lead, and other necessaries, crossbows and bolts for them, bows, arrows, arrow timber, bowstaves, elms, ashes, beeches, alder, birch, holm, and other timber, tanned leather and calfskins, and other necessaries for the ordnance, and all ships and vessels of 16 tons and over and masters and mariners for them.[1]   A William Roose appears frequently in Rymer about this period, a person of importance, who was evidently our man.   He was one of the ' viri circumspecti ' appointed on Sept. 20, 1467, to treat with the Duke of Burgundy on commercial matters,[2] and on Feb. 23, 1469, was named, with others, to assist in an inquiry into the tenure, &c., of certain lands in the neighbourhood of Calais.[3] Later that year, and in 1470, a Mr. Roose is raising men in Norfolk.[4]   William Rosse, ' Vitellarius Villae Calesii ',[5] was

[1] *Pat. Rolls*, 1467–77, p. 494. See the list of munitions handed over to him by Sturgeon at the end of the war cited by Dr. Scofield (ii, pp. 119–20).

[2] *Foed.*, xi, p. 598.

[3] *Ibid.*, p. 641. He seems to have been a merchant of the Staple at Calais, and is described also as late of Bamborough and Oakham (*Pat. Rolls*, 1467–77, p. 290).

[4] *Paston*, ii, pp. 359, 414–15 : July 3 and Nov. 15.

[5] In time of war this was an especially important post, because the forays of the French on land, and the activity of their ships in the Channel, endangered the local and the overseas supply.

nominated on March 4, 1472, a commissioner to settle certain differences with the Duke of Burgundy, and on March 5 to treat with the Governors of the Hanse Towns for a lasting undertaking ;[1] while on June 18 following we find him acting as a commissioner to rectify the Pale of Picardy where it marched with the frontier of the Duke.[2] On Dec. 10, 1472, this ' Vitellarius Villae nostrae Calesii ' is again engaged in the matter of the Hanse Towns,[3] and on May 20 in the succeeding year is one of the commissioners sent to attempt a final commercial arrangement with Burgundy.[4] All grants to him were protected in the Act of Resumption of 1473,[5] and on July 20, 1474, he is once more treating with the representatives of the Hanseatic League for the settlement of certain disputes.[6] Sept. 12, 1476, finds him again a commissioner to deal with commercial disagreements and difficulties that had arisen between England and the Burgundian subjects in the Low Countries ;[7] and in the Resumption Act of 1478 all grants to ' William Roffe Efquier, Vitteler of the Towne of Caleis and Marches of the fame ' are protected.[8] In June, 1481, he is appointed buyer and keeper of all food and munitions of war for the defence of Calais and the Pale at 2s. daily, and 12d. daily apiece for a clerk and a yeoman, and 6d. daily for each of three servants.[9] On June 28, 1483, it was ordered by Richard III that ' William Roosse, vitailler of Calais, contynue in his office '.[10] During the year 1486 he is repeatedly mentioned in connexion with Calais : on

[1] Foed., xi, pp. 739–40.
[2] Ibid., pp. 759–60.   [3] Ibid., p. 766.   [4] Ibid., p. 778.
[5] Rot. Parl., vi, p. 80.   [6] Foed., p. 793 et seq.   [7] Ibid., xii, pp. 32–3.
[8] Rot. Parl., vi, p. 407.   [9] Pat. Rolls, 1476–85, p. 276 : June 2.
[10] Lett. & Pap., i, p. 15.

Feb. 10 and 28, March 8, and Aug. 19, as Victualler of the town
and the marches ; [1] on Mar. 4 as purveyor of the King's 'victuals,
stuffs, artillery, and habiliments of war ' for the defence of Calais
and the neighbourhood, at 2s. a day ; [2] as a commissioner, with
others, to see to the fortifications of the town ; [3] and on March 8
he is appointed surveyor of its defences at 12d., and master of
the works at 10d., per day. [4] On Dec. 15 of the same year
'Willielmus Ros, or Guillermus Roos, Vitellarius Calesii ' is
charged to arrange mercantile matters with Maximilian, King of
the Romans. [5] On Aug. 12, 1488, we meet with him as 'maister
of the King's Ordinaunces ' [6] at Calais, when he has to render
to a commission an account of the employment of a sum of
£273 10s., assigned to him for the last sixteen years, to
be spent on the provision of ' artillarye stuff and ordinaunces '
for the defence of the town and pale. [7] In the summer of
1490 he is adjusting differences with the French King, [8] and
again in the autumn. [9] On Dec. 5 following he is ordered to
assist in preparations for the invasion of France ; [10] while in
1491 'Willielmus Rosse, armiger ', is yet again engaged as a
commissioner in the matter of disputes with the Hanse. [11] Upon
Dec. 6 in that year he is one of three persons commanded to

---

[1] *Mat. Reign H. VII*, i, pp. 288, 323, 378, 543.   [2] *Ibid.*, i, p. 339.
[3] *Ibid.*, i, p. 352 : the month is not stated. For an interesting account of the way
in which money was raised for repairs to the defences of Calais and the Pale, see
Rot. Parl., v, p. 234.   [4] *Mat. Reign H. VII*, i, p. 372.
[5] *Ibid.*, i, p. 319.
                                                          [6] Ordnance.
[7] *Mat. Reign H. VII*, ii, p. 344.
[8] *Ibid.*, ii, p. 453 : June 19.
[9] *Mat. Reign H. VII*, ii, p. 431 : Oct. 8 ; *Foed.*, xii, p. 431.
[10] *Mat. Reign H. VII*, ii, p. 463.   [11] *Ibid.*, ii, p. 441 ; *Foed.*, xii, p. 441.

provide ships, gunners, and crossbow-men, for the coming French expedition.[1] I have been unable to identify with certainty the family of this active and trusted servant of the Crown : possibly he belonged to the distinguished House of Roos.

No. 70. 'The Clerke of the Ordnance Thomas Bonys.' This official does not appear in the Tellers' Roll for the first quarter. The amount of his pay as given in our *MS.*[2] seems to have been 2s. a day. I have not met with his name elsewhere.

No Physicians or Surgeons are mentioned in the *MS.*, but the Tellers' Roll for the first quarter of 1475 [3] states the numbers of them who indentured for this expedition, and their pay for that quarter. Their names are supplied by Grose [4] from a manuscript which he cites. The two authorities combined give :

Master Jacobus Fryle,[5] King's physician, 2s. per day, with two servants at 6d. per day each.

Master William Hobbis,[6] physician and surgeon of the King's body, 1s. 6d. per day, and one assistant surgeon at 6d. per day.

Seven other surgeons at 1s. per day : Richard Felde,[7] Richard

---

[1] *Foed.*, xii, p. 463.
[2] Fol. 4 *recto.*
[3] *Foed.*, xi, p. 648.
[4] *Mil. Antiq.*, i, p. 239.

[5] An error for Fryse. Jakes Fryse was holding the same post in 1464 (*Rot. Parl.*, v, p. 529) ; ' Maifter James Fryfe, oure Phificion ' is protected in Edward IV's Resumption Act of 1467-8 (*ibid.*, p. 597) ; and ' Maister Jakes Frase ' in that of 1473 (*ibid.*, vi, p. 83). He was still King's Physician in 1482 (*Pat. Rolls, 1476-85*, p. 251 : Jan. 29).

[6] On July 3, 1470, he had received a grant of 40 marks a year (*Pat. Rolls, 1467-77*, p. 211). ' Maister William Hobbys ' was excepted from the Act of Resumption of 1473 (*Rot. Parl.*, vi, p. 83) ; and, as Richard III's Physician, was granted £64 a year on Dec. 10, 1483 (*Pat. Rolls, 1476-85*, p. 374).

[7] ' Richard Felde, oure Surgeon ' was holding office in 1464 (*Rot. Parl.*, v,

Elstie, John Smith, Richard Brightmore, Thomas Colard, Richard Clambre, Simon Coll.

Five other surgeons at 6*d.* per day : William Coke, Richard Smythys, John Stanley, John Denyse, Alexander Ledell.

The King's Secretary. Edward IV was attended in his expedition to France, in 1475, by Hatclyffe his secretary, who received 2*s.* per day ; and a gentleman, his servant, was allowed £36 8*s.* for 1 man-at-arms and 13 archers for one quarter's wages. The Secretary's salary was the same as that of the King's Physician and the Clerk of the Council.[1]

The only impression known of the post-restoration seal used by Edward IV for French affairs, as the fleurs-de-lys stops in the legends seem to indicate, is that appended to the Treaty of August 29, 1475, which closed this expedition.[2] It is preserved in the *Archives Nationales* at Paris,[3] and is shown here. The contemporary manifesto announcing to the people of England the terms of the treaty has been published in *Archaeologia.*[4]

p. 529) ; on Oct. 30, 1468, was given the office of Ranger of forests in Hampshire (*Pat. Rolls, 1467–77,* p. 97) ; and was dead by Jan. 29, 1482 (*ibid., 1476–85,* p. 251).

[1] *Proc. Priv. Coun.,* vi, p. cxi ; *Foed.,* xi, p. 848.   [2] Birch, *Seals,* p. 45.

[3] Reference No. $J\frac{5}{648}$.   [4] xxxii, pp. 325–31.

Seal used by Edward IV for French Affairs

appended to Treaty of Picquigny, Aug. 29, 1475

(Archives Nationales, Paris)

INDEXES

I. PERSONS

M

Stanley, Thomas, 2nd Baron, *MS.* 2 *recto,*
22–3, 73, 114 (and see Derby).
—, Sir William, *MS.* 3 *recto,* 48, 63, 73–4.
Stillington, Richard, Bishop of Bath and
Wells, 5.
Stonor, Thomas, 35.
Strangways, Henry, 30.
Sturgeon, John, *MS.* 4 *recto,* 131–3.
Suffolk, Charles, 1st (Brandon) Duke of, 118.
—, John de la Pole, 2nd Duke of, *MS.* 1
verso, 13–14.
Surrey, Thomas, 1st (Howard) Earl of
(and see Howard, Sir Thomas).
Sutton (see Dudley).
Swan, William, 35.

Tailboys of Kettleby, 77.
Talbot of Bashall, 82.
—, Gilbert, 139.
—, Sir Gilbert, 82.
—, Sir Humphrey, *MS.* 3 *recto,* 79–82, 89.
— and Furnival, John, 12th and 10th
Baron, 82 (and see Shrewsbury, 1st
(Talbot) Earl).
— Family, 71.
Talboys, Sir Robert, *MS.* 3 *recto,* 74–7.
—, Sir William, 74.
Tarbock, 23.
Tattershall, John, 70.
Thomasine Fitzwarine, 32.
Trussell, Edward (1469), 117.
—, Edward (1660), 117.
—, Sir Thomas, 116.
—, Sir William, *MS.* 3 *verso,* 116–18.
—, Sir William (ancestor of last), 117.
Tuchet (see Audley).
Tudor, Henry (see Henry VII).
Tunstall, Cuthbert, Bishop of Durham, 95.
—, Sir Marmaduke, 95.
—, Sir Richard, *MS.* 3 *recto,* 58, 80, 86–95,
98.

Tunstall, Thomas, 87.
—, Sir Thomas (Senr.), 86, 95.
—, Sir Thomas (Junr.), 86.
—, Sir William, 87.

Umfraville Family, 76, 77.
Urswicke, ... , wife of Sir James
Harrington, 99.
Ustwayte, Thomas, 127.

Verney, Sir Richard, 125.
Vernon, Sir Richard, 123.
Vescy, Henry (Bromflete), Baron, 62.
Vessey (see Vescy).

Warbeck, Perkin, 2, 101, 103, 122, 124, 125.
Warde, William, *MS.* 4 *recto,* 140–1.
—, Sir William, 141.
Warren, Sir Lawrence, 113.
Warwick, Guy of, 10.
—, Richard, 5th (Beauchamp) Earl of, 71,
79.
—, Richard Nevill, Earl of (1449–71), 26,
32, 52, 53, 62, 63, 121, 128, 129, 133.
Wenlock, John, 79.
Westmoreland, Ralph Nevill, 1st Earl of, 30.
Widville, Sir Edward, 115, 120.
—, Richard, 31.
Willoughby, Sir Robert, 120.
Winchester, Roger de Quincy, 2nd Earl of,
108.
Wood, John, 123.
Worcester, John, 1st (Tiptoft) Earl of, 45.

York, Edward Plantagenet, Duke of, 26,
128 (and see Edward IV).
—, Lord Mayor of, 92, 97.
—, Richard Plantagenet, Duke of, 3.

Zouch of Codnor, John, 30.

II. PLACES

(Counties are added where the place-names occur more than once in England)

III. MATTERS